The Graphic Novel: An Introduction

This book provides both students and scholars with a critical and historical introduction to the graphic novel. Jan Baetens and Hugo Frey explore this exciting form of visual and literary communication, showing readers how to situate and analyze the graphic novel since its rise to prominence half a century ago. Key questions that are addressed include: What is the graphic novel? How do we read graphic novels as narrative forms? Why are page design and publishing format so significant? What theories are developing to explain the genre? How is this form blurring categories of high and popular literature? Why are graphic novelists nostalgic for the old comics? The authors address these and many other questions raised by the genre. Through their analysis of many well-known figures – including Bechdel, Clowes, Spiegelman, and Ware – Baetens and Frey offer significant insight for future teaching and research on the graphic novel.

Jan Baetens is professor of cultural and literary studies at the University of Leuven. His main research areas are modern French poetry and word and image studies, mainly in so-called minor genres such as comics, photonovels, and novelizations. He is the author of some fifteen volumes (among which is a classic volume on Tintin, *Hergé écrivain*, published in 2006) and has published widely in journals such as *Critical Inquiry*, *PMLA*, *History of Photography*, *Poetics Today*, *Yale French Studies*, *Poétique*, *English Language Notes*, *Romanic Review*, and *French Forum*. In 2007–2008 Baetens was the holder of a Belgian Francqui Chair, and the same year he was awarded the triennial prize of poetry of Francophone Belgium.

Hugo Frey is head of department and reader in history at the University of Chichester. He is the author of *Louis Malle* (2004) and *Cinema and Nationalism in France: Political Mythologies and Film Events, 1945–1995* (2014). He has published articles on historiography, cinema, and bande dessinée in journals such as *Contemporary French Civilization*, *Journal of European Studies*, *South Central Review*, and *Yale French Studies*. Recent publications include a critique of the politics of Renaud Camus for Ralph Sarkonak, ed., *Les Spirales du sens chez Renaud Camus* (2010). In the fall of 2013, he was invited to lecture for The Prince's Teaching Institute, London.

THE GRAPHIC NOVEL

AN INTRODUCTION

Jan Baetens

University of Leuven, Belgium

Hugo Frey

University of Chichester, UK

CAMBRIDGE UNIVERSITY PRESS

CAMBRIDGE
UNIVERSITY PRESS

32 Avenue of the Americas, New York NY 10013-2473, USA

Cambridge University Press is part of the University of Cambridge.

It furthers the University's mission by disseminating knowledge in the pursuit of education, learning and research at the highest international levels of excellence.

www.cambridge.org
Information on this title: www.cambridge.org/9781107655768

First published 2015

A catalogue record for this publication is available from the British Library

Library of Congress Cataloguing in Publication data
Baetens, Jan.
The graphic novel : an introduction / by Jan Baetens, Katholieke Universiteit Leuven, Belgium; Hugo Frey, University of Chichester
    pages   cm.
Includes bibliographical references.
ISBN 978-1-107-02523-3 (hardback) – ISBN 978-1-107-65576-8 (paperback)
1. Graphic novels – History and criticism.   2. Comic books, strips, etc. – History and criticism.   I. Frey, Hugo.   II. Title.
PN6710.B235   2015
741.5´9–dc23   2014010130

ISBN 978-1-107-02523-3 Hardback
ISBN 978-1-107-65576-8 Paperback

CONTENTS

ILLUSTRATIONS

ACKNOWLEDGMENTS

We would like to thank Ray Ryan of Cambridge University Press for his support of and interest in this project. We would also like to express our gratitude to the anonymous readers who offered insightful feedback on our original proposal for this work, as well those involved in the peer review of the final manuscript. Roger Sabin and the historian Jean-Paul Gabilliet kindly commented on an early draft of our work, and we thank them here for their time, interest, and encouragement.

Several doctoral students working with us have confirmed to us that graphic narrative is a rich area of inquiry: Ian Hague, Laurike in't Veld, Charlotte Pylyser, Greice Schneider, and Steven Surdiacourt. Special thanks also go to Michael Berry for recalling how and why he wrote about the "British invasion" in the *East Bay Express* and to Mark Daly and Professor Dick Ellis for their lively knowledge of contemporary American literature.

Finally we would like to thank also the "go-betweens" whose work in the ongoing U.S.-UK-France dialogue on the graphic novel has proven inspiring, among them Bart Beaty, David Beronå, Thierry Groensteen, David Kunzle, Fabrice Leroy, Scott McCloud, Paul Gravett, Mark McKinney, Ann Miller, and Benoît Peeters.

1 Introduction: The Graphic Novel, a Special Type of Comics

Is there really something like the graphic novel?

For good or ill, there are famous quotations that are frequently repeated when discussing the graphic novel. They are valued because they come from two of the key protagonists whose works from the mid-1980s were so influential in the concept gaining in popularity: Art Spiegelman, the creator of *Maus*, and Alan Moore, the scriptwriter of *Watchmen*. Both are negative about the neologism that was being employed to describe the longer-length and adult-themed comics with which they were increasingly associated, although their roots were with underground comix in the United States and United Kingdom, respectively. Spiegelman's remarks were first published in *Print* magazine in 1988, and it was here that he suggested that "graphic novel" was an unhelpful term:

> The latest wrinkle in the comic book's evolution has been the so-called "graphic novel." In 1986, Frank Miller's *Batman: The Dark Knight Returns*, a full-length trade paperback detailing the adventures of the superhero as a violent, aging vigilante, and my own *MAUS, A Survivor's Tale* both met with commercial success in bookstores. They were dubbed graphic novels in a bid for social acceptability (Personally, I always thought Nathaniel West's *The*

> *Day of the Locust* was an extraordinarily graphic novel, and that what I did was ... comix.) What has followed is a spate of well-dressed comic books finding their way into legitimate bookshops. Sadly, a number of them are no more than pedestrian comic books in glossy wrappings, and the whole genre, good and bad may find itself once again banished to the speciality shops....[1]

And more briefly, but in a similar vein, these are the views of Alan Moore:

> You could just about call *Maus* a novel, you could probably just about call *Watchmen* a novel, in terms of density, structure, size, scale, seriousness of theme, stuff like that. The problem is that "graphic novel" just came to mean "expensive comic book" ... it doesn't really matter much what they're called but it's not a term that I'm very comfortable with.[2]

Despite this inauspicious welcome, the graphic novel, as an idea and a publishing phenomenon, has endured and has had a significant impact on comics, literature, film, and many other media besides. If awarding a "Special" Pulitzer Prize to Art Spiegelman's *Maus* in 1992 had been controversial at the time, for many reasons one can quietly state today that giving the Nobel Prize for Literature to Chris Ware in 2016, announced in advance here as a scoop by the authors of this book, will no longer be received as a subject of comparable surprise. Today, the graphic novel has escaped the cultural exclusion of much of the comics universe and has gained great respect, not least in the United States, one of the pioneer homes of comics and comic books.

Novelists discuss and refer to graphic novels in their fictional works and critical writings; some, such as Jonathan Lethem and Chip Kidd, have offered narratives for graphic novels, each scripting pastiches to heroes Omega the Unknown and Batman, respectively.[3] Major works such as *Ghost World*, *American Splendor*, *Persepolis*, and *Tamara Drewe* were adapted into highly regarded and award-winning movies, while the overall volume of publishing of graphic novels continues to be strong, unhindered by the rise of digital media, such as Kindle. Indeed digital media seem to expand the realm of the visual rather than contract it. For example, the enhanced e-edition of Michael Chabon's recent novel *Telegraph Avenue* includes additional illustrations by "Stainboy" Reinel and other visual and audio material that are unavailable in the standard hardback first edition. At the time of writing, DC Comics have announced that they will publish the screenplay to Quentin Tarantino's latest film *Django Unchained* (2012) as a graphic novel.[4] Readers, reviewers, publishers, and booksellers (in store and online) have maintained the currency of the graphic novel and continue to use the concept as useful shorthand for either adult readership comic books or single volume comics the qualities (content or artwork) of which distinguish them as exceptional when compared to regularly serialized titles or more generic material (superheroes, sci-fi, or fantasy). In academia the Modern Language Association of America (MLA) has published *Teaching the Graphic Novel*, a guide dedicated to supporting instructors working in the field, mainly focusing on assisting classes or courses taught in departments of literature.[5] Of course Spiegelman and Moore have contributed to this very process of growth and legitimization, but so too have David B., Kyle Baker, Alison Bechdel, Charles Burns, Daniel Clowes, Robert Crumb, Kim Deitch, Julie Doucet, Will Eisner, Neil Gaiman, Andrzej Klimowski, Jason Lutes, Rutu Modan, Frank Miller, Grant Morrison, Harvey Pekar, Trina Robbins, Marjane Satrapi, Seth, and Chris Ware, among many others. In the last three decades they have produced graphic novels that are widely recognized as adding to our culture, and in this study we elaborate a series of analytical frames to better understand their important contributions.

Thus, in this book we return to explore the critical break in the history of the comic book that Spiegelman and Moore were once so skeptical about but gained greatly from, even while being critical. Mindful of their warnings, we certainly do *not* take an elitist stance against the comic book tradition, including the underground comix, nor are we concerned with writing about works that are contributing to the field of children's literature. Rather, we want to use this book to examine how contemporary graphic novels display genuinely significant, although rarely absolute, variation from the preexisting comics and comix traditions, to ask how that change has happened, and to analyze what this means for us as scholars researching graphic narrative, visual culture, popular culture, and literary history.

This book is among the first full and detailed academic elaborations on the graphic novel that openly uses those two, sometimes unloved, words.[6] Many of the best preceding titles in the field avoid the terminological minefield altogether by employing other labels, including, "adult comics," "alternative comics," or "post-Underground." Our shared starting point was that we believed there was something to say about graphic novels and that there was a critical and historical meaning to them, beyond the marketing speak.[7] After all, the graphic novel is being widely used, and there continue to be comics that do not seem like the ones that we read in our respective childhoods. *Maus*, *Watchmen*, *The Dark Knight*, and other important titles in the 1980s (e.g., *Love and Rockets*, *American Flagg!*, and *Swamp Thing*) and their many successors over the last thirty years have found a fixed place in bookstores rather than speciality shops. The graphic novel is a vibrant form of literary publishing, and it merits a critical toolkit to read it better. Indeed, even Art Spiegelman has offered more positive and respectful commentaries that are less frequently cited than are his dismissive remarks from 1988. For example, when speaking with Joseph Witek in 2004, Spiegelman discussed the graphic novel as a genuine subform of comics. Although still declaring he held some reservations, he suggested that for him now graphic novels were works that were "well structured, tempered narrative … this thing of trying to tell a more nuanced story than before."[8]

On the structure of this book

It is noticeable that this book's structure and writing has developed quite organically from our first discussions on the project. After dealing with some basic further definitional questions (here in Chapter 1), we have often found ourselves repeatedly addressing three interlinking concerns: first, the historical and contextual explanation that aims to describe how and when comics were no longer being treated as being "just for kids"

(Chapters 2, 3, and 4); second, mapping out a formal analysis of medium features (Chapters 5, 6, and 7); and third, returning to two important thematic fields, how graphic novels have interacted increasingly with traditional notions of "literature" and how they have commonly become associated with nostalgia and historical representation (analyzed in Chapters 8 and 9, respectively).

Let us say a little more about each of these subjects, so as to explain why they are important for an introduction to the graphic novel. In this chapter we argue for an open definition of the graphic novel that acknowledges how definitional processes are about perception, scales of difference, variety, and impression. In it we aim to explain how in several key respects graphic novels do provide a significantly different set of cultural activities from comics, but that there is no fixed or absolute borderline. On the levels of form, content, and publishing context, graphic novels differentiate from comics. But it is not a case of one rule applying to all, let alone a once-and-for-all definition.

Part I, consisting of Chapters 2 through 4, provides the reader with a historical contextualization. Reviewing the development of adult comics since approximately 1945, these chapters explore the creative contexts out of which serious adult comics developed. Chapter 2 explores the 1950s to 1960s and underlines how creators such as Harvey Kurtzman proposed sophisticated new material. The term "graphic novel" did not have much, if any, popular currency in this period, but works such as *Harvey Kurtzman's Jungle Book* established adult, long-form, complex visual literary material.[9] The Pop Art appropriation of comics is also an important part of our history, for it set out several key ideas later taken up in the graphic novel: irony, appropriation, narrative dualism, and a tension between comics and more elite cultural activity.

In Chapter 3 readers are invited to explore underground comix, the milieu from which several graphic novelists of the 1980s and 1990s first learned their craft. It highlights the work of four important contributors: Jaxon, Art Spiegelman, Will Eisner, and Justin Green. In addition, the chapter points to how developments in sci-fi comics and fiction were promoting early graphic novels. Historical analysis concludes with an overview of the scene in the late 1980s and a discussion of subsequent developments. How British and French graphic novelists impacted the American growth of the graphic novel in the 1980s and 1990s is also described and contextualized here. Chapter 4 concludes by outlining some of the main trends in graphic novel publishing that have developed since 2000.

Part II discusses the formal strategies for "reading" graphic novels. Reviewing and explaining theoretical work, it outlines how to approach graphic novels critically. Thus, Chapter 5 explains the significance of panel and page layouts for interpreting the form. Drawing on critical works from Benoît Peeters and Thierry Groensteen, among others, we show how the visual constructions of graphic novels impact reader response. We do not erect a definitive model but rather show some of the ways through which individual graphic novels can be newly understood. Next, Chapter 6 explores artistic style and how combining word and image in single form have been key aspects for the making of graphic novels. Chapter 7 returns to a more formal analysis of content and narrative than was afforded by the earlier historical analysis.

The final part of the book explores the thematic areas that we suggest are two of the most significant current areas of debate for anyone interested in this subject. Chapter 8 provides an original discussion of the dialogues that are taking place between graphic novelists and more traditional forms of writing, notably literary fiction. This is shown to be a very productive field of activity, with graphic novelists staking a claim to literary material and literary editors adopting graphic novelists into their community, a notable strategy led by Dave Eggers's periodical, *McSweeney's*. In Chapter 9, we suggest that some of the initial tensions that surfaced around the popularizing of the term "graphic novel" have in the long run been played out through, and been sublimated into, the recurrent presence of the theme of nostalgia in several important graphic novels. Comic books are far from dead, but the break that the graphic novel established (if even only symbolically achieved) has prompted much fascination with comic book history, literal and metaphorical.

This has its consequences too, and they merit a detailed reflection for the conclusion to this work.

Our primary and guiding purpose throughout has been to elaborate on each of the aforementioned frames of orientation so that students and fellow researchers will be able to draw on our work and reapply it in their chosen specialism. We can also add that this is a work of meta-commentaries and not of close readings (though we are as precise as possible and have looked to include original insights). We do, however, suggest that the paradigms we elaborate can inform and shape future case work, even if only to stimulate debate and disagreement with our perspectives.

A new definition of the graphic novel

What remains sometimes unclear is what is actually meant by the label "graphic novel." Although we do not believe in a general definition (for there can be no single or definitive one), the objective of the following section is to help bring clarity to the often murky debates on the nature of the graphic novel, which for us is not just a genre but also a medium.

We propose that the graphic novel as a medium is part of other, more-encompassing cultural fields and practices (graphic literature, visual storytelling), and that within these fields and practices there are rarely clear-cut distinctions between types and categories, but rather more commonly scales of differences, that are known by creators and publishers, that are often deliberately exploited to achieve resonance with readers/consumers, and that are rightly contested and debated as part of their public reception. Within the domain of graphic literature, the basic categories are the difference between graphic novel and newspaper political cartooning or caricature (roughly speaking, the distinctive feature is storytelling: the graphic novel is a storytelling medium; short political cartoons or single-image caricatures can tell stories as well, but this is not their primary aim) and the difference between graphic novel and comic books (roughly speaking, the distinctive feature here is not storytelling, for comics as well as graphic novels tell stories, but a whole range of features that cannot be reduced to one single aspect).

We consider then that the graphic novel is a medium, the key features of which can sit on a spectrum on whose opposite pole is the comic book. Roughly speaking, these features can be situated at four levels: (1) form, (2) content, (3) publication format, and, directly related with this, (4) production and distribution aspects. Let us discuss each area in turn before suggesting some more general remarks.

LEVEL 1: FORM

Form is the logical starting point when discussing the properties of a medium, yet in the case of the graphic novel, it is important to stress the complex and variegated nature of form. At this level, differences between graphic novels and comics are not always very clear-cut, as shown by the major works that first introduced the notion of the graphic novel, such as Frank Miller's *Batman: The Dark Knight Returns* (four-issues comic book version in 1986) or Alan Moore and Dave Gibbons's *Watchmen*, the dystopian reinterpretation of superheroes comics (twelve-issues comic book version in 1986 and 1987). That is to say, in terms of form these works started life as comics and then were republished as graphic novels. Drawing style is of course crucial, and many graphic novelists will try to give an individual twist to their work, but here it is more important to emphasize two other, more encompassing dimensions of form: the page layout and narrative. As convincingly analyzed by Thierry Smolderen, the basic model of comics that will be questioned if not replaced by the graphic novel is, apart from the issue of personal drawing style, that of the "grid" and that of "sequentiality." For almost a century, comics have followed the same fundamental structure: their images are juxtaposed in a grid, which intertwines horizontally and vertically organized images that are supposed to be read in a sequential order – that is, a successive way – and that determine the supposedly "natural" narrative status of the medium. Formally speaking, comics are a way of storytelling that is based on the sequential decoding of juxtaposed images that are gathered page by page. Graphic novels can follow all these rules perfectly: first, and as already mentioned, they can borrow the drawing style of the "typical" superheroes comics (to repeat, there at the public consecration of the term with *Batman: The Dark Knight Returns* and *Watchmen*); second, they can also respect the layout rules the comics industry has been using for many decades; third, nothing forces them to abandon the narrative dimension of their juxtaposed images. Yet at the same time, the graphic novel does also *explore* each of these rules, trying to push the medium beyond the limits that have restrained it for so many years. First, the graphic novel tries to foreground more individual styles, although individuality should not be confused with notions such as the beautification of the clichéd comics style; what graphic novelists are craving for is a *recognizable style*, and this does not necessarily mean an "embellished" version of the traditional comics style (which can be very gratifying from an aesthetic point of view, as we all know thanks to the blow-up appropriations by Roy Lichtenstein et al., circa 1962). Certain graphic novelists, for instance Julie Doucet, are even in pursuit of an "ugly" or apparently "clumsy" style, which they consider paramount for the achievement of personality and street credibility. Second, and perhaps more importantly, the graphic novel tries also to turn away from the conventions, including the conventional ways of breaking the rules that characterized the comix field in the late 1960s and 1970s. Hence the generalization that preference is given to either unusual layout techniques, which tend to break the basic grid structure, or the return to classic formats that the comics industry thought too boring to maintain. An example of the first option can be found in the work of one of the founding fathers of the graphic novel, Will Eisner, who liked working with unframed panels, creating a more fluid dialogue between the various images on the page (Illustration 1.a). Examples of the second option are frequent in the more recent production, where several authors seem to refuse any aesthetic upgrade or variation on the grid, preferring a return to layout sobriety in order to avoid any distraction from what they think really matters in their work. After all, a work such as *Maus* displays a surprising appearance of cautiousness as far as layout issues are concerned, especially when compared to the underground experiments of its author in a preceding collection, *Breakdowns*. The same can be said of other great successes, such as Satrapi's *Persepolis*, a rather traditional and easy-to-read work that ironically enough has been produced in the context of the extremely hard-core avant-garde French publishing house, L'Association. Finally, graphic novels may also innovate at the level of narrative (and we return to this aspect in much greater detail in Chapter 7), either by refusing it – a stance illustrated in the so-called abstract comics that used to be ignored as simply unthinkable until quite recently – or by emphasizing a dimension of storytelling that was hardly prominent in comics: the role of the narrator. In the graphic novel, and for reasons that have also to do with issues of content (see our next point), the narrator is much more present, both verbally and visually, than in the case of a comic book, where the story seems to tell itself, without any direct intervention from the narrator.

LEVEL 2: CONTENT

Next to form, *content* is a second element that underlies the divergence between the graphic novel and the comic. Here as well, and perhaps even more conspicuously than at the formal level, the graphic novel has tried to distinguish itself from comics, more specifically from the superheroes comics. Content matter is "adult," not in the sense of pornographic, but in the sense of "serious" and too sophisticated – or simply uninteresting – for a juvenile audience, although of course there have been pornographic works of note, as well as graphic violence on show in some notable examples (one may think here of Alan Moore and Melinda Gebbie's *Lost Girls*,[10] for its steaming eroticism, or Frank Miller's *Sin City* or *Holy Terror*,[11] for their hard-core violence). Graphic novels are also disposed toward realism (here we mean contrary to

Opposite page: 1.a. **The reworking of the classic grid-structure: visual and narrative dialogue between unframed panels.** Illustration from *Dropsie Avenue: The Neighborhood.* Copyright © 1995 by Will Eisner, from *The Contract with God Trilogy: Life on Dropsie Avenue* by Will Eisner. Used with kind permission of W.W. Norton & Company, Inc.

the science fiction or, increasingly, fantasy content of the superheroes comic books), and they are not necessarily restricted to fiction. Many graphic novels are autobiographical or semiautobiographical, and several of them claim to be documentaries, reportage, or history. Let us underline: the three best-known graphic novels, which do not belong to the dystopian superheroes genre, definitely have an autobiographical foundation. Art Spiegelman's *Maus* (1986, 1991), Marjane Satrapi's *Persepolis* (2000–2003, for the original French version), and Alison Bechdel's *Fun Home* (2006) are all personal memoirs, even if the main character is not necessarily that of the "narrating I." Let us recall that Spiegelman's story is about his parents as much as it is about Art Spiegelman; also, Bechdel's account has a double protagonist, *Fun Home* being about the coming out of both daughter and father; and the hero of *Persepolis* is not only Marjane Satrapi but also the whole generation of Iranians (girls, women, boys, and men) exposed to the essentially male, theocratic violence of the Islamic Revolution. It is also the case that Chris Ware's *Jimmy Corrigan: The Smartest Kid on Earth* lends itself to being read alongside its author's life story, a position gestured toward in its end pages where Ware discusses his own father and dedicates the work to his mother. Though this graphic novel begins as a fiction, it is labeled in its conclusion as a "Semi-Autobiographical work of fiction."[12] We can also add that that such is the importance of autobiography as a theme that even creators and works that are not at all directly connected to this issue have reached out to be associated with it. For instance, when publishing a special edition of *Ghost World* Daniel Clowes highlights this aspect, stating: "[O]n another level, Enid (and even more so Rebecca) are all me, and their situation calls upon the dynamics of several friendships I've had over the years."[13] Even the conversation with Frank Miller in the important collection of interviews with creators published in the late 1980s, *The New Comics*, started with the personal: how Miller's changing living environment altered his perceptions. There Miller remarks: "In the *Dark Knight* series, there's a much more direct use of my real life experiences in New York, particularly my experiences with crime."[14]

Other graphic novels are more object- than subject-oriented and may qualify as journalism or history writing rather than autobiography. The work of Joe Sacco is the ultimate example of this approach, but here as well it is easy to add other well-known publications including contributions from Kyle Baker (*Nat Turner*), Alan Moore (*Into the Light*; *From Hell*), Art Spiegelman (*In the Shadow of No Towers*), Will Eisner (*Last Day in Vietnam*; *The Plot*), Rob Morrison and Charlie Adlard (*White Death*), and Ari Folman and David Polonsky (*Waltz with Bashir*). Such categorizations are often problematic in themselves, with several works blending and blurring conventional borders of how critics and scholars organize meaning in the academy. Indeed it is arguably the ability of the graphic novel to work on the borderlines of first-person narrative, history-from-below, and oral history, as well as to introduce fiction with historical meaning (and vice versa), that makes it so fascinating and important a body of work. It would be a pity, however, to be hammering away at autobiography, testimony, memory, and history when discussing the creative possibilities of the graphic novel, as if the preservation of fiction and imagination would imply some genuflection before the "easiness and escapism" of comics. The creation of a compelling story world is no less difficult in fiction than in faction, and there is no reason to decree that it is only by exceeding or circumventing the rhetorical tricks of a fictional environment that the graphic novel can come of age. We hope therefore that through subsequent chapters of our book we will help give an idea of the incredible diversity and variety of content matter of the graphic novel. Indeed we believe such an approach is the only way to provide a helpful orientation, because otherwise only too narrow and limited an analysis would be possible.

LEVEL 3: PUBLICATION FORMAT

At the level of *publication format*, the difference between comics and the graphic novel is both very straightforward and unreservedly complex. It is easy to observe that the graphic novel has a strong preference for the book format, while it tends also to avoid serialization. In other words, the graphic novel tends to adopt a format that resembles that of the traditional novel (in size, cover, paper, number of pages, etc.) and that is immediately recognized as something other than either a comic book (the infamously cheap brochures, where the strips are often truncated with advertising for other merchandise, that do not find their way into quality bookshops and that belong to the newsstand or the specialized comics shops) or the European BD format (close in general to the A4 album format, which could create confusion between graphic novels and picture books for children). In addition, it is also known that the graphic novel prefers the one-shot formula. Just as in the case of the book format, which proved crucial to the expanded cultural acceptance for the medium (the very fact that graphic novels started to be sold in bookshops contributed greatly to their legitimization), the refusal of serialization functions as a symptom of a craving for prestige that aimed at definitively cutting through the possible ties to comics. Moreover, the one-shot approach allows graphic novels to be distinguished from what many see as a classic means of selling out to the commercial demands of the "culture industry," which converts an idea or a character into an endlessly repeated series.

Format and serialization are real issues in the field, yet both aspects are far from raising analogous problems. If the transition from the comic book format to other more booklike formats was nothing more than the amplification of an evolution that was already taking place, the farewell to serialization proved more problematic, as one can see in the diverging attitudes of the graphic novelists themselves, whose current practice remains highly ambivalent in this regard. Serialization is far from absent (see, for instance, Gilbert and Jaime Hernandez's *Love and Rockets* or Chris Ware's *ACME Novelty Library*, among many other examples ranging from Daniel Clowes' *Eightball* to the series *Palookaville* by Seth), and subsequent commercial exploitation in trade form is also not unknown. Most decisive in this regard is the stance that is taken toward serialization/ episodic publishing, certain forms of which might be seen as a mix of the one-shot ideology (typical of the graphic novel philosophy) with the commercial necessities of serialization (inextricably linked with the comics environment). Serialization makes possible the prepublication (and hence the selling) of parts of a work in progress, while simultaneously offering the graphic novelist better possibilities to interact with the living culture of the day.[15] Working on a single, long one-shot graphic novel is by contrast so labor intensive that it inevitably draws a creator away from the world for the long duration of time that is required to complete the book.

A good snapshot of some of the ambiguities discussed here is the career of British artist Charlie Adlard. His oeuvre captures very well the different tendencies about which we are talking. On the one hand, Adlard has collaborated with partners to create two highly prestigious one-shot graphic novels, *White Death* (2002, with Rob Morrison) and *Playing the Game* (1995, with Doris Lessing). These look and feel like the graphic novel format and exemplify what we have just described about the one-shot, book-like format. On the other hand, Adlard is now the famous artist on the hugely successful horror series *The Walking Dead*. These are serialized adventures that have had a commercial afterlife as a popular television series and a video game. However, in fact the borders between these sites of production are very ambiguous indeed. Adlard's artistic style is relatively consistent throughout his works, and one cannot clearly differentiate a major variation based on format. It would also be simplistic to think that the long-forgotten one-shot graphic novels had any more depth than the famous zombie series that is a success precisely because it does contain intellectually stimulating material alongside its horror genre thrills (Illustration 1.b and 1.c).

LEVEL 4: PRODUCTION AND DISTRIBUTION

The fourth point of our discussion, generally speaking, suggests that the asymmetry of graphic novels and comics is once again very present. One cannot stress enough the importance of independent publishing in the rise of the graphic novel. After the do-it-yourself period of self-publication and distribution during the high days of the underground comix tradition and the not-always-very-successful attempts by Will Eisner to force a breakthrough in the general bookstore market, around 1980, the

1.b and 1.c. *The Walking Dead:* a work where philosophical questions about society are implicitly explored through a reworking of the genre of horror comics. Illustration with kind permission from the artist, Charlie Adlard.

production and distribution of graphic novels depended essentially, first, on the efforts of small independent publishers and, second, on the existence of specialty shops or head shops offering a mix of comic books, gadgets, and graphic novels, often with very limited sales figures (Spiegelman's 1977 *Breakdowns*, for instance, was met with relative indifference).[16] Things had changed, although less rapidly than in later years, by the time of the publication of *Maus I* by Pantheon, as well as the launch of a new "line" (Vertigo) of more serious works by the comics publisher DC. Crucial in this regard is the manifestation of the new player in the market, Pantheon, whose industrial impact on the book market should not be underestimated in the success of the graphic novel. It is always difficult to interpret history for fear of seeing too much of the present in the past, but it does not seem absurd to think that the independent publishers that dominate today's graphic novel market, Seattle-based Fantagraphics and Montreal-based Drawn & Quarterly, owe something, despite the qualities of their backlist and their exceptional commitment to the field, to the commercial *force de frappe* of Pantheon, Penguin, Faber and Faber, and some other major publishers, first in 1986–1987 and then again through the 2000s. Once again, however, it would be absurd to reduce the work and the publishing practices of all graphic novelists and all companies publishing graphic novels to one single template. Various patterns compete, and what matters is to stress the possible impact of a given pattern on a given work. The degree of creative freedom given by Pantheon to post-underground figures such as Spiegelman or fiercely independent artists such as Ware (we return to the role played by Pantheon's editor Chip Kidd in Chapter 8) is light-years away from what is often said about the culture industries' intellectual and ideological disposition for the mutilation of creativity. And similarly, not all the works released by independent houses are examples of superlative creativity and personal thinking.

In beginning to knit together the four aspects that we have just discussed in isolation, another element to stress is that we do not necessarily embrace a definition of the medium in terms of "auteur theory," although artists themselves believe and use this fantasy, as do publishers, who frequently publish auteur-style collections of interviews. The difference between comic books and graphic novels is *often* (it would be silly to deny it) but *not always* the difference between the collective and Taylorized way of working in the cultural industry (attacked and parodied by Will Eisner in his 1985 graphic novel, *The Dreamer*) on the one hand, and the personal and subjective mode of the individual artist who manages to pervade all possible aspects of his/her creation, on the other hand. Although subjectivity and personal expression are important in this debate, one has to admit that even within the comics industry certain authors find their way to deeply individualized creations (good examples are Jack Cole's *Plastic Man*, a figure invented in 1941, to whom Art Spiegelman has paid an impressive homage, and Jack Kirby's *Fantastic Four*, launched in 1961 by Marvel to face the competition with DC's more numerous and better established superheroes series) and that, more generally, the style and universe of the superheroes comics, to which the comics are often reduced, remains open to all kind of creative reappropriations in the graphic novel field. Furthermore, it would be naïve to think that all graphic novels are examples of the auteur ideology. In quite a few graphic novels, even those made singlehandedly by fiercely independent creators, there are many traces and aspects of popular mass culture and the culture industry. And as an author such as Charles Hatfield has highlighted, it may not be a smart move for the graphic novel to run away from its commercial and industrial roots, for the split between the (supposed or intended or imagined) elite culture of the graphic novel and the numerous constraints but also opportunities of popular culture may prove to be a dangerous evolution for the viability of the former.[17]

Indeed, Hatfield and others have expressed significant doubts around the comics/graphic novel split we discuss in this book. In the field of comics and graphic novel scholarship, Hatfield represents, in a very convincing and coherent way, the suspicion toward any too strong or sharp division between comics and the graphic novel. His arguments, advanced in his books *Alternative Comics* and *Hand of Fire*,[18] are threefold. First, Hatfield stresses the very impossibility of maintaining a sustained and professional graphic novel production outside the

economic context of comics, where the existence of a broad audience
and the possibility to prepublish graphic novels in serialized comic
books offer the financial conditions no independent artistic production can do without. Second, he fears the elitist excesses and dead ends
that may arise from the abandonment of the popular world of the comics. Third, and more positively, he has demonstrated that the economic
constraints of the popular market can be important triggers for invention and creativity. In this regard, his position is close to that of many
specialists of the modern cultural industries (not to be confused with
the monolithic vision of the culture industry introduced by Adorno
and Horkheimer after World War II), who defend similar stances on
the productive aspects of the market.[19] We are glad to take Hatfield's
(and others') point, but believe also that our open approach toward the
graphic novel leaves always the possibility to discuss the differences
between comics and graphic novels in nonessential, context-sensitive
ways. It also seems a little counterintuitive for a critical community
(comics scholarship, visual studies, and cultural studies) to reject a
concept and an idea that is being so widely used, even if in all sorts of
different and changing ways, just because it has a loyalty to the world
of comics. There is a danger of being left behind by practice and letting
journalists, publishers, and booksellers make all the running, purely
because of hairsplitting around terms.

Making room for differences: an open definition of the graphic novel

In summary, we contend that the graphic novel, though not necessarily a sharp break at the level of form or market conditions, represents
at least some level of self-knowing "play with a purpose" of the traditional comic book form, and in some cases a radical reformation of it.
Individual graphic novelists respect or disrespect form to their own
ends, and a variety of approaches range from near to complete removal
of grids altogether (e.g., Will Eisner's rejection of sharp panel edges
and speech bubbles, or more recently Kyle Baker's *Nat Turner*, which

at points looks closer to a woodcut or illustrated storybook than a comic) to high aesthetic modeling to achieve maximal readability (e.g., Spiegelman's formal comics page layout approach on *Maus*). Regarding content, graphic novels have had some propensity for autobiography, reportage, and historical narrative. Underground comix established the autobiographical potential for text-image work (e.g., groundbreaking comix from Justin Green and Harvey Pekar and his collaborators), and they also expanded graphic narrative into historiography, not least in the work of Spiegelman but also in the work of figures such as Jaxon (penname of Jack Jackson), comix pioneer and lifelong fellow of the Texas Historical Association, who did not want to publish under his own name the historical graphic novels that offered a complementary vision to his own academically published research on the history of Native America and Texas.[20] However, the graphic novel does not equate exclusively to what could be called postmodern historiography or quirky history for countercultural academics interested in provoking their more earnest undergraduates. Works from Clowes, Seth, Ware, and many others show how graphic novels are capable of sophisticated fiction, as much as memoir or alternative history writing. Furthermore the worlds of literature and graphic novel-making have for the past decade moved much closer together than ever before (see our discussion on this in Chapter 8). Moreover, novelists have always been fascinated with symbols and images, and rich interactions exist between literature and comics that prepared the way for the graphic novel. For instance, E. E. Cummings appreciated George Herriman's *Krazy Kat*, John Steinbeck wrote on *Li'l Abner*, and Dashiel Hammett wrote Alex Raymond's *Secret Agent X-9* script.

For many commentators the publishing format has been inextricably linked to definitional questions of naming publications as either graphic novels or comics. Thus, for some purists, graphic novels are always and exclusively so-called one-shot, longer narrative works that have no prehistory of serialized publication in shorter, episodic comics. That format and production have contributed greatly to the invention of the graphic novel tradition goes without saying. However to establish the novel-like one shot as the critical or exclusive criteria for labeling a graphic novel a graphic novel is reductive and counterintuitive, especially when considering how many now-famous seemingly one-shot graphic novels have long publishing histories as (regular or infrequent) serializations,[21] or, for that matter, how these fanzines have themselves been the exclusive auteur-driven publications exhibiting a sole creative achievement and are no longer collections from multiple creators, although these editions do also continue.[22]

Although the times of self-publication and special forms of distribution have changed a lot since the period of the underground comix, there still exist major differences in the ways comics and graphic novels are published, printed, distributed, reviewed, and marketed. In our discussion, we try, however, to critically engage with the superficial opposition between independent publishing and publication by major trade publishers, who are now playing an important and creatively very challenging role in the development of the graphic novel.

Finally, and most crucially, to define does not automatically mean to reduce or to fix, for there are ways of defining that are perfectly compatible with an open approach. What we are looking for in this book and in this chapter is not a closed list of essential features of the graphic novel, and their systematic opposition to those of comics (itself a much more heterogeneous domain than is often acknowledged), but to open up new spaces and offer new tools for the critical analysis of what is being published in this dynamic and rich field. For this reason, we do not mean for our definition to be taken as a universal or eternal approach of the graphic novel (this may have been the error committed by some comics scholars, who quite shortsightedly have been proclaiming the paramount importance of the one-shot publishing format as a quintessential feature), but admit – and appreciate! – differences in time and space (although for practical reasons we shall concentrate mainly on U.S. production).[23] The graphic novel is something that changes all the time, although not always at the same rhythm, and that is characterized moreover by strong cultural variations. In short, and to repeat, we are context-sensitive to both space and time.

Regarding spatial variations, the field of comics/graphic novels follows three great models or traditions: the U.S. model (with rather sharp distinctions among cartoons, comics, and graphic novels), the European model (in which these distinctions are more blurred; the European model might be called the *bande dessinée* or BD model, although it is much broader than just the French corpus), and the Japanese model (massively dominated by the local equivalent of comic books, namely mangas). It is true that globalization has abolished some of the frontiers between these three models, but in practice the relationships between the U.S. and the European models seem to be more powerful than the ones between the U.S. tradition and mangas. For this reason, in this book we will focus more on the former than on the latter,[24] not because mangas are not important in the American market (on the contrary, mangas have been booming business for more than a decade, and their success is still growing), but because, contrary to the BD tradition, they have played a rather marginal role in the rise of the graphic novel. The fact that mangas clearly influenced Frank Miller, Chris Ware, and others proves that a creative and challenging dialogue between the U.S. and Japanese production exists, yet this does not imply that it has the same intensity, depth, and breadth as the almost-continuous exchange with European models. For that reason, and to repeat, our approach, while concentrating on the American graphic novel, will not neglect those interactions that have proven capital to the development of U.S. practices: the influence of the French BD world and the surprising story of how the British comics and graphic novel scene made such an impact on the graphic novel (see Chapter 4). As readers no doubt will appreciate, these international dialogues have been hugely rich, longstanding, and too often overlooked in histories of American comics.

Regarding temporal variations, we reject any transhistorical or essential approach toward the graphic novel. We foreground instead the dynamic aspects of the medium, making room for *retrospective* reading; although the notion of the graphic novel is quite recent (the term was coined in the late 1970s by Will Eisner, among others, although he was not the first to use it), we consider it incongruous to state that there had been no graphic novels before that period.[25] The very existence of the label "graphic novel" enables modern readers to reinterpret works and models of the past that had not been read as such but that clearly belong to the same universe. Good examples include David Beronå's archaeology of the woodcut novel tradition (1920–1950 and beyond), which he sees as a forerunner of the graphic novel,[26] and Jonathan Lethem's self-assessment of his fascination with Jack Kirby's *The Fantastic Four* and Marvel comics as a way of reading "comics as graphic novels" before the graphic novel era.[27] This does not mean that one should be anachronistic; instead, we argue that the origins of the graphic novel are ably mapped in U.S.-American history through the 1950s to the 2000s.

PART ONE

HISTORICAL CONTEXT

2 Adult Comics before the Graphic Novel:
From Moral Panic to Pop Art Sensationalism,
1945–c.1967

This chapter introduces a period in the history of comics when the idea of the graphic novel barely existed. In retrospect, the 1950s and 1960s nevertheless represent a crucial backdrop to the subject of this book. It was in the early part of this period that the comics tradition was accused of pandering to base themes of violence and even encouraging criminality in the young. Familiarity with the anti-comics crusade is instructive because the period has become a significant theme in present-day production, the memory of the period still proving influential on the graphic novel. It is also the case that censorship of horror and crime comics forced publishers to tackle new themes, notably adult satire on culture and societal values, and it is here that one finds antecedents to the graphic novel in work from Harvey Kurtzman. As the 1950s drew to a close, it is a moot point whether Roy Lichtenstein's, Andy Warhol's, or Mel Ramos's appropriation of superhero, war, and romance comics for their Pop Art "saved" comics from the cultural margins. What is significant for us is that while comics received a new burst of creative energy, significant parts of that process influenced future graphic novel production, opening up classic comics to freewheeling reinterpretations, narrative dualism, and appropriation.

Censorship and renewed creativity

A picture can be worth a thousand words, and this is surely the case of press photography dating from the late 1940s that shows groups of cheering young American people, boys and girls, gathered around huge trash bins that contain burning papers. These types of image are powerful because they play with our existing historical assumptions. On the one hand, the image of burning pyres of paper materials and a moblike crowd taps into our collective memories of similar historic scenes from Nazi Germany, where the totalitarian state organized the destruction of books deemed dangerous to readers. On the other hand, the youths pictured are clearly dressed in North American garb, and there is not a single Swastika or military uniform in the pictures. In fact, this scene is from 1949, Bennington, New York, and it portrays to how pupils at the St. Patrick's Academy set about burning their comic books in a public display of contempt and self-purification. It is an iconic image that speaks to the moral panic that surrounded children and comics in the United States in the late 1940s and that was to recur and remain powerful long into the 1950s. Historian David Hajdu explains this sometimes-forgotten episode from postwar American history in his work *The Ten-Cent Plague: The Great Comic Book Scare and How It Changed America*: "The panic over comic books falls somewhere between the Red Scare and the frenzy over UFO sightings among the pathologies of post war America"[1] (Illustration 2.a).

The events in Bennington in 1949 were just one of several comparable scenes, with previous comics burnings taking place one year earlier. Who was provoking this public crisis, and why were comics being so stigmatized? From the early days of comics in the 1930s, some educationalists and journalists had denigrated them as worthless or as a lesser form of literature, dangerous for literacy and children's intellectual development. Comparable hostile attitudes grew after the end of the Second World War, and it was a loose coalition of teachers, parent-teacher groups, educationalists, journalists, and psychologists who repeated these negative claims about the dangers of comics. No single dramatic event sparked a controversy in a simplistic fashion, but rather an incremental

2.a. The cover art work of Charles Burns captures the contemporary fascination with the 1950s and the censorship of "dangerous" images. Cover illustration from Burns for Hajdu, *The Ten Cent Plague* (New York: Farrar, Struass and Giroux, 1999). With kind permission from Farrar, Strauss, and Giroux.

rise in public discourse against comics – published in scaremongering articles in weekly family magazines, newspaper articles, and news stories – sometimes linked youth crime with reading strips that had excessively violent content. Others claimed that reading comics would end improvements in literacy and that comics were making a generation of illiterate youth. From there, the burnings and some more official censorship campaigns followed, including Senate investigations.

One name is associated repeatedly with the anti-comics campaign: Fredric Wertham. Wertham was a practicing psychologist and public intellectual who genuinely feared that the violence and implicit sexuality of some comics was negatively impacting children's values and behavior. In articles and his later extended study, *The Seduction of the Innocent* (1954), he developed a now-notorious critique of comics. Media scholar Bart Beaty further nuances our understanding of this period in his meticulous consideration of Wertham's life and work, *Fredric Wertham and the Critique of Mass Culture.* According to Beaty, Wertham's critique of comics is far more complex when one starts to look at him more closely and to unpick the political subtexts of his whole career. For Beaty, Wertham is an important public intellectual, a radical psychiatrist who was more a leftist than a political reactionary.[2] Wertham's denigration of comics did not derive from a conservative position but rather from a liberal-social concern for improving society.

This is not the time or place to add much further on the anti-comics crusade. Suffice it to say that between 1948 and 1954 comics were systematically marginalized and the industry was placed into retreat, eventually creating its own censorship regulations, the Comics Code (1955), that prohibited much of the existing content. In short, a generation of comic writers, artists, and publishers were ground down by accusation, rumor, and conjecture. No one was sent to the electric chair for producing the horror and crime strips that attracted so much critical attention, but nonetheless, numerous careers were blighted, and some people never got over how their field was so publicly denigrated. Infamously, Jack Cole, the creator of the character Plastic Man, took his own life in August 1958, although it is not clear why exactly. Art Spiegelman is also unable to resolve this mystery in his and Chip Kidd's fascinating appreciation of the artist.[3] Whatever the cause of that tragic event, the rich and anarchic world of comic strip creation was censored and pushed into retreat. This retreat meant self-regulation of the Comics Code and a relative change away from the genre of extreme horror and crime to safer genres such as romance, war, and superhero material, much of which future star artist at Marvel and then DC Jack Kirby worked on in the early 1960s.[4] In his work on the anti-comics campaigns, David Hajdu's sympathies clearly lie with this repressed community. For him the churchmen, literary critics, politicians, and psychiatrists who denounced the crime and horror comics were figures from a conservative and unattractive past. According to Hajdu, what these philistines detested was an emerging younger generation of creative people and readers who were "developing their own interests and tastes, along with a determination to indulge them."[5] For Hajdu the comics and their readers were evidence of the revolutions in taste and society that were to follow in the 1960s. A specialist in folk and rock music, he identifies in the comics scene the beginning of the path to Elvis Presley, Bob Dylan, Woodstock, and a more liberal society. Furthermore, he adds that just as the attack was starting, comics were themselves developing into more sophisticated forms. He explains that by the 1950s more ambitious young artists and writers were already experimenting with longer, single book-length strips. For example, in 1950, Arnold Drake, Leslie Waller, and Matt Baker published *It Rhymes with Lust*. Marketed as a "picture novel," the work was, according to Hajdu, "a pulpy mix of leftist social realism and melodrama," and it announced the birth of the graphic novel, "a literary-artistic form that would not come to fruition for another thirty years."[6]

More generally speaking, writing in *Projections: Comics and the History of Twenty-First Century Storytelling* Jared Gardner productively situates the anti-comics moral panic as well as literature such as *Seduction of the Innocent* alongside wider social concerns in 1950s America. He explains that comics were seen as another influential device that could brainwash, akin to corporate advertising denounced in Vance Packard's contemporary bestseller, *The Hidden Persuaders* (1957), and similar too to the world depicted in Richard Condon's Korean War-inspired novel *The Manchurian Candidate* (1959). Gardner represents the 1950s as a period of deep conservatism and paranoia, where images – good or bad – were taken very literally to influence the public mind, and by implication the life of the nation. Standing back, as historians must, we can state that this collective scare was probably not only because of the social-political pressures of the Cold War. It can equally be interpreted as a slow, much longer aftershock from the previous period of state propaganda and social control organized through the "hot" war years of the Second World War, 1941–1945.

Before moving forward in history, let us pause briefly to underline two important aspects about the anti-comics crusade that pertain to the graphic novel. First, while Wertham's theories were damaging to comics and comic creation, they did imbue the medium with great public significance and import. The later, longer development of the graphic novel occurred against this backdrop. Comics being stigmatized so powerfully pushed creators to challenge the marginal position from which they now started. *Grosso modo*, adult comics and graphic novels can be understood as an antithesis to the stigmatizing emphasis of the postwar moral scare. It is also the case that the destructive impact on comics would clear the field for different types of creativity. It is a complicated matter, but at the least, a historical line was drawn before and after the anti-comics episode.

Second, Wertham and the anti-comics crusade are a recurrent theme in modern graphic novel production. Artists as different in style as Art Spiegelman, Daniel Clowes, Spain Rodriguez (Illustration 2.b), and Charles Burns have all made works that depict the 1950s moral panic. For example, writing a single-page strip for *McSweeney's San Francisco Panorama Comics Supplement* (*McSweeney's* Issue 33), Spiegelman mocks the sinister attack on comics in the 1950s. The final image of the strip underlines his particular message. Here, Spiegelman draws himself as a toddler reading his own *Maus*, held upside down. He informs the reader of his thoughts through a classic speech bubble: "Funny thing about comics – First they kill off literacy, and now they're the last bit

2.b. An example of Spain Rodriguez's interpretation of reading the 1950s horror comics so despised by Fredric Wertham. From the collection of strips, *Cruisin' with the Hound* (Seattle: Fantagraphics, 2012).

of print culture still flourishing." Although Spiegelman is being ironic about the great success of the contemporary graphic novel, it is also evident he is proud that the form he loves is now appreciated by at least some cultural opinion formers and other cultural elites, if not everyone. Similarly, Spiegelman's work with Phillip Johnston, *Drawn to Death: A Three Panel Opera*, has created a musical history of the rise and then collapse of comics in the 1950s. Why such a repetitive concern for the anticomics purge of the 1950s? It seems that the violent treatment of comics still haunts creators and that they see this moment as having meaning for their own history and so return to it in their works. The recurrent critical treatments of Wertham indicate some residual concern that the graphic novel could be again in the future vulnerable to moral panic and censorship. Here an early Daniel Clowes strip, published in *Blab!* in 1988, is significant. Titled "Seduction of the Innocent," it concludes with a satirical portrait of a Werthamite "moral father figure" next to text from Clowes that didactically, but ironically, comments, starting with a quote from Wertham:

"Children are like flowers. If the soil is good they will grow up well enough. You do not have to punish them any more than the wind and storm punishes flowers. But there are some things you have to bring them. The most important of these is reading ..." Ahhh ... fuck that shit! Kids don't read comics anymore anyways, and the gimps who do are the lamest bunch of suckers to ever come down the pike.... Let's just drop it, okay.

Thus Clowes asserts that there must be no return to Wertham-like censorship. This was as much contemporary political comment as historical discussion. At around the time Clowes brought out this strip in 1986, some recent comics and graphic novels were being criticized in the press for their adult content and especially for their violent visual content.[7] Writing and drawing about Wertham represents a sophisticated way of defending graphic novelists' freedom of speech.

Superficially then, the 1950s are an inauspicious time to discuss the roots of the modern graphic novel. Yet the period was more rich and diverse than might be imagined. Entertainment Comics (EC), responsible for some of the lurid crime and horror comics that were attracting so much hostility, also published works that are today greatly admired for their special sophistication: the historical and war comics printed in *Two-Fisted Tales* and *Front Line Combat*. These works stand out because of their meticulous detail and in particular their subtle narrative content. Joseph Witek describes them in his very important study *Comic Books as History*:

> The EC war comics, with writing, layouts, and often finished art by editor Harvey Kurtzman, featured no … graphic gore. They were instead the first antiwar comics in the history of the medium and the splash page from "First Shot" … illustrates Kurtzman's commitment to traditional standards of historical accuracy and his determination to produce works that would, in his own words, show "the utter horror and futility of war."[8]

Kurtzman's was a brave and powerful intervention – so soon after the Second World War (1939–1945) and the Korean War (1950–1953). The strips offered powerful and moving scenes that depicted the stupidity of conflict. Take, for example, Kurtzman's cover art to *Two-Fisted Tales*, number 28, from July–August 1952. It portrays two men crouching in fear before an exploding tank. The figure looking at the reader exclaims, "No! the Tank carrying the wounded … it hit a mine!" The picture not only captures the violence of combat but also underlines how casualties result from error and misjudgment as much as direct attack. Similarly there is the famous strip reprinted in Les Daniels' *Comix: A History of Comic Books in America* titled *Big 'If'!* and first published in 1952.[9] It describes the inner feelings of a combat soldier who has witnessed his colleague randomly killed by a shell. It is neatly told in a series of flashbacks exploring the tiny variables that place Paul Maynard in line to lose his life. What is important about the material pertaining to the Korean War is that these are not history comics but rather contemporary (fictional) reportage speaking to a war still being fought. They announce a tradition picked up years later in graphic novels by Joe Sacco and several of the very recent works that reflect on the international crisis post-9/11 that we will return to in Chapter 4.[10] The point is not to create a hierarchy of great works from the past, but rather to appreciate that in the early 1950s significant work on similar themes seen in present-day graphic novel production was occurring. Besides its pacifist content, already distinctive is how in *Big 'If'!*, Kurtzman uses the comics page to frame and manipulate narrative time, with individual pages including images of retrospect, and then narrative flashback developing the main plot. Kurtzman was not present in his own work, and the material was framed in a format closer to a short story or morality tale than to an autobiography.

It was also at EC that in 1955 one finds probably the first comic strip to address the theme of the Nazi death camps decades before *Maus*. Thus, Bernie Krigstein's *Master Race* is today considered by many, including Spiegelman, to be an important classic, a forerunner to how present-day graphic novelists address all possible subject maters, including history and genocide.[11] It too is presented in a short format and uses flashback frames to show how a former camp commandant now living in contemporary New York is haunted by guilt and fears capture.[12] The piece is set on a subway journey, and the frames of the windows of the train neatly echo the panels used to sequence the narrative. Again past and present are neatly represented, not only through the flashback panels, but here also in a single frame image where camp victims loom up on the walls of the underground, haunting the Nazi, Carl, who runs away from a survivor who may have recognized him.

The moral panic around comics also pushed EC publisher Bill Gaines to develop his interest and investment in a satirical humor title, *Mad*. First published in 1952, it gave the press a means to make witty pot shots at the moral crusaders against comics, as well as at comic strips themselves, such as *Superduperman!*, which mocks DC's superhero, and *Mickey Rodent*, which teased Walt Disney's famous mouse. A cover from October 1954 mocked the moralizing panic around comic strips. It is a faux newspaper story that highlights the absurdity of thinking that cartoonists could be considered as equivalent to common gangsters or drug dealers. Its text reads: "[T]hese comic book artists were rounded up today at their hideout, where they had stored a sizable amount of brushes." In a drawn fake news photograph above the text, the crime cartoonist is depicted in a straightjacket and exaggeratedly shown to be insane, while the science fiction artist is pictured as a friendly but frightened alien, complete with three eyes and four ears.

Quite quickly, *Mad* represented a safe new investment, and Gaines developed it from comic book format into a full-fledged adult satire magazine. Success followed, as did many imitation titles (over the years, many came and went, including *Eh!*, *Whack*, *Crazy*, *Wild*, *Riot*, *Unsane*, *Trump*, *Humbug*, and *Help!*), often created by and providing employment for the original EC talent pool. Most veterans of the later underground comix period (1968–1978, discussed at length in Chapter 3) acknowledge their debt to *Mad* and in particular its driving creative force, once again, Harvey Kurtzman. For a period Robert Crumb was a protégé of Kurtzman, working with him on his *Mad*-like *Help!* (1964). Numerous other comix artists and future graphic novelists had similar apprenticeships (e.g., Gilbert Shelton, Jay Lynch, Skip Williamson, Denis Kitchen, Terry Gilliam, and René Goscinny), and it is difficult to imagine the underground comix existing without the satire magazines that preceded them. When *Mad* celebrated its twenty-fifth anniversary in 1977, *The New York Times Magazine* ran an extensive article noting its influence on a generation of artists and writers from across the media, including Crumb, but also writers, journalists, alternative comedians, and children's entertainers such as founders of *The Muppet Show* and *Sesame Street*. The same article highlights the magazine's most important feature as taking no sides and being willing to attack both left- and right-wing culture.[13] This was a lesson plainly learned by Robert Crumb, whose two most famous underground comix characters, Fritz the Cat and Mister Natural, were really blunt satires of beat culture and the hippy/New Age movement, the same milieu that was reading underground comix.

It is also important to draw attention to Kurtzman's book-length publication from 1959, *Harvey Kurtzman's Jungle Book*.[14] Like later graphic novels, this is a one shot published in booklike format by a mainstream press, Ballantine Books. It includes four different original strips, each of which is quite extensive and several of which could have been published individually. Perhaps more important, Kurtzman's work displays significant literary and visual innovation. The narrative content mocks modern fashions and cultural styles, as well as genres such as detective fiction and the western. Though superficially amusing, it addresses clearly political themes, notably in the fourth and final tale, "Decadence Degenerated," which treats the subject of small town racist violence (lynching) in the Deep South. What is clever is that this section of the work mocks racism but then also teases how cinema so often fails to depict it appropriately or to really fully speak out against it. Kurtzman's page layouts and drawing style support and advance his satire. They offer close-up shots of protagonists but also provide splash-page single images and more detailed close-ups. Compared to comics of the period, fewer frames are used, and there is a greater willingness to offer close-ups on characters rather than more distant framing. In fact, there is a great confidence and stylishness evidenced in every frame. There is also some quite original experimentalism; for example, nighttime sections are colored entirely black with only speech bubbles indicating the presence of characters, and there is even a pastiche drawing of Grant Wood's famous painting *American Gothic* (1930). However, this rare example of a graphic novel did not sell well on its first publication. There seemed to be no significant market for longer length original work, and Kurtzman continued his satirical vision through the character Little Annie Fannie in *Playboy* magazine. In hindsight, it is odd that such an important work for the history of the medium has only ever received one major reprinting, yet it is appropriate that this reprinting was at the height of the breakthrough of the graphic novel in 1986.[15]

Somewhat comparable to *Harvey Kurtzman's Jungle Book*, *The Underground Sketchbook of Tomi Ungerer*, the work of a young European graphic artist then living in New York, was published in 1964 by literary publishing house Viking Press. It is debatable how to classify this title since it is composed entirely of pictures without words and does not use frames. Ungerer's focus is, however, quite clear: the horror of war, everyman's vulnerability to totalitarian power, and the proximities among human cruelty, desire, and sexuality. From our point of view, the title is worth noting quickly here because, rather like Krigstein's *Master Race*, it evidences cartooning on subjects later associated with the graphic novel. Indeed, even on its publication readers were already guided to interpret Ungerer as a serious political-historical commentator. In his preface, Jonathan Miller guided the reader: "In one sense at least the art of Tomi Ungerer is a derivative of sixty years of modern mechanized warfare. He is the artistic offspring of Passchendale, Stalingrad, Auschwitz, and Algeria."[16] Although not made explicit at the time, the work was also implicitly autobiographical: Ungerer grew up under the brutal Nazi occupation of his hometown, Strasbourg, and this experience clearly was seared into his imagination. His career continued with famous posters, design work, illustration, and children's literature.

Regarding the late 1940s and 1950s more generally, it is also worth recalling that educational strips were frequently produced and that text-image art was being regularly used for instructive purposes without any controversy whatsoever. Comics were not always considered dangerous, and indeed the form was used for some quite useful – if conservative – purposes. Famously, for an extended period, one of the future father figures of the graphic novel, Will Eisner, worked on illustrations for the American Army, including instruction manuals to assist military personnel to avoid accidents with equipment. Similarly, a future doyen of superhero art, Neal Adams, produced a comic history of the National Guard to attract recruits. The Health Services and Park Authorities also used short comic strips to inform readers on issues of safety.[17]

Comics too were regularly being published to draw younger readers into the world of classic literature. The famous *Classics Illustrated* series were an important genre of comics, and they worked as a bridge toward serious literary fiction, with their tagline advertisement from 1950 onward being "Now that you have read the *Classics Illustrated* edition, don't miss the added enjoyment of reading the original, obtainable at your school or public library."[18] Issues of *Classics Illustrated* were released to coincide with the start of the new school year, and the Boy Scouts of America recommended their titles in their 1957 manual.[19] Nonetheless, Fredric Wertham held reservations about their imagery too, targeting the cover of a *Great Expectations* adaptation, and dismissing a positive review for the series that was featured in *The New York Times*.[20] Be that as it may, numerous otherwise minor authors from a previous generation of literary fashion were kept alive by the adaptations, when otherwise their work was going unread (e.g., Jane Porter, Anthony Hope, W. H. Hudson, Talbot Mundy, and the like).

In summary, it is therefore a little too easy to interpret the 1950s as being exclusively a period of repression or suppression of adult comics or proto-graphic novels. Alongside the attacks and later self-regulation, comics were starting to tackle serious historical subject matter in publications such as *Front Line Combat* and in the satire magazines that provided powerful parodies of contemporary society. The 1950s are often misread as a time of exclusively conservative dominance, and it is all too easy to forget that this is the same decade that first produced work that challenged that very dominance. Publications such as *Mad* and *Harvey Kurtzman's Jungle Book* stand in comparison with the bestselling *Peyton Place*, the novel and *succès de scandale* by Grace Metalious that in 1956 also exposed the hypocrisies of the decade. Wertham too remains a fascinating figure, a recurrent focus of attention in recent work who will remain significant so long as there are public debates on the appropriateness of content in adult comics and graphic novels.

Pop art: the influence of an ambiguous revival of comics

Historian Jean-Paul Gabilliet highlights that the early to mid-1960s witnessed a general renaissance of superhero comic strips, with all the major publishing houses either reinventing characters or creating new ones.[21] In addition, collectors fairs began at this time (1964), and in 1965, encouraged by editor and novelist E. L. Doctorow, Jules Feiffer offered his essay and reprints of comics from the 1930s and 1940s, *The Great Comic Book Heroes*. Around the same time, mainstream publisher Ballantine reissued two collections of EC horror comics, the source of all that cultural conservatives like Wertham once had thought was wrong about the form.[22]

It is tempting to read Pop Art's recuperation of comic strip images in fine art as a significant cause of some of the above change in comics' fortune. For example, Thomas Crow writes that it was Roy Lichtenstein who rescued comics from the Wertham era, describing comics after Wertham as "ghosts of the dead" that were "left to Lichtenstein to trace the patterns of their residue painstakingly in order to lend them a new, enduring life under the aegis of fine art."[23] Similarly, Adam Gopnik narrates that it was Pop Art that influenced Stan Lee at the Marvel publishing house, and Lee in turn did the most to reorient comics to more adult readerships.[24] Pop Art did make an important contribution to reviving public interest in comics; however, whether this was ever quite so simple as the arguments summarized above is doubtful. Marvel comics were themselves demonstrably changing from within. Innovative titles such as *The Fantastic Four* were created in 1961, a little before Lichtenstein's major works. So, the post-Wertham resurrection of comics toward a more serious and engaging mode was probably underway before Pop Art's full ascendency. And, as we described earlier, it would be a pity to not recall Kurtzman's role in advancing the content of graphic narrative in the earlier period.

Nonetheless, the Pop Art phenomenon did reposition how one can understand comics, and indeed all mass consumer products. To summarize briefly, it is helpful to quote at length from Andy Warhol's memoir, *Popism*. Writing about a 1963 road trip from New York to California, he explains the essence of how he and others reinvented perceptions:

> The farther West we drove, the more Pop everything looked on the highways. Suddenly we all felt like insiders because even though Pop was everywhere – that was the thing about it most people took it for granted, whereas we were dazzled by it – to us, it was the new Art. Once you "got" Pop, you could never see a sign the same way again. And once you thought Pop, you could never see America the same way again. *The moment you label something, you take a step* – I mean you can never go back again to seeing it unlabeled. We were seeing the future and we knew it for sure. We saw people walking around in

it without knowing it, because they were thinking in the past, in the references to the past. But all you had to do was know you were in the future.[25]

For us the quotation is illuminating, especially the phrase we placed in italics. It illustrates how Warhol as artist-observer transformed popular culture and mass media into a new and significantly different item — Pop Art. Motel road signs, advertising boards, everyday objects (such as Coke bottles and soup and soap tins), and comics are transformed when labeled as something other than mass objects and implicitly made part of an expanded world of art. No longer are they functional objects or, in the case of comics, popular genre fiction; instead they become statements on society, indicators of the emptiness of America, signifiers of the banality of culture. Post Pop Art, superhero comics were open to this same questioning and reinterpretation by readers and also, just as importantly, creative reworking by artists. Not everyone made these connections when reading the superhero strips, but significant changes in perception and production had taken place when compared with the past. At the least the labeling process inherent in Pop Art meant that comics were being taken fully away from the earlier definitions imposed by those who stigmatized them as being associated with either low educational attainment (illiteracy) or social delinquency. Warhol's and Lichtenstein's blowups and reinventions of strips made one rethink all assumptions about what comics meant, including undermining the social-psychological stereotyping that had marred them in the late 1940s and early 1950s.

In the end, it was probably the pop-informed *Batman* television series adaptation of the comics that did most to make comics seem part of the wider Pop phenomenon and to push them away from categorization as (good or bad) juvenile literature. On the evening of January 12, 1966, the American Broadcasting Company (ABC) launched the prime-time adaptation of the Batman strip. Starring Adam West as Batman and Burt Ward as Robin, the series screened twice weekly for three years. The hugely successful *Batman* television series popularized and played with the new Pop Art sensibility. As in the fine art work of Andy Warhol, Roy Lichtenstein, and others, *Batman* adapted the premise of a comic book to a new medium, television. In addition, producer William Dozier chose to highlight the more absurd and surreal aspects of the strip so as to make it plainly comedic for adult audiences, while retaining enough seriousness for child-fan viewers to enjoy the action and adventure. The series underlined the camp aspects of the original strip and turned the previously potentially transgressive subtexts (loathed by the likes of Wertham) into explicit and fun amusement. The *Batman* television executives saw their product as tapping into the new Pop Art scene, and they recruited from that world to launch the first television episode. Famously ABC set up several New York-based events specifically designed to evidence support of pop artists for the series. First a drinks party reception was staged at Harlow's Discotheque. Andy Warhol was among the guests who put in an appearance. This was followed by a premiere of the first episode for the art fraternity at the York Theatre. There one observer remarked that the "lobby was adorned with Batman drawings and stickers that sported slogans proclaiming their status as 'authentic pop art.'"[26] Apparently Andy Warhol and Roy Lichtenstein were also shown the first episode of the series in an exclusive hotel room screening.[27] In addition, the star of the show, Adam West, was swept up by the hype, instructing readers of *Newsweek* that "*Batman* will be considered pop culture in the time continuum of our society. Talking in art terms, I guess you could say that I am painting a new fresco. If you twist my arm I will say that I'm the pops of film pop culture."[28] Furthermore, the release of the series chimed precisely with when Warhol and Pop Art were gaining mass media attention. It was in the autumn of 1965 that Warhol and the Factory hit headlines and gained national media attention. That year in Philadelphia a Warhol show opening witnessed frenzied crowds, with four thousand kids packed into two rooms. By December 1965, just weeks before the *Batman* series launch, the National Broadcasting Company (NBC) broadcast a feature documentary titled *Hollywood on the Hudson*. This was the program that Warhol himself felt made him a national celebrity.[29] Certainly, the *Batman* series, Pop Art, comics, and Warhol were newsworthy and interchangeably hip signifiers circa 1966 (and one might add that the spirit of the times also included an air of European surrealism too, with a major René Magritte exhibition staged at the Museum of Modern Art (MOMA) in New York in 1965).

It is important to avoid historical anachronism, and in the main pop directly contributed to the revival of comics and did not signify a trend for publication of graphic novels. One or two book-length publications with original and innovative content did develop in its backwash, however. Notably, there is the success of the American translation of the French sci-fi pop satire by Jean-Claude Forest, *Barbarella* (first published in France in 1962). It was published and translated in the literary periodical *Evergreen Review* alongside other examples of French avant-garde literature. In 1966 *Evergreen Review*'s publisher, Grove Press, brought out the complete work.[30] In the periodical itself, Michael O'Donoghue scripted and Frank Springer drew the sadomasochistic sex romp *Phoebe Zeitgeist*. It is fascinating for many reasons, not the least of which is how it set up a publishing process commonly associated with later graphic novels. This work is a good early example of how serialization, reprinting, and one-shot concepts can be blurred categories. *Phoebe* was first run episodically in *Evergreen Review* and gained cult popularity there. However, following this success, it was next revived as single book-length publication. This new one-shot book of *Phoebe* combined earlier material but then included original new narration and art to provide a more sophisticated backstory for the heroine. The finished and complete *The Adventures of Phoebe Zeit-Geist* was also published by the Grove Press in 1968 and is another example of the avant-garde literary publishing house supporting a long-length graphic narrative.[31]

Parking these two exceptional cases to one side, the importance of Pop Art for the graphic novel is not so much in terms of establishing a list of exemplary publications but rather in its more subtle and strategic impacts. Generally speaking, pop attitudes and dispositions freed up comic materials for all manner of remediatization. Of course, comics had always been used by other media (radio, cinema, stage, and musicals), but pop's radical questioning and probing showed little respect for the original context and demonstrated that comics could be reworked however one wanted and twisted to attract new and different readerships or audiences. This lesson has been hugely influential ever since, and when today's graphic novelists reinvent superheroes through placing them in all manner of original narrative interpretations, it is a device that was a fundamental part of the Pop Art revolution.

Moreover, two rhetorical tactics at the core of Pop Art's reinventions of comics are frequently returned to in graphic novel work. We will detail each in turn.

The first tactic is dualism and multiple levels of narrative. The *Batman* television series was founded on the notion that comics-inspired material could be read safely by children and then more wisely and knowingly with even some quasi-explicit straight and gay sexual content by adults. As stated above, satire on superheroes was not new. *Mad* had done it in strips such as *Superduperman!* and *Mickey Rodent*; similarly Superman's own publisher had run a series that was rather tongue in cheek alongside its mainline characters (*Ma Hunkel*, June 1939), and the early sex comics – the Tijuana Bibles – had reused superheroes for their purposes, too. But what was unique about the ABC series was that it could successfully hold together irony with seriousness to achieve significant mass resonance. We can add that following Charles Hatfield's work in *Hand of Fire*, this kind of dualism was also something Kirby and Lee were developing in Marvel comics at around this same period. Hatfield underlines that "the operative principles of Marvel were irony and graphic energy."[32] Just dipping into sample *Thor* strips confirms that passages were created to achieve dual-level meanings, often through crude innuendo or doublespeak. One interesting example evidences an early challenge to Comics Code censorship of drug-related themes. This is the case in the Comics Code-approved Thor story "Journey into Mystery" (1963). Attributed to Lee and Kirby, the tale introduces Thor's sworn enemy Loki, who inhales burning magic leaves so as to "tune in" on Thor's progress on earth. The text is worth citing: "Narrator: 'The God of Mischief then takes some strange leaves and covers them with the sap from a sacred tree.' Loki remarks: 'According to the ancient ritual, I subject the leaves to fire.... And as the smoke rises I concentrate on my foe Thor.... Thor ... He appears!'" And then the text reads: "Editor's Note: Loki has tuned in on Thor during his adventure last month, 'Thor prisoner of the reds!'"

Establishing dualism of narrative content (sometimes very coded, or sometimes very explicit as in the Thor example) is important for a history of the rise of the graphic novel. Creating equally valid multiple levels for reading works has been a fundamental strategy in so many publications, either by playing with reader assumptions about genre or through playing with contrasting visual techniques with literary-textual plots to establish levels of communication inside single works. For example, in the so-called postmodern superhero graphic novels of the 1980s, the content is often a mosaic of signifiers pitched at multiple reading groups (*Watchmen* and *The Dark Knight Returns*, to note two famous examples). Furthermore, even graphic novels with little connection to superheroes make use of now highly sophisticated forms of dualism. For instance, a good example of such an advanced dualism can be found in the work of Daniel Clowes. Throughout his oeuvre, the comicslike look of his artistic representation (what we will later analyze as "graphiation" in Chapter 6) plays out against a more melodramatic, mournful type of narrative.[33] Here one reads the images for their reassuring, traditional comicslike look while one also explores the works for their essentially pessimistic depictions of youth culture that are closer to the world of Bret Easton Ellis's fiction about the ennui of rich Californian teenagers (*Less than Zero*) than to anything one might find in a mainstream comic. More generally, dualism brought an adult knowingness about formal questions to comics that had not been so clearly present before, and this remains a factor in many graphic novels (Illustration 2.c).

Pop Art also popularized the comparable and interlinked concept of appropriation as a suggestive and powerful visual tactic. As we saw above, this had always existed; note, for example, Kurtzman's reworking of *American Gothic* in *Harvey Kurtzman's Jungle Book*. Nonetheless,

2.c. *Ghost World*: wherein Clowes appropriates the literary imagination of writers such as Bret Easton Ellis. Reproduced with kind permission of Fantagraphics, Seattle.

Lichtenstein and Warhol made the strategy well known and part of an artist's common repertoire. It has been a significant element in so much work ever since, almost so that by the 1990s it became something of a cliché. This was the tenor of the discussion on appropriation when journalist Andrea Juno discussed it in her conversation with Chris Ware. Ware notes his dislike for theorization or academic concepts that limit or exaggerate understanding, but goes on to suggest that "[a]rt and culture may naturally 'appropriate' but it's silly to turn it into a self-conscious, mechanical thought process. I never think, 'Here I am overlapping images.'"[34] Throughout a work such as *Jimmy Corrigan: The Smartest Kid on Earth*, Ware redesigns scenes from small town America originating in popular advertising and the works of Norman Rockwell and Edward Hopper, and places them as the setting to his main narrative. His subjects and images are not always fully new, but they are made to look fresh by the new rendering, elaborate frames and frames within frames, use of bold color and clear line renderings, and juxtapositions of styles from different periods on a single page or sequence of pages. Not everyone takes such an open and free-floating approach to appropriation as Ware does. Sometimes it is a case of mixing up narrative content with formal expression and blending traditions to create new looks. For example, new works from DC and Marvel have made independent creators associated with underground comix take their traditional heroic characters and redraw them in comix style. Pulling visual material from one place and mixing it with another has become a staple of a significant amount of graphic novel creation. That is not to say that there are no original auteurs but that many of these auteurs are highly aware of existing aesthetic styles and images and search out useful ones for their own creative purposes. The example illustration is from Bryan Talbot's cover art and is a powerful reworking of the design model created by Beatrix Potter in her famous children's books. As one can quickly spot, *The Tale of One Bad Rat* is a social commentary that works through the idealized views of youth so often signified in "pretty" or "nice animal" stories (Illustration 2.d).

This appreciation of appropriation as a legitimate strategy in the graphic novel is some distance from how comics artists first reacted to

2.d. Talbot's cover art reinvents the famous imagery of the world of Beatrix Potter. With permission from the artist.

seeing their work taken up in Pop Art. Irv Novick, who had served with Lichtenstein in the Second World War, was angered by Lichtenstein's use of his war comics in paintings such as *Whaam* (1963).[35] Nonetheless, the genie was out of the bottle, and the comics artists already themselves started craftily stealing back their own images from the artists in what Lawrence Alloway rightly identified as a "feedback loop." For example, in the late 1960s and early 1970s, DC Comics designated Novick to the Batman strip. Whether intentionally or not, in his own post-Lichtenstein work on Batman, Novick returned to create quite comparable images to those Lichtenstein had reused from Novick's earlier war comics. For example, in his work for the Batman comic *This Murder Has Been Pre-recorded* (March 1970), he redeployed imagery quite close to *Whaam*. Similarly, there are other neat comic book recuperations of Pop Art elsewhere in Batman comics. Alloway highlights how the comic book *Batman: Beware of Poison Ivy* opens with a half-splash image of a "Sensational 'Pop Art' Show."[36] It includes three faux fine art images of female supervillains that are possibly pastiches of Mel Ramos's fine art work, and in another panel there is a glimpse of a Warhol-like soup can. *Batman: The Art Gallery of Rogues* (a very interesting title!) is another example, in which the third panel on its first main page is an image quite close to Lichtenstein's *Drowning Girl*.[37] This is the story that follows the strip *Two Batmen Too Many*, which is about the creation of a fake Batman. Such material does encourage one to read between the lines to see some dialogue develop around the Pop Art appropriation theme. The evidence does indicate that the comics world was itself reactive to Pop Art and that the intervention from Lichtenstein and others had effects on the strips themselves, making them more reflexive and open to ambiguous "insider" readings.

Pop Art's long-term influence on the graphic novel also worked by inspiring significant countertendencies. Batman's campy, satirical tone on television inspired a backlash that had long-term reverberations for adult comics. The comics industry and its readers grew to dislike the satirical edge to the representation of Batman and Robin in the camp television reworking and in turn moved to develop its antithesis: darker, more serious strips that looked gritty and real. Thus, at DC in the early 1970s, it was clear that superheroes should be reconstructed with more seriousness and that comedy and camp were alienating readers. Editor and storyteller Dennis O'Neil and artist Neal Adams oversaw this new mode that was the antithesis to some aspects of the preceding pop revival era. Batman returned again in the early 1970s as a bleaker figure, a disposition usually associated with graphic novels of the 1980s. Similarly, besides a darker edginess, new nods to social realism were developed in comics to place superheroes in real-world contexts where they confronted exploitative capitalists, deranged religious cults, and ecocatastrophes. These were all themes that were developed by O'Neil and Adams in the Green Lantern strip. Batman too was repositioned at a maximal distance from its television rebirth. At Marvel, there were comparable moves to break from pop levity to more complex adult-world themes. As Les Daniels highlights in his still informative *Comix: History of Comic Books in America,* in an issue of *Spider-man* dating from 1971, an explicit drug crime reference was included, thus fully breaking the Comics Code ban on this subject. Similarly, other Marvel characters such as Black Widow were used to situate comics in contemporary political settings.[38]

Saga of the Swamp Thing, Watchmen, V for Vendetta, Sin City, The Killing Joke, and other graphic novels from the late 1980s were notable for their tendency for adult cinematic-style violence. However, this was an intervention that was working in a preexisting trend that was itself an earlier reaction to the mid-1960s campy comedy style. What was still distinct about the noir turn in mainstream comics in the late 1960s and early 1970s was that this narrative shift remained classified within the comic book field, rather than breaking out into the more literary publishing and distribution formulas of the future graphic novel. However, what is important to underline here is that graphic novels with adult violence dating from the late 1980s were just a completion of a longer reaction against mid-1960s camp comedy.

Conclusion

It is always important to avoid historical anachronism, so let us begin by underlining that few if any of the works discussed above or their creators thought of themselves as graphic novelists. Just occasionally phrases such as "picture story" gestured toward describing comics to signify something longer in length and closer to conventional literature. The examples of *Harvey Kurtzman's Jungle Book* and *Barbarella* stand out as unique contributions from author-artists that were longer works distributed by two mainstream publishing houses. However, as we have illustrated, the 1950s and 1960s were significant periods with examples of comics artists producing sophisticated work that remains much admired today and that did start to attract adult readerships. To repeat, Kurtzman's many contributions remain a key point in most chronologies of the history of adult comics and can be seen as a major site in any archaeology of the graphic novel. What was strikingly different from today's graphic novels? First, there were women artists at work on comics, but they were hidden inside male-run offices. Second, explicitly autobiographical work was not being developed at all. The reportage or historical works from EC did not refer to or bring in the creator's explicit own stories, though by implication the selection of themes suggested authorial-artistic independence. Third, with rare exceptions, publishing formats were dominated by comics or magazines and not novel-like one-shots.

It is also worth repeating that Fredric Wertham seemingly haunts today's graphic novel, reappearing with regularity to exemplify how bad the past was and to remind readers that censorship is a wrong-headed turn. Ironically, the seriousness with which Wertham viewed comics also chimes with graphic novels' quite earnest thematic interests and repeated claims to be taken seriously. In comparison, even though Kurtzman is still highly regarded, his historical memory does not feature so emphatically. Sadly there is no contemporary modern-day equivalent to the perceptive and beautifully drawn satire on culture that is *Harvey Kurtzman's Jungle Book*, not that there is a shortage of subjects to mock in contemporary culture …

Pop Art, the golden age of Marvel, and Batmania are fascinating episodes from recent history. The mid-1960s marked a revival for comics, and they gained new, campus-based, older readers. Pop made the material seem chic, and production at Marvel chimed with this. The comics revival taught future graphic novelists lessons of irony, playfulness, and revisionism. Narrative dualism and appropriation are two key lessons well learned by our contemporary graphic novelists. Neil Gaiman and Andy Kubert's *Marvel 1602* is a classic example of the appropriation style. This title uses the Pop Art technique of redrawing and reframing comics into new forms to a maximal degree. It uses the superheroes the X-Men and then redeploys them into a historically (reasonably accurate) world of reformation Europe and the European colonization of America. Thus, we find characters familiar to us from the comic book transported into a completely new period (early modern history) and drawn up in near-pastiche images of woodcuts and prints from the seventeenth century and merged into a faux-historical narrative that references the Reformation, the Inquisition, and the discovery of America. All the while, the original characterizations and themes from X-Men are cleverly reframed into the historical setting.[39]

3 Underground Comix and Mainstream Evolutions, 1968–c.1980

This chapter continues the historical analysis of the development of the graphic novel in further chronological order by taking our narrative forward from the 1960s into the 1970s. In it we underline the role of the underground comix in changing the form and the creation of its first cultural star, Robert Crumb. While no clear notion of the graphic novel existed in the public mind for much of this period, one can very clearly put forward for discussion works that would be hugely influential on future creativity, such as Justin Green's *Binky Brown Meets the Holy Virgin Mary* and Jaxon's *Comanche Moon*.[1] Equally, it is important to describe how the pioneer graphic novelists Will Eisner and Art Spiegelman were greatly influenced by the milieu of comix.

The chapter does not therefore propose any revisionism in the standard history of comics, and in fact we here recommend several important existing histories written by Jean-Paul Gabilliet, Charles Hatfield, Paul Lopes, Mark James Estren, and Patrick Rosenkranz.[2] However, in its concluding paragraphs, we discuss how some parallel developments outside the world of the comix were also leading to the contribution of long-length, adult-focused comics quite similar to our present-day graphic novels (e.g., newspaper strips in collected editions by Charles Schulz and Garry Trudeau), and how in a corner of the sci-fi community there were also ambitions for longer, implicitly more literary works, which gave rise to insiders from this world labeling some works as graphic novels or the similar term "illustrated story." By the end of the 1970s, there was no full consensus on when to use "graphic novel," but in works such as Eisner's *A Contract with God: A Graphic Novel* (1978) and Archie Goodwin and Walter Simonson's *Alien: The Illustrated Story* (1979), people were producing and reading works with close relation to today's publications.

Comix: foundations for the graphic novel

We do not propose to write a new history of the underground comix scene but rather to summarize briefly how that culture fed into the graphic novel. What is important to recognize is that in the mid- to late 1960s, it was on university campuses (Michigan State, University of Texas-Austin, and University of California, Berkeley, to name some of the better-known) and in the radical districts of major urban spaces (including Haight-Ashbury and the Village in New York) that graphic narratives aimed at adults, and with little or no connection to superheroes (including pop and the post-pop noir variants) were first circulated, printed on the new off-set presses that facilitated self-publishing and small press endeavors. Robert Crumb, Gilbert Shelton, Kim Deitch, Jaxon, and Justin Green, among others, produced new amusing, sexually explicit, and often satirical strips in self-produced magazines or in supplements to student newspapers. Their work was self-conscious, sometimes quasi-autobiographical, and utterly irreverent. For them, no topic was taboo. Sex, race, hippies, old mainstream comics, and the alternative drop-out scene itself, as well as targets in straight and conservative America, were all fair game for satire.

College humor magazines created a network of venues and distribution for young satirical cartoonists. Similarly, nationwide humor magazines (e.g., *Mad* and *Help!*) featured clever one-to-two-page satires from unknown artists who had not worked for superhero or other mainstream strips (see also Chapter 2). In 1965 free newspapers and magazines such as *East Village Other*, *LA Free Press* and *Oracle* developed and provided alternative noncommercial newspapers for students and anyone else interested in alternative media perspectives. Momentum was then gained in 1968 when three individual artists self-published landmark comix. In San Francisco, Gilbert Shelton created his *Feds 'n' Heds* and Robert Crumb made *Zap*, while in Chicago, Jay Lynch and Skip Williamson completed *Bijou Funnies*. These three publications heralded a revolution, and within a relatively short period a booming self-sufficient market could sustain three hundred different titles, with new material being printed in runs of twenty thousand.[3]

The underground comix changed preexisting assumptions of what comics could achieve. Both in style and in subject, they laid the groundwork for the alternative comics and the breakthrough of the graphic novel in the later years of the 1980s. Charles Hatfield explains further in his landmark study *Alternative Comics: An Emerging Literature* that the underground artists addressed topics that would become subjects of graphic novels in years to come; notably, autobiography and introspective strips about creators' lives and outlooks (original exponents being Crumb and Justin Green, as well as women's underground strips that didactically asserted selfhood and gender interests in counterpoint to the sexist objectifications in much of the male-produced work). Hatfield also underlines in *Alternative Comics* that the comix scene created a market of production and consumption outside of mainstream superhero comics. Here the artists owned their own work and were not employees for a commercial comics concern. The underground community demonstrated that artists could achieve success without becoming entangled in the formal comics industry. The comix culture also disproved the notion that comics had to be based on extended runs of serialized plots, either in a daily or weekly newspaper or in a weekly DC/Marvel comic. Hatfield implies that this shaking up of the form of comics was significant. It prepared artists, publishers, and readers for graphic narratives to be available in almost any mode, including the longer form of the one-shot "novel." We can add too that undergrounds – exiled outside of the mainstream comic book industry – could deal directly with literary publishing houses that had different distribution approaches and royalty schemes than the old industry did. In other words, the most successful underground titles were carried in some mainstream bookstores as well as the head shops that were the sale points near campus or in the alternative communities nearby.

Let us next discuss a little further the direct significance of Crumb's career. *Grosso modo*, in the figure of Crumb the underground and the mainstream media that reported on him created their own star comic artist and writer, and in so doing established a public framework for appreciating individual creative talent in the field. In short, the very success of Crumb in the late 1960s and early 1970s prompted the idea of the comix artist as a figure of comparable significance to a novelist, filmmaker, or any other important cultural worker. Though based on his depiction in the biographical movie *Crumb* (director Zwigoff, 1995) it is easy to imagine Crumb as a socially marginalized outsider producing absurdist – and often offensive – comix, it is also the case that his comix broke through from small circulation campus-level material to gain significant national prominence. To put it simply, Crumb became a legend in his own time, a star graphic novelist, *avant la lettre*. His originally self-published work from venues such as *Zap Comix* was relatively quickly anthologized and repackaged by mainstream publishing houses. For example, Viking Press brought out a first mainstream anthology in 1968, and then two years later Ballantine provided a new version of the earlier underground collection *Head Comix*. In 1969 Ballantine also marketed its collected edition of Crumb's infamous *Fritz the Cat* strips. Simultaneously, Crumb's work broke into at least the margins of the fine art scene. It was exhibited as part of a wider underground art event at Berkeley and was also featured in a Whitney show dedicated to the "Grotesque in American Art" (October 1969–March 1 1970, Whitney Museum of American Art, New York, and University Art Museum, University of California, Berkeley). This fascinating event shows how Crumb and two others were briefly penetrating the fine art circle. Its catalogue, *Human Concern/Personal Torment*, includes samples of comix from Crumb alongside work from S. Clay Wilson and Spain Rodriguez.[4]

The music scene was also part of the consecration of Crumb. Famously, Janis Joplin recruited Crumb to provide cover art to her album *Cheap Thrills*. In 1970 the Grateful Dead released the song "Truckin," after the phrase "Keep on Trucking" that Crumb had popularized in his strips.[5] Crumb himself became part of a blues and folk band, "The Cheap Suit Serenaders." Equally important is the fact that cultural commentators recognized Crumb as an important figure. The novelist Terry Southern noted that Crumb continued where *Mad* magazine left off. Others added further praise, with art historian Robert Hughes describing Crumb in an essay for *Time* magazine (May 22, 1972) as "a new world Breughel." National newspapers caught the mood of interest in Crumb and popularized him further beyond the underground. New publications coming from academia were not far behind when an early issue of *Journal of Popular Culture* (*JPC*) featured Harvey Pekar's essay on the artist. There Pekar highlighted the fascinating nature of Crumb's work and guided scholarly readers: "Crumb is a very hip guy with big eyes for what's going on around him."[6] Such material is all the more important in the invention of Crumb precisely because *JPC* was a serious academic journal that, though interested in popular culture, was being edited to high scholarly standards and aimed to be taken seriously by sociologists, literary scholars, and historians.

The adaptation to cinema of *Fritz the Cat* added greatly to Crumb's fame. *Fritz the Cat* – the movie (1972) – was a critical and commercial success. Though Crumb hated the work and subsequently blamed his then-wife for selling the rights to the picture, Ralph Bakshi's animation was hugely successful. Reading through the original press reviews, one can see quite clearly how Fritz and his creator had broken out from the counterculture to become a radical element inside the mainstream. Indeed, within a short period of time the first movie had spawned a sequel, *The Nine Lives of Fritz the Cat*. And for a while radical cartoon animation was available in cinemas. Director Bakshi followed up his work with two original features of his own, *Heavy Traffic* (1973) and then the controversial *Coonskin* (1975). Art Spiegelman's achievement of a special Pulitzer Prize for *Maus* in 1992 was awarded some thirty-eight years after Fredric

Wertham's *Seduction of the Innocent.* Let us not forget that in the intervening years Robert Crumb found almost instant cultural legitimacy and for while in light of his success, comix were a relatively mainstream part of popular culture (in select quarters and obviously not with everyone).[7]

For the future graphic novel, the collapse of the underground comix scene in the mid-1970s is itself quite as significant as its first emergence. Underground publishing was severely impacted after the United States Supreme Court ruled in June 1973 that the definition of obscenity should be left to local authorities. Moreover, the heady atmosphere of the late 1960s and early 1970s could not be sustained. With the war in Vietnam ending and the wider counterculture contracting, the underground had given birth to a handful of powerful and determined artists, but now they had no audience or fixed place for publication. For example, discussing the negative situation in 1979, the young Art Spiegelman raised the case of Mark Beyer in an interview piece for *Cascade Comix Monthly.* This innovative artist had been working on a book-length work, and he was finding publication frustrating. According to Spiegelman, five years earlier there would have been no problem publishing Beyer's project, but now the "traditional undergrounds" were facing too much economic strain, and those in the business were only interested in commercially reliable works, the paradoxical beast of "mainstream underground" comix to which Beyer did not conform.[8] In addition the head shops were no longer so popular, and they were less and less fashionable locations for bohemians. The slow and sometimes painful end of the underground left a vacuum that was filled only slowly by figures such as Spiegelman and publications such as his and Françoise Mouly's magazine of collected strips, *RAW* (first published in 1980 and discussed further in Chapter 4). And, generally speaking, the same cultural space of the underground continued to be redeveloped when, in the 1990s and 2000s, graphic novel publishing houses republished and commissioned new works from veterans Kim Deitch and Robert Crumb.[9]

In summary, the underground comix invented formats and contents for future graphic novels, and then their own slow death presented a cultural-economic gap to be filled, albeit over the course of several years.

In self-produced short comix such as *Zap*, *Head Comix*, *Feds 'n' Heads*, *Bijou Funnies*, and *People's Comix*, among others, a generation of artists and writers cut their teeth, experimented, and worked out a direction and purpose to their art. More than anything, the revolution allowed artists to practice, draw, redraw, design, narrate, and then publish. The majority of graphic novelists born before 1960 and whose careers became publicly and widely recognized as being of literary-cultural interest in the 1980s and 1990s (Crumb, Deitch, Trina Robbins, Spiegelman, and others) learned their trade through the underground. For a short while Crumb had taken comix out of the underground and into the mainstream, setting up future possibilities for their wider recognition.

Between comix and graphic novels: four exemplary figures

The lines between the underground scene and the emergence of the graphic novel can be drawn directly and straightforwardly, just as surely as one can chart some of Miller's and Moore's works of superhero violence back to being an antithesis to the pop camp of the *Batman* television serial. In particular, works from Justin Green, Jaxon, Eisner, and Spiegelman are worth discussing further here. These creators were preparing material in the late 1960s to 1970s that established themes later to be associated with the graphic novel. The borderlines – at this historical threshold – are understandably fuzzy. Late comix look forward to what within years is publicly constituted as graphic novel work, while early publications that sported the label graphic novel were clearly shaped by underground aesthetics. Maybe ultimately what these examples indicate is that what a production is labeled is not as significant as what its common properties are. What works from Green, Jaxon, Eisner, and Spiegelman share is innovation, original content, extended length of narrative, and a push for the material to be considered as somehow richer than its antecedents, including comix.

The less well-known figures Green and Jaxon produced great work for the underground comix/alternative press scene. Their works in underground comix stand out because these figures were two of the first to be producing longer-length comix that marked up content that would be greatly taken forward in graphic novel creation: autobiography and history. In 1972 Green published the relatively long, critical self-exploration of a Catholic education *Binky Brown Meets the Holy Virgin Mary*. In a preface to the recently reprinted edition, Spiegelman highlights its importance to him and the later creation of *Maus*. Two aspects are noted. First, at forty-four pages in length, for its time, this was an unusually long one-shot comix that, with the benefit of hindsight, Spiegelman describes as "epic." Second, the intimate autobiographical, sexual details that form the narrative content of the work were distinctive. Spiegelman is again helpful. "Justin turned the comic book boxes into intimate, secular confession booths and thereby profoundly changed the history of comics," he says of this "pioneering work." In the afterword to the same reprint, Green offers a modest summary of the influences that had shaped him: "Autobiography was a fait accompli, a low fruit ripe for the plucking. Binky's story was contingent on my having seen the early work of other underground cartoonists. In addition to Joyce's *Portrait of the Artist as a Young Man*, I was also aware of Philip Roth's *Portnoy's Complaint* and James T. Farrell's *Studs Lonigan Trilogy*. J. D. Salinger, too, was a hero from an early age. His *Catcher in the Rye* was a literary touchstone for my generation." Of course what these novelists could not achieve, but that Green could through the comix, was to combine narrative of anti-Catholic, teenage sexual angst with powerful explicit and implicit metaphorical images. The explicit content was not very new, nothing much more shocking than could be found in an average early 1970s comix, but rather its insertion as part of a self-reflexive, everyday, extended discussion of a teenage education was different. Dream, nightmare, satire, and self-obsession blur together into a complex meditation on Binky's life. The colorful depictions of writhing snakelike penises were not especially radical for the world of comix. The emphasis on Green's childhood daily reality was, however, new. So too were the more banal and semi-realist frames that underlined the combination of boredom and oppression of a conservative upbringing surrounded by the requirements of strict Catholicism.

Jaxon's work also stands out from the deluge of crude comedy comix of the period, and like Brown's, it points the way to content now more commonly mined in the contemporary graphic novel. A father figure of underground comix and press in Texas, by the later 1970s Jaxon was using graphic narratives to write extended historical treatments on the story of his home state. These are remarkable pieces (e.g., *Comanche Moon*, 1978) that reject the crude drawing style and content of the majority of the comix in exchange for extended, highly detailed, long, and thoroughly researched depictions of the nineteenth-century Southwest frontier. What is interesting here is not only how clearly Jaxon was influenced by the comix revolution but also how his aesthetics revived precision and detail from earlier comics such as EC horror and war material and *Classics Illustrated*. On the one hand, Jaxon's narrative radicalism is clearly inspired by the alternative, anarchic politics of the underground. On the other hand, visually the work is conservative, detailed, and meticulous. The black-and-white hatching, obsessive detail, and careful, clear shaping of backdrops suggest some influence and mutual respect toward Crumb; more important though are the very stable and conventional page layouts which provide sequences of repeated framings and often wider panels for landscapes prior to close ups. *Comanche Moon's* approach to aesthetics harks back to the educational comics and *Classics Illustrated* of the 1950s, as well as to EC horror comics that, although violent in content, maintained very regular and controlled layouts and panel usage.

Published in 1978, *Comanche Moon* is described in its title page as "A Picture Narrative about Cynthia Ann Parker." The phrase is historically interesting because it underlines that Jaxon and his publisher, Rip Off Press/Last Gasp, recognized that the material was not comix (the immediate past/context) or comics but somehow required a better label for marketing and general description. The term gestures toward the need for something akin to the label "graphic novel," but probably because Jaxon did not want his material associated with fiction, "Picture Narrative" was deemed more appropriate. Others, such as Joseph Witek, have called the work a "trade paperback," which again notes the departure from existing kinds of graphic narrative and hints implicitly to something akin to conventional literary publishing. As we know, by the later 1980s, "graphic novel" was the phrase that stuck; what is more important is that in work from Jaxon and Green, graphic narratives were shifting out of the comix conventions, becoming longer, addressing new subjects, and being published in book-length formats. The comix heritage was, of course, ever-present in their work, yet they were also creating work distinctive from common or garden-variety "sex and drug"-themed short strips.

One of the most fascinating and sometimes overlooked examples of the fuzzy lines that exist between underground comix and the development of the graphic novel is the case of Will Eisner, the man who in the same year *Comanche Moon* was published started using "graphic novel" to try to distinguish his work from other forms of comic or humorous publication (satire or joke books). In retrospect, one can see clearly that Eisner's *A Contract with God – A Graphic Novel* (1978) developed straight from the underground milieu, despite the originality of its subtitle. Eisner, long retired from his work on mainstream comics in the 1930s and 1940s, became associated with the underground world in the 1970s, and it was that milieu that sparked his return to creating. Attending a comix's convention in New York in 1971 (New York Comic Art Convention) and meeting some of the young artists, he was slowly inspired to rethink making comics and found contacts willing to reprint his earlier superhero-style work from the 1940s (*The Spirit*), notably Denis Kitchen of Kitchen Sink Press. Eisner recalled: "To a buttoned-down type like me, this should have sent me running in the other direction. However, it didn't take great genius to see that what was afoot was a reprise of the frontier days of 1938."[10] Looking back on the 1970s, Eisner recognized that it was through mixing with these people that he could begin to imagine how he could return to graphic narratives and make something new and different. It was because of discovering the underground approach to comics that Eisner was able to conceive of returning to making comics for adult readers. The summation of this encounter was, then, his publication of *A Contract with God*, the first significant work to describe itself as a graphic novel on the title page of its paperback edition. Taking a closer look at that work, one can see some direct influences shading through from Eisner's encounter with the underground. Though not directly autobiographical, its subject was close to Eisner's heart: the struggles and hard times faced by the migrant Jewish community in New York during the Depression. Moreover, the title story in the collection addressed the theme of a father losing his adopted daughter to illness, the terrible experience suffered by the Eisner family. Eisner did not explain this on publication in 1978, and it was only in providing a preface to a new edition in 2004 that he articulated in public the full autobiographical scope of the story: "The creation of this story was an exercise in personal agony.... My grief was still raw. My heart still bled. In fact, I could not even then bring myself to discuss this loss. I made Frimme Hersh's daughter an 'adopted child.' But his anguish was mine."[11] Alongside that hidden autobiographical aspect, the collection also featured the "Cookalein" short story, a piece on growing up and youth culture that contained relatively explicit imagery of sexual encounters. Again Eisner was learning and adapting from the underground by drawing on his own experience and memories rather than using fiction/genre or the comics tradition to which he had so contributed. This section was richly informed by Eisner's own experiences and captures the New York Jewish community's annual vacation and how teenagers thrilled at the opportunities for fun it brought. Finally, the new underground comics influenced Eisner's art for *A Contract with God*. Now, Eisner abandoned any formal grid page layout and preferred a looser, more relaxed, and more radical mixture of layouts.[12]

In summary, Eisner saw *A Contract with God* as radical innovation: "A Graphic Novel." However, its themes and style drew on underground preoccupations. Eisner reorganized them into a nonsatirical, explicitly ethnically positioned narrative (Jewish) with historical setting disguising its tragic autobiographical content. He clearly saw it as distinct from comix, and in many ways it was. However, as with Green's or Jaxon's works, Eisner's work from the later 1970s was on the cusp between comix and something new, and Eisner wanted that break to be underlined in its subtitle and classification in bookstores.

Students should also appreciate that Art Spiegelman's *Maus* directly developed out of the world of underground comix. It was here in an underground collection that his original vision that first pointed to *Maus* was published. This is found in the four-page strip Spiegelman contributed to the underground collection *Funny Aminals* (1972). Similarly, the "Prisoner on the Hell Planet" sequence from *Maus* that so brutally narrates Spiegelman's mother's suicide was first published in the underground collection *Short-Order Comix* (1973) and again in *Breakdowns* (1977). The very spirit of *Maus* was also more subversive than many critics have imagined, and here again one can see comix bleeding into the graphic novel (Illustration 3). Its dominant frame, "a comic about the Holocaust," was as provocative a move as any seen in the underground. Moreover, Spiegelman made readers consider attitudes and think about their own prejudices toward history and the Holocaust. His use of mice as a metaphor for Jews is most telling and double-edged. Certainly it is a clever attack on the Nazis's own anti-Semitic mindset that identified Jewish people as vermin. Yet it was also a way of making contemporary readers ask why they were comfortable and sympathetic to Holocaust victims when imagined as gentle mice, yet were maybe less willing to come to terms with the scale of the crimes of the Nazis when presented with straightforward images or detailed historical documentation. Before *Schindler's List* (1993), Hollywood had rarely addressed the Holocaust, and for years after the war many Americans preferred not to think about anti-Semitic genocide, as evidenced by the 1959 Hollywood adaptation of *The Diary of Anne Frank* removing contextual reference to Anne's religion. Often the critical and subversive politics of *Maus* are hidden because Spiegelman also wanted to tell a straight story and guide his readers through his experiences (on one level). Nonetheless, the more radical mode breaks through to disturb and provoke, often in highly memorable single images or short passages of narration. Thus, there is the famous image of Spiegelman at work drawing, sitting at his desk atop a pile of corpses. That is a picture that opens to a more radical and violent politics in the work that asks what images mean and why some are comfortable and others not so palatable. Or in the deeply ironic passages that follow, there is the section that describes the Spiegelman family driving their car, with father Vladek abusing a black hitchhiker, while the reader is left to decode the pretty-looking gaslike images coming from the tailpipe. It is a juxtaposition of images and themes redolent of a terribly sarcastic humor on Spiegelman's part. These images in comix would no doubt have been presented more crudely and with greater directness, yet nonetheless, they are something one can associate back to that tradition. This is not to say that *Maus* is influenced only by comix or evokes only that aesthetic. Not discussed significantly in this book, the "silent" woodcut art book narratives from Lynd Ward, made in the 1930s, were also an influence on Spiegelman's work.

Repackaged newspaper comic strips and the "serious" sci-fi

Alongside the underground, the graphic novel also developed out of other centers and peripheries of graphic narrative. Mainstream newspaper comics (e.g., *Peanuts* and *Doonesbury*) have had a long tradition of hugely successful republications in individual single-volume editions, therefore looking similar to graphic novels, *avant la lettre*. Although not graphic novels per se, these works were single-authored graphic narratives that gained huge commercial success and no doubt assisted in the legitimization of the longer form comic. Already in 1962, Schulz's collection *Happiness Is a Warm Puppy* was a national bestseller, and by the end of the 1960s, some thirty single-volume *Peanuts* titles were charting in the book-sales league tables alongside books by high-powered novelists and biographies of U.S. presidents. In addition, the newspaper strip inspired a successful off-Broadway musical that then toured across the States. This was itself a prototype for holiday-themed television animations that gained appreciative audiences through the 1970s and early 1980s.[13]

In addition, Garry Trudeau's *Doonesbury* merits acknowledgment for its influence in creating a reading culture disposed to adult strips with serious themes. Through the 1970s and to the present day, collected daily newspaper strips have been sold as single-volume, themed collections, the first being *Still a Few Bugs in the System*, released in a pocketbook formula in 1972. The *Doonesbury* format of republication next started to look more like European *bande dessinée* strips, with strips appearing in larger collected formats that gathered together several years of work in one place. These *Doonesbury* reprints were made legitimate by the inclusion of prefaces and introductions by important writers whose professional credentials were unrelated to the world of graphic narratives. For example, Gary Wills, a journalist and historian, introduced the first extended collection. As with Crumb and Schulz, Trudeau's work also gained further public legitimacy through its re-presentation in multimedia forms. Now long forgotten, *A Doonesbury Special*, a twenty-five-minute long animated film, proved a hit at the 1978 Cannes Film Festival and the Academy Awards. Similarly, Robert Altman worked on a television series, *Tanner 88*, that was inspired by the strip. In 1975, Garry Trudeau was the first graphic narrator to be awarded a Pulitzer Prize for editorial cartooning.[14]

The successes of Schulz and Trudeau illustrate that the rise of graphic novels in the contemporary period is established against a background of some remarkable previous achievements in the closely related text-image forms of newspaper cartoons (of which we just mention one or two notable examples here). Trudeau is particularly important for us to recognize, as his work has so often shifted from the short satire on daily life/politics of the original newspaper format into long-running, complex, and implicitly serious plot lines. Given the already slippery and contested nature of the term "graphic novel," it is appropriate to note his longstanding contribution. Indeed, Trudeau's career is in many respects close to that of the more widely discussed Crumb, Spiegelman, or graphic novelist Joe Sacco. As with them, his work has engaged with contemporary issues, including war, human suffering, and loss (not least in Trudeau's depictions of U.S. military deployments post 9/11). Also like them, his work started in what might be broadly defined as underground cartooning, with the first versions of *Doonesbury* created by Trudeau for the Yale student magazine *Yale Daily News* (1968). One can say that a direct influence on Sacco can be quite precisely traced. Trudeau and Joe Sacco cover modern warfare in some detail, the one (Trudeau) offering bleak satire through extended daily episodic stories about U.S. troops, diplomats, generals, and spies, while the other (Sacco) writes and draws what he has encountered while living and reporting from conflict zones. Their mediums are similar, and their general subjects almost identical, although their style of drawing is significantly different, with Sacco evoking the grotesque body shapes of Crumb (not exclusively) and Trudeau using clean, almost European, clear line characterizations with little or no backdrops and – because of his strip's original context of newspaper publications – including no larger images (so-called splash pages).

When Schulz and Trudeau were popularizing the power of comics, few if anyone was using the term "graphic novel." While graphic novel-like collections of *Doonesbury* and *Peanuts* were being widely read, re-mediatized, and publicly acclaimed, it was only in the margins of the underground scene that the term itself was gaining currency. Before Eisner picked up and used the label to describe the paperback edition of *A Contract with God*, it was writers and publishers working on genre comics close to the underground scene who were first touting the phrase to distinguish their works from both comics and comix. R. C. Harvey underlines that it was Richard Kyle who first used the phrase "graphic novel" to describe his contribution to sci-fi comic magazine *Wonderworld*.[15] Kyle then continued to use terms such as "graphic novel" or "graphic story" to describe serious narrative comics with better quality art. Thus, when in 1976, he and a colleague published George Metzger's sci-fi strip *Beyond Time and Again*, they used the label "graphic novel." Also in the intersections between underground comix, sci-fi, and illustration, Byron Preiss was frequently using words such as "graphic novel" and "graphic story form" to describe his illustrated and reconceptualized science fiction publications. For instance, Howard Chaykin worked with Preiss to produce what they called a "Graphic

Story Adaptation" of Alfred Bester's science fiction short story *The Stars My Destination* (1979). This was an original piece of graphic design. It was plainly not a comic, since it eschewed any standard page layout panels or speech balloons; however, it was also something more than an illustrated work of fiction. Thus, rather than separating Chaykin's imagery from Bester's words, Preiss instead melded them together by bringing text and image into unusual and abstract sequences that were more than conventional illustration but less formal than a comic. Prior to publication, *The Stars My Destination* was previewed in the sci-fi comic magazine *Heavy Metal*. Similarly, Preiss had worked with Jim Steranko on a comparable project, *Chandler*. Later he would become one of the first to see the possibilities of multimedia publishing, leading in the field of early online material.

A standard style even developed for these sci-fi illustration-graphic novels. There are, for example, great similarities between Preiss and Chaykin's aforementioned *The Stars My Destination* and Richard Corben's adaptation of a Robert E. Howard story, *Bloodstar*. Published in 1976, this title was maybe the first of its kind to use "graphic novel" as a marketing concept. Its preface begins: "*Bloodstar* marks the great leap forward for the art of the comic strip through its revolutionary synthesis of ideas and artforms. In this book, the imagination and visual power of comic art are wedded to the complexity and depth of the traditional novel, producing an enthralling hybrid which might best be labeled – the graphic novel."[16] What follows again aims for a kind of visual seriousness: pages are not filled with panels but include some strategically placed across a page next to empty white spaces. Speech bubbles are shaped in relatively consistent forms and avoid all extravagant wavy lines that might hint of comics or comix. Text sits alongside the images or in the space of the page, and not in very comic-like panels. In retrospect, it looks very crude and unsophisticated, whereas it was intended to be radical, modern, and distinctive.

By the turn of the decade, it was a Hollywood film that inspired a highly successful one-shot that was very close to the titles described above, but rather more stylish and modern-looking by our standard. This was Archie Goodwin and Walter Simonson's *Alien: The Illustrated Story*.[17] Rereading this title reveals the clear sophistication of the material compared to either relatively contemporary comics or standard comix. While the narrative provides a loyal adaptation from the film script on which it is based, the visual presentation in the extended "illustrated story" format is distinctive. Simonson's work – in particular, panel and page layouts – provided a careful and coherent shape to the work that brings the characters and tension of the plot to the greater attention of the reader. This is achieved by offering some standard panel frames but then quite regularly breaking images outside of the panels and organizing the page in this more free-form style. More traditional grid panels are present – unlike in, for example, Eisner's *A Contract with God*, where there are none – but frequently these disappear or are reduced, and then representations of characters and backdrops, without framing, lend the work a confidence and readability that is impressive. Similarly, this free-flowing but highly planned approach prepares for three double splash pages of major scenes that present the discovery of the spaceship where the Aliens are first encountered and two passages of violence when the Alien attacks. Similarities with Eisner's recent work can also be seen in the rendering of the people. Simonson avoids making any body shapes or lines too comic-like and instead draws sketchy, "realistic" depictions of the crew of the spaceship, Nostromo. The balance of these – often close-ups – and then the larger-scale double-page horror sequences is a powerful device. The reader is invited to engage with the characters and to then, as in the movie, be shocked at their quick and violent demise. Of course, the work is genre based and derivative, but the form developed makes it impressive and powerful.

Thus, through the 1970s, the idea of graphic novels was gaining some currency in paraliterary areas where illustration had always been important. It was being used by innovative creators looking for alternative ways to create fiction for fans attracted to visual as well as textual material. This was plainly the case in the subfield of science fiction, where television and cinema had asserted the importance of visual narrative for some extended period – Kubrick had completed *2001* in 1968, and *The Planet of the Apes* premiered in the same year (both features also inspired comics, the former drawn by Jack Kirby). However, in the mid-1970s, this usage was relatively limited, and it was not being applied to the far more commercially successful book-length compilations of newspaper comics, despite work such as *Doonesbury*, which was charting terrain close to that of the graphic novels of the present era: world politics, history, the blurring of fact with reality, student and youth culture, and imagining average middle-class American life.

Conclusion

The underground comix established themes and publishing structures that were influential on subsequent production. It was out of this context that self-publishing, distinct from publishing inside the traditional comics industry, fully developed in the most significant way, and the comix graphic narratives were explicitly produced to be read by adults. In the figure of Robert Crumb, the United States generated an art-media celebrity, a paradigm to be emulated. Because this history of comix is so interesting, rich, and important, newspaper cartoons and their reprints of extended storylines are often neglected altogether. This chapter has started to fill this lacuna and underlines the historical role of Schulz and Trudeau. Trudeau remains a fascinating figure, and his work is illustrative of how coming to fixed definitions of what is or is not a graphic novel can be rather reductive. More important to note is that his political satires form a long and powerful force in book-length cartoons and that repeatedly their content has reflected some of the most serious contemporary themes, including in recent times post-combat stress and rehabilitation.

This chapter has also highlighted works from the complex middle years of the 1970s, titles between comix and the recognizable graphic novel of the late 1980s. Works from Green, Jaxon, Eisner, Spiegelman, as well as works from the sci-fi world, all indicate how graphic narratives were enriched by comix practice, and yet individual creators were pushing material in new directions away from the more clichéd and crude humor strips. Likewise the publishers of these works shared a common appreciation that the titles were not comix but something different, precisely because they were lengthier, more serious, reflexive, and sophisticated. This breach between comix and different, implicitly more serious works is how the need for a label such as "graphic novel" essentially arrived. This may not have been the best term (the word "novel" too often implies fiction, when common a subject matter of graphic novels is autobiography or history), but it did gesture helpfully toward a new classification for works that were not slavishly sticking to preexisting conventions.

4   **"Not Just for Kids":** Clever Comics and the New Graphic Novels

Between the late 1980s and the present day, the graphic novel has become an accepted medium for literary and visual creativity and storytelling. This successful development cannot be attributed to a single cause or effect, and to attempt to locate such a thing would be reductive. When in 1986–1987, Moore and Gibbons's *Watchmen*, Spiegelman's *Maus*, and Miller's *Batman: The Dark Knight Returns* were picked up in the media and soon described as the "big three" graphic novels, it was after years of development of adult comics. This chapter (1) makes a series of arguments to try to unpick further some of the hidden wiring behind the breakthrough of the graphic novel in 1986–1987, and (2) discusses some of the dominant strands in more recent production: history and reportage, autobiography, women creators, and revival of genre-driven works. The chapter ends with some more general suggestions as to the lessons provided by history.

1986: the breakthrough of the "big three"

It is first important to emphasize that the successes of Spiegelman, Moore and Gibbons, and Miller had their roots in the threshold period of the later 1970s, which we analyzed in Chapter 3. It was in that period that comix were slowly changing into a new, less frivolous format, and the concept of the graphic novel first gained some common usage and initial public interest. We can add here that both Spiegelman and Moore had been working on developing adult comics for much of the 1980s before their names became famous as founding figures of the graphic novel.

As stated in Chapter 3, parts of *Maus* were first printed in underground comix titles. Similarly, it was in Spiegelman and Françoise Mouly's *RAW* magazine that full episodic instalments of the graphic novel were published in serial form (1980–1992). More generally speaking, *RAW* worked as a forum for leading post-underground artists to publish original and new work. It provided a space for younger artists to get themselves known to new readerships (such as the New York arts and literary scene and noncomic readers first interested by *Maus*), and when Spiegelman's work became famous, his editorship provided an imprimatur of quality for those who had featured in *RAW*. Besides original narrative content, the magazine emphasized a belief in eclectic artwork and published pieces of differing styles that showed off the diverse possibilities of graphic narrative. Among the artists who would in later years come to contribute greatly to longer form graphic novels, *RAW* published Charles Burns, Kim Deitch, Ben Katchor, Chris Ware, Alan Moore, and Gary Panter. As we explain in more detail later in this chapter, it also provided a space for non-American artists to publish and influence the post-comix scene in America. For example, over the years the magazine published work from Tardi, Joost Swarte, Ever Meulen, and Baru, among others.

Coeditor Françoise Mouly grew up in France and moved to New York in 1974. It was her experience of self-publishing guidebook maps to Soho that provided her with vital early experience of graphic design, while later she would become art editor on *The New Yorker*. For what it's worth, Spiegelman also supported himself through outside professional work, at Topps Greeting Cards, where, as an employee for twenty-two years, he became steeped in the world of bubble gum cards and their history.[1] Meanwhile, *RAW*, whose history we will not retell in full detail here, was the project that enabled Spiegelman to become more than just a (self-published) comix cartoonist. Directly inspired by what was being done in France, his work on *RAW* moved him away from a certain type of crude underground comix, while steering him into the direction of something more sophisticated. He explains:

> In the mid-'70s, Bill Griffith and I edited a magazine called *Arcade*. R. Crumb did most of the covers. Crumb and I had interesting arguments about the whole "genteel versus vulgar" tension of comics. After *Arcade*, he went off and edited *Weirdo* comics. I went off and did *RAW* magazine. *RAW* was doing a Little Nemo trip. It was definitely tugging things toward a more elegant presentation, selecting work by people who were conscious of themselves as artists. That's very different than *Weirdo*, a good magazine, but more interested in printing the jokes that were on toilet rolls as their fill-in material whereas *RAW* would print Gustave Doré. I must admit, it's more glamorous to be on the vulgar, *Weirdo* side of the argument.[2]

To repeat, each issue of *RAW* aspired to offer a showcase of the adult comics of tomorrow, as well as to create a not-yet-existing audience for this kind of work. The commercial success of *RAW* was moderate, although it was far from a failure – after all, the magazine was kept alive for more than a decade. But although *RAW* was not a bestseller, it proved one of the major seedbeds for what would become the graphic novel movement. It brought a new style, it kept an eye open for politics, it was keen of graphic experiments, and it pioneered many new forms of storytelling, a crucial element that established a clear difference from both comics and comix, in which storytelling was either highly formulaic or subordinate to excessively crude style or thematic content.

Alan Moore's influence on DC and the mainstream comics similarly preceded the hype that surrounded *Watchmen*, to which we will return to shortly. In hindsight, it was his run on the DC horror comics serial *The Saga of the Swamp Thing* that is of special historical significance. It was when writing for this comic in new and original ways that Moore signaled to readers that he was a radical innovator who was unconstrained by existing genre conventions or public expectations around the nature of comics and their content. Through 1984, Moore turned in a series of stories, brilliantly illustrated by Stephen Bissette, that took the strip away from being a simple genre piece and made it a more significant and challenging work that was clearly aimed at readerships wanting more than simplistic action or mystery tales. Thus, issue 29, from October 1984, included explicitly violent plot material that meant that the series no longer included a Comics Code censorship certification on its cover. Shortly after this it was rebranded as an "Adult Suspense" title, becoming the first DC title to openly market without reference to the Code. Next, Moore went a step further and added a new twist when the Swamp Thing falls in love, and even makes love, with the heroine. This famous romance issue, "Rite of Spring" (March 1985, no. 34), broke all sales records and provided a radical departure for comics, not in having some sexy content to please the male gaze, but in making the entire strip narrate the before, during, and after of the monster and girl's surreal intercourse.

Comparison between *The Saga of the Swamp Thing* and *RAW* is not as spurious as one might first imagine. Just as Spiegelman made *RAW* a site for showcasing experimentalism and modernism, notably through publishing varieties of form of graphic narrative (including many works with very differing styles, page layouts, and narrative subjects), in a subtle way Moore and Bissette used several issues of their comic in a comparable method. Through the course of the groundbreaking year of 1984–1985, they referenced numerous graphic narrative traditions in different issues of *Swamp Thing*. For example, the famous romance episode brought into a DC strip original artwork that had more in common with poster or fantasy-fiction illustration than it did with other comics. Similarly, the psychedelic aspect of that same issue harked back to the underground and swirling page layouts from creators such as S. Clay Wilson. The range of references was, however, regularly changing and never limited. Issues from the same period directly used and paid homage to EC horror comics, and a later issue brought Swamp Thing into an encounter with characters from the children's newspaper strip *Pogo* (the original by Walt Kelly). Moore and Spiegelman were being similarly experimental in their respective publications, where they were able to play with and replay their versions of the history of comics and their aesthetics. Spiegelman and Mouly's publication was quite explicit in its aim to raise the standard and intellectual quality of the preceding comix. While Moore and Bissette did not make such explicit claims, it is the case that they were exploring how to develop comics culture and readerships in new directions.

Moreover, similar modernist experimentation was shaping other parts of the comics world at this time. Two long, adult, independent comics narratives that anticipated the graphic novel were *American Splendor* and *Love and Rockets*. Both titles offered new narratives and visual styles for adult comics, and both were in their different ways able to become "talking points" that suggested adult comics were changing and contributing new, more sophisticated material. Harvey Pekar had started publishing his diary-style accounts of life in Cleveland in 1976. However, it was in the mid-1980s that the series was "discovered" by the mass media, notably when David Letterman hosted Pekar on his popular television talk show. Pekar made several appearances with Letterman before publicly falling out with the host on a live show broadcast in 1987. His reportage strips on his daily life experiences, drawn by different collaborating artists, continued and were published in a graphic novel-style anthology format by Doubleday in 1986. *Love and Rockets* was first published as a serialized post-underground strip in 1981 and established a long-running series by Jaime and Gilbert Hernandez. Both titles share an interesting localism embedded in a strong sense of place and its subculture – post-industrial Cleveland for Pekar and suburban punk Southern California and Central America for the Hernandez brothers. Both also reside on continuity of characters – Pekar himself in his autobiographical world, and *Love and Rockets* narrating the lives of a cast of young, mainly female characters across two different, long-running narrations that were spliced with shorter material. Compared to traditional mainstream comics, they each have slow, almost boring narratives that twist through repetitive and knowing variations aimed at cognoscenti readerships that have followed long runs of their episodic printing. Compared to comix, they provide sophisticated melodrama rather than the one- or two-page "joke" strips. Maybe precisely because of their strong focus on people and places, rather than on the immediate narrative rewards of fantasy or adventure, they have gained very loyal readerships (*Love and Rockets* was especially popular in the 1980s UK youth scene) but were not able to create the wider recognition that welcomed the more coherent one-shot narratives from Spiegelman, Miller, and Moore and Gibbons. At times *American Splendor* and *Love and Rockets* are painfully slow to read: the eye has to adjust to the many paneled pages of mixing of realism and retro-1950s art in *Love and Rockets*, and the brain needs to adjust to Pekar's endlessly repetitive, ordinary daily routines. Trapped in long serializations, they did not provide the accessibility of a novel or the soon-to-blossom graphic novel. However, as with *RAW* and *Swamp Thing*, their modernism was a hugely influential change in contemporary graphic narrative, and in particular the look of page after page of *Love and Rockets* (black-and-white, clear line style applied to contemporary youth culture rather than superheroes – though they feature too, along with robots, dinosaurs, wrestlers, space ships, and other cult film genre references) initiated a pathway that is still used today by many contemporary graphic novelists, including Daniel Clowes, Chris Ware, and Charles Burns. Moreover, the "difficulty" of initially getting into the two works made another significant correction to the idea that graphic narratives were only ever good at simplification of communication. These are not base works, of either comix-style provocation or educational manual pedagogy.

Marvel also pushed material in new directions and was among the first to use "graphic novel" as a title for a long-form, first publication series. The first title of this kind, dating from 1982, is Jim Starlin's *The Death of Captain Marvel*, and it does warrant revisiting. Although drawn and presented in fairly traditional comics format, for the period, it includes an original and modern plot: the superhero is dying of cancer. Given the graphic novel's subsequent achievements in exploring difficult social and political life issues, this is an important text to review. If one sets aside the fantasy, Starlin does rather touchingly and slowly narrate

Captain Marvel's very human battle against the disease. It also offers snapshots of how he has to cope with his friends' knowledge that he will not survive. It is an effective summation of everyday human mortality, transposed to a sci-fi fantasy context. Similarly, commonly glossed over by most historians, Marvel also included in this same eclectic series a touching autobiographical graphic novel: Sam Glanzman's *A Sailor's Story*. Published in 1987, it is not as slick as the DC graphic novels, nor as original as Spiegelman's work. After all, it is drawn in rather an old-fashioned manner, including 1950s-style conventional layouts and meticulously crafted "realist" drawings of the characters. It does, however, still make a strong case for the argument that graphic novels are able to capture the life stories of individuals and to map them neatly in relation to world historical themes. In this case, it is a summary of Glanzman's experiences as young serviceman in the U.S. Navy during the Second World War. Such contributions can run the risk of kitsch, but Glanzman's work avoids this. It is a pity it has been overlooked in the secondary literature, and the same can be said of the ambitious Marvel comic run *The 'Nam*. It too was published during the 1980s graphic novel craze and aims to offer snapshots of the history of the Vietnam War. *The 'Nam* attempted to be more experimental than other Marvel titles, claiming to be narrating in "real time" the monthly experiences of troops on a tour of duty. In hindsight some of the caricature work looks quite dated, but it also achieves a sense of the horror of war, the naivety of young soldiers, and the friendships they develop. It also aimed at historical accuracy and in one early issue, a short, more formally framed and drawn section provided a balanced and fair description of the causes of the conflict. *The 'Nam* also has a good sensitivity to multiple viewpoints and shares some of the qualities of Will Eisner's own later collection *Last Day in Vietnam* (2000).

Of course, Roger Sabin is right to argue that it was the quality of the better known works of the late 1980s that produced a "big three" media popularization of *Watchmen*, *Maus*, and *Batman: The Dark Knight Returns*. In the end, the conclusion he draws on the "big three" still rings true:

In essence, they were what they said they were: novels in a graphic form. More specifically ... in book form with a thematic unity ... what made it appealing both for readers and creators, was that it opened up fresh storytelling possibilities. Put simply, in a longer narrative there was more scope for building up tension, generating atmosphere, developing characters and so on. At the same time, the visuals could often be superior to the usual comics, because the status of the work was supposedly to be higher.[3]

It is also the case that American cultural-political context played a role in making these particular publications feel especially relevant. Spiegelman, Moore and Gibbons, and Miller engaged in different but equally powerful ways with the late 1980s zeitgeist. This type of historical analysis is necessarily slippery and hard to prove, but it is clear that the works were voicing deeper public trends from the period.

For example, historian Peter Novick suggests in his groundbreaking *The Holocaust and Collective Memory: The American Experience* that it was the 1970s and 1980s when the United States collectively started to remember and publicly discuss the meaning and legacy of the European genocide of the Jewish community.[4] Spiegelman's work became a major part of that wider discussion and gained attention through its central themes (Illustration 4. See over). The 1980s marked significant international commemorations and anniversaries, including the fortieth and fiftieth years after the Second World War and the Holocaust. In addition, Holocaust denial; the Kurt Waldheim scandal; President Reagan's controversial speech at Bitburg, West Germany; and the capture and trial of Klaus Barbie, "the Butcher of Lyons," and revelations as to American involvement in his initial escape from capture after the war punctuated the decade and added to further public concern over the meaning of history.[5] It was in this context of active collective memory of the 1940s that Spiegelman gave his unique testimony as a son of Holocaust survivors. As the graphic novel underlines, in the immediate postwar years it had been necessary and easier to rebuild and not reflect on what had happened. Now, with some distance, Jewish and non-Jewish communities were rediscovering and assessing the memory of the Holocaust. *Maus* was an honest, readable discussion of many of these issues, and its own creation is one part of the extensive processes of postwar reflection that were central to public life in the 1980s.

Furthermore, it was among the intellectuals and historians working on themes relating to the collective memory of the Holocaust that some of the most favorable reception of *Maus* appeared. Indeed, it was writers from this scholarly community who did much to draw powerful academic notice to the work, including in perceptive analyses from Dominick LaCapra and James Young.[6] It was also the case that public intellectuals concerned with how the Holocaust should be mediated found the work more acceptable than other U.S. interpretative modes, notably Steven Spielberg's *Schindler's List* (1993). At a *Village Voice* round table debate dedicated to that film that included Art Spiegelman as a significant commentator, it was implied that his graphic novel/metaphorical strategy was a more sensitive and ethically appropriate mode of historical representation than the melodramatic and often exploitative movie. Thus, Ken Jacobs, academic and radical filmmaker comments that:

> Spielberg says the SS threw babies out of windows and shot them like skeet. But he wouldn't show so terrible a thing, not even stage it using dolls. So this unpleasant truth doesn't reach the audience. But why not for a moment stop turning out these crazy-making counterfeit-reality movies, and do it with dolls, obvious stand-ins for the real thing. Like Art's drawings of mice, alluding to, indicating without attempting to re-present.[7]

Miller's *The Dark Knight Returns* and Moore and Gibbon's *Watchmen* spoke quite firmly to the late Cold War period in which they were published. Thus in *The Dark Knight Returns*, Miller directly included a

---

IT WAS NOT SO EASY TO GET FREE FROM LUCIA.

17

satirical depiction of then-President Ronald Reagan speaking in a press conference about an imagined international relations issue (the "Corto Maltese Crisis" is an insider reference to the *bande dessinée* of the same name by the Italian Hugo Pratt). More generally speaking, Miller's deconstruction of vigilante superheroes Batman and Superman provides a wry comment on Reagan's media image as a cowboy-style hero able to cut through bureaucratic red tape or liberal baloney to speak to the people and address their concerns. Moore has explained that he intended a similar layer of political commentary in his work but was careful not to include direct statements on contemporary politicians; thinking of Reagan he used instead the now "safer" ex-President Richard Nixon. The work is, however, not as politically subtle as that disclaimer suggests. In effect, Moore and Gibbons loaded *Watchmen* with themes and images that chimed with contemporary U.S. Cold War politics and society, as well as references to the history of the conflict. It is even reported that when the Oliver North, Iran-Contra scandal developed, publisher DC rang Moore to congratulate him and tell him that the Tower Commission inquiry on Iran-Contra had even coincidentally used the original classical reference to the "Watchmen" that would also conclude the comic and graphic novel. Such coincidences were not magic but rather a testimony to Moore's sharp narrative eye on the warp and weave of late Reagan era politics. The brashness of its coloring and some of the backdrop art is also of its time. And, certainly besides the Cold War references, Moore's narration on an unknown, possibly sexually transmitted disease connected to experimentation on Dr. Manhattan plainly evoked the AIDS virus and its devastating effects. For what it's worth, Moore was already well-versed in producing strips that linked to their period of production: the first publication of *V for Vendetta* in the UK magazine *Warrior* coincided with the year 1984, forever linked to the commemoration of George Orwell's novel, from which Moore had freely borrowed, and it spoke to Margaret Thatcher's proudly draconian contemporary approach to government.

Finally, although this is a point rarely made and we are not art historians, it is also the case that the timing of the success of the graphic novel has some parallels with development in the contemporary fine art scene. Writing on comics and contemporary art, John Carlin and Sheena Wagstaff underlined that "by the early eighties there was a resurgence of comic quotation."[8] They go on to note works from Alexis Smith, Vernon Fisher, Steve Gianakos, David Salle, and Suzan Pitt as examples of new Pop Art. Also highlighted in the same essay is the significance of graffiti art as well as work by Keith Haring and Kenny Scharf. These people were not directly part of the rise of the graphic novel, but it is worth more than a footnote to point out how comics were becoming trendy in the art world at the same time they were gaining renewed street credibility elsewhere through graphic novels. Twenty or so years after the first Pop Art recuperations, this younger generation of artists kept some bohemian attention on comics, and this helped the graphic novel along as well.[9] And in some ways these artists' uses of classic figures such as Mickey Mouse and The Thing were less earnest and more playful than their predecessors' uses and often were featured in multimedia works rather than straightforward blow-ups from comic to canvas. Certainly graphic novel artists in the period – one thinks first, for example, of Bill Sienkiewicz – were visibly influenced by graffiti art.

Underlining the cultural change: promotion and trans-nationalism

Besides reviewing works and suggesting their original quality, the media welcomed the graphic novel through a variety of other discourses. Sometimes these were critical and noted the graphic violence of titles, such as Brian Bolland and Moore's *Batman: The Killing Joke* (1988). On the whole though, there was media excitement that a new kind of graphic narrative was being created. Several further promotional discourses circulated: debates occurred that explored how serious topics could be addressed through a "simple" form; the graphic novel was promoted as a new kind of literature with new "authors;" and its cosmopolitanism was underlined in commentaries that highlighted the influence of British and French comics. Let us talk about each of these interpretations in turn.

Whether or not the new label "graphic novel" was needed, or appropriate, to describe adult comics from the late 1980s was a topic that consistently drew media attention. The long-running debate on "what is" and "what is not" a graphic novel garnered much press interest, and this popular debate has only helped the field become more appreciated as being "important." For example, that *Maus* was hard to categorize and that this became a matter of correspondence between Spiegelman and *The New York Times* when that paper described the work as fiction, gained the author and his work increased publicity. Similarly, when others question the helpfulness of the label "graphic novel" because they prefer comics as a tradition, it adds to the idea that this is a significant cultural phenomenon at hand, that there is a public debate to be had on it. Had the new comics of the late 1980s–2000s passed without controversy about what they were doing and what they meant for culture and society, then the field would not have developed as it did. For the contemporary media, the graphic novel was newsworthy precisely because there was disagreement as to its meaning and the seeming disjuncture and contradictions among its form (visual and light), its content (serious social and personal themes), and the history of the graphic narrative medium (dangerous material of the 1950s; children/young adult literature).

A specific sub-literature even developed to explain and educate – and therefore mediate and preach on behalf of – adult comics or graphic novels.[10] By collecting interviews with creators together in single volumes – such as Gary Groth and Robert Fiore's *The New Comics* (1988), Stanley Wiater and Stephen R. Bissette's *Comic Book Rebels: Conversations with the Creators of the New Comics* (1993), or Andrea Juno's *Dangerous Images* (1997) – artists and writers with lesser profiles than Spiegelman, Miller, or Gibbons and Moore were brought to public attention alongside these big stars. Often overlooked, these important products from the late 1980s and 1990s kept attention on the emerging graphic novel, provided artists with a venue to elaborate on their oeuvres, and added to the wider media attention graphic novels were already receiving. Moreover, they produced a template of the artist interview that would be much repeated subsequently. Alongside these texts that taught people how to read and understand adult comics and graphic novels, there was even a cinema-released documentary film: director Ron Mann's *Comic Book Confidential* (1988). It is a very standard work that combines a brief historical backdrop with short interviews with artists. Nonetheless, when graphic novels were first "making it big," the film too was treated with some reverence. For instance, in London, it was screened at no less a venue than the prestigious arts center the Institute of Contemporary Arts and received some coverage in the daily broadsheets. The film was the high point of a fairly extensive para-literature that sold key early works such as *Maus*, *Watchmen*, and *Batman: The Dark Knight Returns* to U.S.- and UK-based readers, booksellers, librarians, and educators. Moreover, these titles were translated and became publishing successes in continental Europe as well. For instance, it was crime novelist and sometime *bande dessinée* writer Jean-Patrick Manchette who provided the French translation of *Watchmen*. Infamously, it was the Polish edition of *Maus* that proved the most controversial to achieve because Spiegelman's metaphorical depiction of Poles as pigs was viewed as offensive. It was eventually published there in 2001, still with some protests.

Bound up with all of this sometimes helpful and sometimes purely commercial discourse on the graphic novel, two theoretically inflected works became keystones for explaining the sophistication of comics and also how to begin to understand their mechanics as text-image works, again suggesting by implication that comics were not just child's play. These works are Will Eisner's *Comics and Sequential Art* (1985) and Scott McCloud's *Understanding Comics* (1993). These were the high points of the explanatory literature (including short guides, catalogues, interview collections, and picture books) that emerged to trumpet the graphic novel's importance. Certainly they are the stand-out texts from the era, and they include fascinating material, yet one can suggest that their significance would have paled without the biotope of the wider "what is a graphic novel" subculture of which they were also a prominent part.[11]

The mainstream media depiction that "comics were not just for kids" was complemented further with extensive commentary on the role and positive influence of foreign comics traditions on the U.S. scene, notably British and French (Francophone) interventions. In particular, Moore's highly original work for DC was quickly represented as being more than a one-off episode, and reporters searching for a different angle on "the arrival of the graphic novel" started suggesting that there was "a British invasion" of the U.S. comics scene.[12] This analysis was given greater traction by the fact that DC themselves were actively recruiting other British writers and artists to try to repeat Moore's innovative contribution on other series. It was further fueled by the success of Neil Gaiman who revived *Sandman*, turning the series into a publishing hit that transcended the comics market to attract younger women readers, Goth music fans, and fantasy fiction acolytes, as well as others. Subsequently, DC's Vertigo imprint became a virtual home away from home for British writers, and the series made the British presence one of its unique selling points. The lavishly produced art book *Vertigo Visions* (2000) that celebrated the series is illustrative – in more ways than one. Throughout it the watchwords are as follows: Brits, surreal, humor, metafiction, dark, unsettling, literate. Reflecting on this heritage in an interview with Julia Round dating from 2008, *Vertigo* editor Karen Berger highlighted how it was Moore and the British writers who had followed him to work for DC that were the significant force for making DC publish more sophisticated works, their takes on the graphic novel. She explained to Round:

> It was totally writer-led, and if anything it was really Alan Moore who changed the perception of writers in comics. He just turned the whole thing around, I mean he brought a respectability to the form, you know, by his sheer genius and talent and storytelling abilities. And such an intelligent and passionate human writer and he really showed that you could do comics that were, you know, literary, but modern and popular, but could really stand next to a great work of fiction, of prose fiction, and that really changed everything. There was really no going back after Alan did *Swamp Thing*, that's my feeling, and then *V for Vendetta* obviously sort of started before, and then finished with us, and *Watchmen*, obviously, was in a class of its own.[13]

En passant, we can add that quite a lot of the claims of a British invasion exaggerated the quality and scale of the actual contribution. Moore himself described his stardom in appropriately phlegmatic terms: "Nobody wanted to say 'he's talking rubbish,' they all sort of said, 'He's an English genius, and you must be a fool if you don't see it' which did me well for a while."[14] It is also the case that the idea that the British brought more radical political agendas was an exaggeration. Moore's reinterpretations of the history of the Deep South in *Saga of the Swamp Thing* are sometimes unsophisticated and repeat stereotypes.[15] The republishing of *V for Vendetta* as a color graphic novel arguably undermined its more original, stark black-and-white rendition. For historian John Newswinger, there is a reactionary subtext to some of the British comics where Moore cut his teeth.[16] Claims to Moore's originality are also a little exaggerated. The plot of *V for Vendetta* closely resembles that of *A Clockwork Orange* as well as 1970s trash fiction stories about right-wing conspiracies and coups. The famous smiling badge from *Watchmen* featured previously in Alex Cox's cult movie *Repo-Man* (1984). Still, it was easy to see how the discourse about a British invasion of talent gained currency. Moore and Gaiman were deservedly "hot" names for several years, and Grant Morrison and Dave McKean's *Arkham Asylum* (1989) is regularly noted as another landmark publication. That title felt like a punchy British invasion, the creators repositioning Batman into a high art-looking visual world that referenced English literature as much as Pop Art. To reverse some criticism leveled at the idea of the graphic novel, would it be quite right to call it a comic?

In precisely the same period, French and Francophone comics were equally feted – not only by Spiegelman, but also by the likes of Will Eisner, Harvey Kurtzman, Stan Lee, Jaxon, and others. It was *RAW*'s republishing of European talent that established the mood for Francophilia in the later 1980s. As noted earlier, *RAW* had showcased works from Tardi, Baru, Swarte, and others, and when it published a collected edition of its first issues, Spiegelman portrayed Hergé's famous hero, Tintin, falling through skyscrapers on its cover. However, regarding the French presence in the United States, due acknowledgment should also be made to the magazine *Heavy Metal* (*HM*). Originally created in France by a number of artists wanting to escape from the banality and social and political pointlessness of mainstream comics found in the journal *Pilote* (created in 1959 and home to the thriving series *Astérix* and *Lucky Luke*), the French *Métal Hurlant* (literally: "Roaring Metal") was:

> a glossy produced monthly showcasing the openly erotic and visually stunning work of a number of European creators. They included Philippe Druillet, Enki Bilal and, above all, "Moebius" (the pen-name for Jean Giraud[17]), whose richly surreal strips "Arzach" and "The Airtight Garage" were instantly recognised as adult classics.[18]

Launched in the United States in 1977, the American version of the magazine was not a straightforward translation of the European original and was in many respects a poor relation. A co-owner of the journal himself, Moebius did nothing to hide the differences between the French and American *HM*:

> Our model was the American underground press. But we didn't realize that it would take a radically different direction there, because of the differences between the audiences. In the United States it remained marginal, and bogged down into a sterile situation, while in France, it rejoined an old literary tradition, which is simply that the avant-garde explores a new territory and once that territory is open, everyone heads in that direction.... Listen, as an artist and a critic, I find *Heavy Metal* idiotic. It's a hodgepodge. There are no lines in the magazine. It's really an absurd catalog, with no coherence whatsoever, of all sorts of tendencies. One can criticize them for that.[19]

Nonetheless, it was Moebius who was invited to craft a Silver Surfer graphic novel for Marvel (in 1987), implicitly to compete with Moore's work for DC. Simultaneously, Marvel translated, had colored, and reprinted several of his major works as new graphic novels. They were less accessible than Moore's work, which always has narrative force, whereas Moebius's mix visual styles and have a more absurdist, science-fiction-meets-surrealism imagination. And when in 1993 Robert Crumb moved to live in France, there was no greater confirmation that France was the land of the future, and the richest past. It did not matter that this was a complete oversimplification of how influential the earlier U.S. comix underground had been on changing French production itself (as pointed out by Moebius above) and pushing it in new, more serious directions, let alone how a decade earlier in the 1950s it was Harvey Kurtzman's *Mad* that had influenced René Goscinny before he created *Astérix*.

To summarize, what is important to realize here is that an injection of cosmopolitanism was part of the graphic novel's rising fortunes and its public media persona. Spiegelman working with Mouly provided a bridge to European comics, while Moore had developed his unique angle on U.S. comics from his own vantage point of coming out of the UK "arts lab" and sci-fi/alternative comics tradition. These interventions also meant that existing domestic traditions started to look more permeable and less fixed, with figures such as Moore and Moebius clearly being influenced by both comics and comix and not one more than the other. In other words, the space for creation was being enlarged and its content put in greater flux because the outsiders did not know unwritten but significant rules of the game, or did not feel any special loyalty or rational reason to continue to play by those rules. As outsiders they also looked more like freewheeling international writers or fine artists than commercially hired "production line" employees, an image sometimes put to the test in the reality of the economics of publishing houses and media organizations. (*En passant*, the third creator associated with the "big three," Frank Miller, is equally cosmopolitan. Japanese action-adventure comics and films are an inspiration for him.) All these influences started appearing roughly at the same time and were discussed publicly alongside the new graphic novels. As such the graphic novel became associated with a greater cultural openness than comics, and it was through dialogue with outside, sometimes prestigious partners that the graphic novel enhanced its institutionalization. As a corollary, nonwhite American creators also saw a greater space developing for their contributions. Writing in *Your*

Brain on Latino Comics, Frederick Luis Aldama suggests that it was the cultural turmoil inspired by the 1980s' rise of graphic novels that shook things up enough to start to expand and diversify the types of narrators and artists being published. Aldama writes:

> [W]ith these twists and turns in the storytelling form in the '80s and '90s, the opening up of the readerly canons, and the pounding on publisher's doors by the author-artists themselves, a path began to clear for the creation and production of Latino comic books and comic strips.... great strides have been made.[20]

A growing sense of independence: from the 1990s to the contemporary period

Immediately after 1986–1987, some more titles were translated from French, and there were hit series such as Neil Gaiman's *Sandman*, but there was not a further burst of activity that matched the initially huge expectations for and interest in graphic novels. For a while the medium followed a series of different – at times, seemingly quite different – and even contradictory directions. As noted above, DC pushed trade paperbacks and did well with the uncanny tales and original artwork in the Vertigo imprint. It is widely agreed that *Watchmen* and *The Dark Knight* also inspired many violent and unsophisticated superhero revisions. Moore and Bolland's *Batman: The Killing Joke* particularly pushed readers beyond their comfort zone, with its inclusion of quite miserable scenes of torture in the Batman story world. Meanwhile Moore also worked on new, more serious material, and with DC's publication of *V for Vendetta* and Knockabout's publication of *From Hell*, he was established firmly as a significant writer and not just a writer of comics. In contrast, Spiegelman and Mouly developed a "*RAW* One-Shot" imprint that tended toward avant-garde adaptations from recent well-regarded literary fiction (see also Chapter 8). *RAW* itself ceased publication in 1992. Nevertheless, further new and significant works were printed in the 1990s, including titles such as Jason Lutes's *Jar of Fools* (1994), John Wagner and Vincent

Locke's *A History of Violence* (1997), Max Allan Collins and Richard Piers Rayner's *Road to Perdition* (1994), and the surreal horror anthology series *Taboo*, which arguably attempted to make a better quality *Heavy Metal*. Also, there were some serious political-historical works, notably Joyce Brabner's *Real War Stories* magazines and her work on the collaboration *Brought to Light* (1988), which was critical of American foreign policy. The success of Joe Sacco was also a very important highlight for this period. Although his work is quite different from either Moore's or Spiegelman's, he provided another new and distinct voice and vision for the 1990s and has continued to publish major works ever since.

During this time, production may have been patchy, but it was important, because unlike on other occasions in the past, the graphic novel did not mutate back into the world of comics or comix. Instead, there was enough original production for it to remain a unique literary-artistic format. In fact, quite a lot of titles that were to become well received and reprinted in the 2000s were first published in the 1990s, including the aforementioned work from Lutes and also titles from Ben Katchor and, of course, Daniel Clowes. Moreover, "graphic novel" became common usage and remains the catchall label for inventive, serious graphic narratives published in paperback or hardback book formats. As Chris Ware noted in an interview published in 1997, contemporary work looked quite sharply different from comix. He stated:

> I read in an interview with Crumb where he stated that he couldn't create anything that wasn't funny. I think there are a lot of younger artists who are perfectly willing to do something that's entirely not funny at all. There seems to be a new generation creating a more "mature" form of literature. At least that's what I'm trying to create.[21]

Compared to the 1990s, graphic novel production in the 2000s has expanded and is more diverse than ever before. This is easily measured when, for example, one returns to Roger Sabin's *Adult Comics*, written and first published in 1993, more or less still during the initial breakthrough period. In that work Sabin could review graphic novels by highlighting the then-most significant figures who were producing work: Will Eisner, Dave Sim, Bryan Talbot, Raymond Briggs, Art Spiegelman, Howard Chaykin, Frank Miller, and Alan Moore. Today one is no longer in a position to adopt an individual-by-individual perspective. Of course, several of these figures remain at work and have continued to make important and prize-winning works. What Sabin could not anticipate was how so many new and different creators would publish works that have achieved significant public recognition. Nor could he foresee how the graphic novel would benefit from interactions with the literary community (see Chapter 8) or that the trade paperback, and especially series of it, would become so central to DC and Marvel comics.

That is not to say that a new and changing star system among the most popular or critically acclaimed creators has not continued and evolved. Any updated list of graphic novelists would now need to include Chris Ware, Daniel Clowes, and Alison Bechdel, as well as the most successful new European imports, Neil Gaiman and Marjane Satrapi. What has changed in that elite talent pool is that the BD-in-translation breakthrough has borne significant fruit (Satrapi and also David B. and Joann Sfar). However, this has been primarily through works from the avant-garde L'Association and not the mainstream publishing houses. Also, the graphic novel has proven more open to women writers and artists, and the importance and influence of Bechdel and Satrapi is a very significant development since 1987. In the early to mid-1990s, graphic novels were sometimes identified simply as comics created by better writers. In contrast, grosso modo, today's contemporary graphic novel is more associated with visual sophistication. The text-image balance makes up much of Part II's discussion of form. For now, it is sufficient to note that the renewed success of graphic novels in the 2000s has oriented around works where narrative and page design have combined powerfully and in innovative ways. Chris Ware's work here is exemplary, and it invites a visual reading as much as a traditional literary one. That is one movement in a new direction away from the 1980s: Spiegelman, Miller, Moore, and Gibbons were highly sophisticated in making their art cohere and serve narrative, whereas Ware seems to take the graphic novel in the alternative direction.

In addition, the theme of international politics/reportage/autobiography has been very strong. When introducing *In the Shadow of No Towers*, Spiegelman described his experiences of being caught up in the 9/11 attack on New York in a very compelling passage:

> I tend to be easily unhinged.... Before 9/11 my traumas were all more or less self-inflicted, but out-running the toxic cloud that had moments before been the North Tower of the World Trade Center left me reeling on that fault-line where World History and Personal History collide – the intersections my parents, Auschwitz survivors, had warned me about when they taught me to always keep my bags packed.[22]

Though not of course accounting for all graphic novels, the phrase "that fault line where World History and Personal History collide" is a telling summary of much current production. As Hillary Chute also perceptively noted, graphic novels have made significant interventions when they are works of reportage, historical reflection, or personal testimony. She writes:

> For instance, three of today's most acclaimed cartoonists, Spiegelman, Joe Sacco, and Marjane Satrapi, work in the nonfiction mode: Spiegelman on World War II and 9/11, Sacco on Palestine and Bosnia, Satrapi on Iran's Islamic Revolution and war with Iraq. This is not a coincidence. We may think of graphic narrative, in the innate, necessary formalism of its narrative procedure – in its experimentation with the artificial strictures of the comics form – as calling our attention to what Shoshana Felman and Dori Laub call "textualization of the context": "the empirical content needs not just to be known, but to be read ... the basic and legitimate demand for contextualization of the text itself needs to be complemented, simultaneously, by the less familiar and yet necessary work of textualization of the context" (xv). Graphic narrative accomplishes this work with its manifest handling of its own artifice, its attention to its seams. Its formal grammar rejects transparency and renders textualization conspicuous, inscribing the context in its graphic presentation.[23]

What Chute is suggesting here is that it is no coincidence that the personal and historical are terrain for graphic novelists. The page layouts and frames that are a part of the form provide multiple spaces for dialogues to develop between individual narration and its context; or, to put it more crudely, graphic novelists can pull close together in nearby images their own feelings, and situate them quickly next to broader sociological/political/historical themes. Novelists can do this but not in such a straightforward, clear, symbolic, and literal manner.

And this format of blending autobiography and history/reportage has seen many major contributions in the past decade. In particular there have been numerous works that have attempted to take stock of the international world politics of the 2000s by treating the topic through small and personalized stories. This is seen in works from creators in the United States but also notably in translations from graphic novelists based in the Middle East and North Africa. Besides the noted contribution from Sacco and Satrapi, one should also acknowledge strong works from Rutu Modan, Ali Folman, and Magdy El Shafee and Lamia Ziadé. Titles from each of these creators have combined eyewitness reportage with family history. They are achieved in quite different styles but share a sense of authenticity and place.

Moreover, post 9/11, it is understandable that stories and visualizations of experiencing violence and sudden terror should grab our attention. In some small way, in the television, Internet, and multimedia age, we are all able to witness terrible and violent events previously only read about or discussed by political elites. On the one hand, this is democracy, while on the other hand, much of what is witnessed is truly terrifying and depressing. The re-mediatizing and re-presenting of these kinds of experience into graphic novels is a most effective way of thinking through and considering what has occurred. The directness of drawn images and small, localized narratives – what graphic novels are good at – is a powerful combination that breaks down seemingly unfathomable and complex political catastrophes into a more manageable and human form. While literary fiction sometimes tries to do this kind of work, that has not always been fashionable. Moreover, the combination of visual and textual representations provides space of sensitivity and also direct-ness that can appear clichéd in the novel and especially in film. It is also the case that the personal-historical faultline that Spiegelman discussed feels more accurate and honest, given that standard media reporting is sometimes banal and may reflect snap assumptions that are politically colored. It is not too far-fetched to note that mass media or television strategies to "embed" journalists in conflicts or sites of political revolu-tion are in some ways a commercial mimicking of the tropes we are dis-cussing in the graphic novel. What is different is that the embedded are themselves edited by other television employees, while graphic novelists can self-publish or be supported by creative publishing houses.

It has been quite common to explain the success of this material, as well as other intimate-themed work, around the concept that graphic novels slow down time and make readers approach the page as a single picture, a space to meditate on the gaps between the images and heart-wrenching stories. However, it could also be precisely the opposite. Graphic novels can be read rather fast, the eye pushing to understand the plot from the pictures while quickly comprehending the text. This higher speed of reading is arguably helpful for responding to emotional material; it means one engages with the creator's imaginary story world quite directly and strongly to get meaning, but one does not slow or suf-fer from sensing any cliché or overly emotional kitsch.

Adding further to Spiegelman and Chute's correct claim that graphic novels can provide stories and images from where history and the per-sonal collide, we state that this process is shared in many different socie-ties, offering uniquely individual and culturally specific interpretations, many of which are being translated into English. At times a risk is that the material does not create much of a significant dialogue between the differ-ent perspectives that are narrated in the various titles. Autobiographical works have yet to develop into a more community- or group-based form of discussion, although Spiegelman has been at the forefront of shared creation, not only editing *RAW* but also coediting a collected narrative from some sixty-nine artists, *The Narrative Corpse*. Nonetheless, the cur-rent of work has been productive and proportionately diverse. There is a quite high proportion of women graphic novelists who are making their voices heard in this format. That there is no shared visual style to support some of the common narratological underpinnings of autobiographical reportage is, for us, also a sign of confidence and positive diversity.

It seems that gender-balanced social history from below is a significant territory for the graphic novel. As we will discuss later, this may be so because of the graphic novel's formal properties: drawing suggests authenticity and intimacy, while narrative opens to what some may label old-fashioned devices such as character and place. We also should note that genre works have been major players in the field. Horror titles have made a powerful return to the scene. Yet these works are also coded reflections on the political anxieties of the present. Titles such as *The Walking Dead* are successful not because of their old-fashioned horror violence but because of their careful metaphorical replaying of scenarios of sudden terror (scenarios seemingly reflecting 9/11, other terror attacks, or national environmental disasters). They provide a political discussion too, but this is muted and left as a fictional experiment. The fun provided by old-style horror such as *Hellboy* is, of course, another site of reassurance. When old stories are appropriated and remade, the reader is comforted.

Finally, there has also been some distinct differentiation between graphic novels as films and comics as films. Whereas major film studios have created hugely profitable franchises from superhero comics characters, more independent filmmakers have made works based on graphic novels. Daniel Clowes and Terry Zwigoff's reinterpretation of *Ghost World* (2001) was a significant example, and it was followed by another Clowes-inspired film, the comedy *Art School Confidential* (2006). *American Splendor* (2003, directed by Shari Springer Berman) offered a similar offbeat, quirky interpretation of modern America and included clever aesthetics that evoked its autobiographical and comix-graphic novel origins. Animations have not been popular at all, but this assisted, paradoxically, the success of the French-produced *Persepolis* (2007, directed by Satrapi and Vincent Paronnaud), which gained acclaim as a work of cinema because of its originality. Joann Sfar's biopic *Gainsbourg* (2010) is another fascinating work; it does not use animation directly, but rather creates a story world where comiclike masks reveal how characters perceive themselves and how other people view them. In short, the relationship between cinema and graphic novels is distinctive from the role and impact of superhero works. Of course, as ever in our approach, the borderlines are never clear-cut: Miller's and Moore's famous works from the late 1980s inspired many later superhero franchises. Industrial and legal issues are also paramount. Independent graphic novelists can play some part in how their creativity is adapted on screen. DC and Marvel sit inside publishing, media, and filmmaking conglomerates that own and push strategically viable titles. Warner Bros owns DC, while Marvel Entertainment/Walt Disney is the parent company to Marvel Comics.

Conclusion

The public acclaim given to three graphic novels in the late 1980s was a culmination of many years of comics being taken more and more seriously by adult readers. These three graphic novels also marked the fruition of works from earlier in that decade, including *RAW* and *Heavy Metal*, and cult titles, such as *American Splendor* and *Love and Rockets*, as well as long-forgotten Marvel graphic novels. Cultural change was also encouraged by the presence of influential outside voices, perspectives coming to graphic narratives from outside the U.S. tradition from Britain, France, and Japan. It is also worth underlining that the basic wager of a title like *Maus* – to tell a serious life story in a serious mode, through texts and images – set up a model repeated in significant future productions, including, of course, autobiography and journalism-reportage titles. The many examples of recent "crisis" comics and Spiegelman's own *In the Shadow of No Towers* confirm the current vibrancy of that trajectory.

Three themes are useful to further highlight as we conclude Part I:

1. Graphic narratives, whether being accused of stimulating juvenile delinquency (1950s) or being presented as insights on international

politics (post 9/11), consistently are viewed as a significant and somehow potentially special or unique mode of communication that is important for American society. This means that understanding some of the basic functions of how they work to communicate their message is an important task, and that is the theme we turn to in Part II.

2. For reasons of space we have only occasionally related how adult comics developed in relationships to other media; however, this is an important and recurring theme (note the role of the *Batman* television series, Pop Art, and film adaptions such as *Alien*, as well as the links between music communities and the alternative press scene).

3. Adult comics and graphic novels are a form that are especially capable of making meta-commentary and reflexive references to existing titles, creators, and even whole genres. Not only can stories resemble other stories and refer to historical and biographical material, but the very images and page layouts, lines, and structures can also innovate or refer back to older styles. Arguably, much current production blends and plays with older traditions, often explicitly weaving different strands together to form complex but rewarding new meta-texts. As noted above, this is quite a common tactic for contemporary horror genre works, where much of the reader's pleasure is derived from understanding the pastiches at work. In other cases it has been an explicit commercial gambit, with DC and Marvel both producing collections where they opened their franchised superheroes to be recrafted and reinvented by artists working in more underground-comix style. This propensity has its dangers, potentially making works readable only to those familiar with the codes, but it has also helped sustain the production of graphic novels for nearly the last thirty years.

PART TWO

FORMS

5 Understanding Panel and Page Layouts

What are the basic formal aspects of the graphic novel, and how do we suggest one can read them for critical purposes? Rather than answering these questions by listing the features that we consider essential, we offer here and in the subsequent chapter some reflections on three fields of interest that are a necessary and an inevitable part of any graphic novel: the organization of the drawings in multipanel pages, issues of word-image combination, and questions of style. These three chosen areas have the advantage of being connected in one way or another to the narrative dimension of the graphic novel that is always, even in its nonmainstream forms, a crucial aspect of any work.

Any productive discussion of the medium can begin with understanding one of its vital and most fascinating properties: panel and page layout. As we explain below, this aspect has received extensive critical attention from scholars working on American and European comics and graphic novels, with Benoît Peeters, Thierry Groensteen, and Charles Hatfield making important contributions.[1] Here we present their approaches and discuss them with reference to notable examples such as Art Spiegelman's *In the Shadow of No Towers* and Alison Bechdel's *Fun Home.* Gradually we will move to offer a synthetic conception drawing on the existing theorizations that is weighted to neither privilege production nor reader reception.

Page and panel composition

As we all know, every picture tells a story, and there does exist something as simple as a single-frame narrative, not only in narrative painting or narrative photography,[2] but also in cartooning. *Dennis the Menace* is a good example of little stories told in just one captioned panel. However, the kind of narratives that we will discuss here are multiframe narratives; a graphic novel is basically conceived of as a story told by a multiplicity of panels, even if this *a priori* does not entail that a panel must contain more than one image. Many graphic novels that do not question the formal structures of the medium fundamentally do include pages or even double pages with no more than one drawing, as happens, for instance, in Bechdel's *Fun Home* at the moment of the postmortem discovery of Bechdel's father's "illicit photographs" (pp. 100–101). There the usual grid form page layout is interrupted, and what pops up is a double spread made of one panel covering all the available space, including the margins of the book. Other graphic novelists make a more systematic use of this technique, such as Frank Miller in *300* or the avant-garde graphic novelist Martin Vaughn-James in *The Cage*. And let's not forget that several of the historical forerunners of the contemporary graphic novel used this system as a kind of default option: we find it in the wordless woodcut novel, as well as in the first weekly plates of Outcault's *Hogan's Alley* (featuring the Yellow Kid) and the engraving series by William Hogarth such as *A Harlot's Progress* (1732), often mentioned in surveys of the medium. All these examples are not single-frame narratives but rather multiple-frame narratives presenting single-frame segments, which is, of course, something completely different.

How then are the panels of a graphic novel organized? In general, and regardless of any detailed discussion of their context (see below), one can argue that this organization includes and combines three levels or layers:

- the strip or tier, which can be organized in different ways (horizontally, vertically, or a combination of both);
- the page, which can have a wide variety of sizes and formats (it can be the last page of a newspaper, as in the Sunday comics supplement, but it can also be the page of a small comic book or the A4 page of a BD magazine); and
- the book (the book not just as a compilation of pages but as a three-dimensional object, including aspects such as its dust jacket and spine), and here also size and format can diverge widely, from the small pocket book format of Frans Masereel's wordless graphic novels to the giant format of Spiegelman's *In the Shadow of No Towers*, a book whose pages are as thick as the coverboards of a hardback.

Two special cases have to be added:

- first, web comics and digital graphic novels, and
- second, the insertion of graphic novel-inspired drawings in "beyond the book" installations, where the graphic novel itself becomes part of a different artistic practice closer to public architecture or installation art (these are a dimension that we will not deal with in any detail in this study[3])

These basic distinctions coincide partially with the distinctions among newspaper narratives, weeklies and magazines, and books. They may even suggest an historical evolution, from tier to page to book, although this is more doubtful; even in the nineteenth century, Rodolphe Töpffer issued his work in the form of the book.

Why is the description in terms of strip/page/book then not sufficient? Two reasons come to mind. The first has to do with the fact that the contact between the frames can, at each of the three levels distinguished above, be just sequential (one reads first this and then that, even if the order between these two panels is not necessarily chronological[4]) or more like a single picture than a sequence (as the many "checkerboard" pages of *Watchmen* make immediately clear: the rows and panels of these pages are meant to be read both one next to another and all at once, in order to highlight the underlying grid). Sequential organization is necessary, given the basic need of putting images next to one another in order to keep the story going. Nonsequential reading is inevitable, given the impossibility for the human eye to separate the panel from the page. In other words, the sequential structure of the images is made more complex by a second type of organization, which some scholars call "tabular" (Fresnault-Deruelle),[5] but which can be called perhaps more cautiously "translinear" (Thierry Groensteen, who has most convincingly written to establish the importance of this dimension, uses the metaphor of "braiding"). At the level of the page, the reader notices that there is in the checkerboard pages of *Watchmen* (and many other examples we will analyze later) a more generalized use of these tabular/translinear elements. We notice, for instance, an attempt to achieve a certain kind of chromatic balance or a certain kind of alternation of action and stasis. These elements are not incompatible at all with sequentiality; rather they are intermingled with it, and both enrich each other.

There is, however, a second reason, on top of the inherent tension between linear and nonlinear uses of the frame organization, to try to exceed the initial triad of strip/page/book. This reason has to do with the fact that the relationship between image and "level" (strip/page/book) is never fixed and definitive. First of all, most graphic novels are not published in one single format but instead have an editorial trajectory that engenders shifting relationships between the unit (the image or the panel) and the whole (strip/page/book). In many cases, graphic novels are serialized before they are printed in book form, if they ever are (and with Porter Abbott,[6] we have to admit that certain stories have no endings, since they can continue eternally, at least long as there is a public that is interested in them; for instance, Frank King's soap opera strip *Gasoline Alley* has continued for numerous decades). Many authors – Hergé is a good example, and Chris Ware no less so – develop all kinds of strategies to make their work function at various levels (that is, in various editorial contexts such as installments as well as books). Second, the publication business of the graphic novel is such that between two editions, formats can change quite dramatically. A simple example of this is the reprint in one volume of the original four books of Marjane Satrapi's *Persepolis*: the reading of the translinear effects is inevitably different because the page length is different (far longer in the single edition). And the same applies to, for instance, reissues in pocket book form that alter, and often destroy, the original page layout. But even if the modern publisher tries to respect as much as possible the original layout, the results are not always successful. Take, for instance, the book version of Milton Caniff's *Terry and the Pirates*. This adventure strip from the 1940s, which can be read as a primitive form of graphic novel, was not supposed to be reprinted in book format; it was meant in the first place to be an exciting installment narrative, and therefore Caniff repeatedly employed cliffhangers at the opening of each new daily strip. The book version publication makes this device appear odd and tiresomely repetitive. Here, it is harmful to the immersive reading experience of the new reader.

Much more than the novel, here then is the graphic novel differential. Marjorie Perloff describes the migration of literary works in the multimedia environment of cyberculture: "[Differential texts are] texts that exist in different material forms, with no single version being the definitive one."[7] Novels and graphic novels, as well as films, games, oral histories, and so on, merge increasingly in one global novelistic continuum – a subfield of the all-encompassing field of narrative. Differentialization of the graphic novel can be easily observed and, as we suggested above, has been a long-standing feature in a field where relationships between image and page have been subject to variation because of differing and multiple publication venues.

Some fundamental taxonomies

Following Fresnault-Deruelle's pioneering discussion of linearity versus tabularity, there have been many attempts to further describe the relationships between image and strip/page/book. Here we first present and discuss the two most important "formal" descriptions, the one given by Benoît Peeters in "Four Conceptions of the Page"[8] and the one given by Thierry Groensteen in his book *System of Comics*, which we illustrate with North American examples, since most works studied by these authors are European. Then we compare this still rather formal reading method with the more reader-oriented vision advocated by Charles Hatfield in *Alternative Comics: An Emerging Literature*. Finally we propose an integrated approach in order to give a more complete analysis of the dialectic relationship between the image and the "rest."

In "Four Conceptions of the Page," probably the most important theoretical contribution to the discussion on page layout in comics and graphic novels, Benoît Peeters rejects any purely formalist analysis of the division of the page, articulating a taxonomy based on the various relationships between two basic elements: narrative (the graphic novel as storytelling device) and composition (the graphic novel as a device for the production of images, visual patterns, and spatial forms). For Peeters, either form can be dominant (at the automatic expense of the other: the more we follow the story, the less we notice the visual components of the panels and vice versa), and the connection between narrative and composition can be either autonomous (in that case, there is no direct interaction between both dimensions) or interdependent (in that case, both dimensions will influence each other). Thanks to these elementary principles, Peeters can then distinguish between four modes of panel utilization:

	Narrative/ Composition: Autonomy	Narrative/ Composition: Interdependence
Narrative: dominant	*Conventional use*	*Rhetorical use*
Composition: dominant	*Decorative use*	*Productive use*

But what is meant by these modes, which have the double advantage of being both very simple (and the simpler a system and its components, the more elegant and user-friendly it is) and universal (in principle all possible kinds of panels and page utilizations fall into one of these four modes)? The *conventional* mode (which may also be called the "regular" mode) is based upon the systematic repetition of the same structure and form of tiers and panels, independent of any content, style, or author; the same panel or the same tier is repeated over and over again, tier after tier, page after page, book after book. This system has no visual or pictorial ambition; storytelling is the dominating mode, and since the grid (for all conventional types are variations on this figure) always preexists any possible content, the relationship between the two dimensions is one of independence. In such a conventional mode, the panels are not necessarily always the same (for instance, a tier may be composed of one larger and three smaller panels), but what counts is the fact that the tier structure (in the newspaper strips) or the page structure (in Sunday strips, magazines, albums, and books when the basic unit is no longer the tier but the page) remains always the same. Examples of this are numerous: most pages of *Watchmen*, various short stories of Adrian Tomine's *Sleepwalk*, and most pages in abstract comics often have a strong preference for the gridlike character of this layout type. As Peeters observes, it would be a mistake to believe that this model is typically "primitive," in the two senses of the words. First, it does not belong exclusively to the early years of comics, but is used in all periods of the medium (the graphic novel, for instance, proves extremely sympathetic to this form). Second, regularity does not mean lack of sophistication, as is well known by all readers of *Watchmen*, which sticks closely to this model. An appealing example is also given by Simon Grennan's adaptation of Anthony Trollope's *John Caldigate* (1879), a work-in-progress that is to be published on the occasion of the 2015 Trollope bicentenary. Aiming at drawing the reader into an experience of the nineteenth century, the graphic novelist has adopted a number of narrative rules that cleverly match his decision to adopt a conventional page layout, with a simple grid composed of three identical tiers, each of them aligning two identical images. What may seem at first sight a rather uneventful decision becomes dramatically meaningful and efficient once linked with the key narrative rules of the book, which show only a very limited range of distances between viewer and scene, while only representing whole actions, not divisions of actions, and following throughout the whole adaptation a waltzlike rhythm in its narrative kernels. Thus the narrative motivation of the elementary grid appears very powerful. The recurring six-image page layout helps install a three-time rhythm. It enhances the representation of a whole action (each sequence of six panels coincides with a separate part of the overall story). This perfect match of page structure and repetition of distance between reader and character makes it possible for the former to become part of the represented world of the latter, reinforcing the readerly involvement in the story world. The reader of this graphic novel adaptation feels that there is "room" for him or for her in the development of the story (the reader can become a kind of silently present witness), and he or she also realizes that there is time to find his or her place in this world (the repetition of a number of narrative and visual features guarantees that the reader, during the act of reading, is really invited to join the fictional universe of the characters). (See Illustration 5.a.)

The second mode, the *decorative* use of the page, emphasizes the visual properties of the layout, independent of any given content. The artist creates first a new and idiosyncratic page organization that is then filled in with content. The narrator is in the first place someone who treats the page as a painterly canvas, and the ideal decorative use of the panel structure implies the desire to modify the visual composition in each new page. Well-known examples of this include *The Plot Thickens* (1980) by Bill Griffith, in which each new row shrinks (vertically) while adding a supplementary panel. Just as with the conventional mode, decorative panel structures can be found in all periods; comics historians will not hesitate in reminding us of the decorative use of the page in Outcault's *Hogan's Alley*, the forerunner of what is considered the first newspaper strip with a real impact on the field, *The Yellow Kid*. It should, however, not come as a surprise that this is certainly *not* the most frequently used format in the graphic novel, given precisely the dominant position of narrative in this form of drawn literature (when the graphic novel experiments with forms of abstraction when treating

Opposite page: 5.a. A match of three-time rhythm and six-panel grid: sample page from Simon Grennan's adaptation of A. Trollope's novel *John Caldigate*, to be published with Jonathan Cape in 2015. Used by kind permission of the artist.

narrative content and related issues, as we study in Chapter 6, the situation changes dramatically).

The third mode, the *rhetorical* use of the panel/page structure, is the most widespread. As Peeters notes: "The panel and the page are no longer autonomous elements; they are subordinated to a narrative which their primary function is to serve. The size of the images, their distribution, the general pace of the page, all must come to support the narration." Here, it is the narrative that preexists and that informs, selects, and shapes the panel and page structure that helps best convey the narrative meaning of the work. Examples are numerous. Thus, one can turn to Julie Doucet's *My New York Diary*, where the small departures from the underlying grid system give a maximal impact to the variations in panel size, or Art Spiegelman's *Maus*, where a comparable mechanism of small but meaningful variations on a basic pattern is followed throughout the whole work.

As equally observed by Peeters, the rhetorical use of page layout does not concern only the size and form of the panels. No less important is the place of the panels on the page, or even on the double page (in the case of a cliffhanger, for instance, a traditional, if not overused, aspect of multipage visual storytelling is the difference between left and right, which is crucial: certain effects can be destroyed if the cliffhanger is placed at the bottom right of the left page). This importance of place, which is a compositional element, indicates how relative the dominant position of the narrative always remains, even in works where storytelling is definitely the leading dimension. We might add briefly that for students working on graphic novels, this approach – and the thinking that lies behind it – represents almost a natural way into achieving a critical reading. This is because it allows one to write about content and form and to map a relationship between the two. For example, although going beyond page layouts as a formal issue, this is essentially the way that one of us explored the work Yvan Alagbé in a recent essay for *Yale French Studies*.[9] Of course, that is not to say that all graphic novels are open to this approach, but it is a very good starting point since it connects narrative with form.

The fourth and last mode, the *productive* use of panel structure and page layout, is not only dominant (as in the decorative mode), but it even produces the story itself. As Peeters suggests: "[I]t is the organization of the page which seems to dictate the narrative. A particular arrangement generates a piece of narration." It is, in other words, as if the form of the page structure helped the author invent a story that appears to be the consequence of a preexistent formal structure. Since this type may be less familiar to the reader, we will not just quote some examples but also give a brief analysis of a famous occurrence, namely the cover of *In the Shadow of No Towers*. (See Illustration 5.b.)

An illustrated cover normally includes two elements: an image (which can be full page) and a certain number of written or printed para-textual units, most often horizontally reproduced (the paratext, as later examples will specify in more detail, refers to the written and visual elements that present and accompany a work on the cover of a book and its first and last pages). Spiegelman does not break these rules, he transforms them, first by reducing the image to a gigantic but barely visible black on black image (the two towers are more haptically than optically present: they become palpable through the partial plastification of the cover, which leaves the background unplastified), and second by not compensating the quasi-absence of the image in this unusually large book with the help of a more prominently visible paratext (the title of the book and the name of the author, both in white, are dwarfed by the rest of the page). The great tension between black and white, great and small, vertical and horizontal, constructs a third element, the central box with color in the upper center of the page. This element has a typically intermedial status, for it combines elements of image and text: the former determines its iconic content, while the latter suggests that the sequencing of the small characters can be the structural equivalent of the letters of a word, or the words of a sentence. Whatever the interpretation of this intermediate solution may be (image or text), it is for many obvious reasons the central element of the composition, and it is on this fragment that analysis must concentrate.[10]

The horizontal presentation of the color image, stressed by its frame as well as by the sequencing of its components, is a layout element that can be endowed with a productive meaning, in the sense of Benoît Peeters, for it brings to life an alternative vision of the basic iconic

5.b. Spiegelman's cover is one example of the "productive" page: an aesthetic that creates narration. Book cover, copyright © 2004 by Pantheon Books, an imprint of the Knopf Doubleday Publishing Group, a division of Random House LLC; from *In The Shadow of No Towers* by Art Spiegelman. Used by permission of Pantheon Books, an imprint of the Knopf Doubleday Publishing Group, a division of Random House LLC. All rights reserved.

5.b. *(continued)*

figure behind the whole scene. First, the clash between extremes (black and white, horizontal and vertical, reality and representation) engenders a leap into what may appear the absolute opposite of the 9/11 attacks: no facts, but fiction, and no Great Tragedy, but "low" pop culture fun and entertainment in full color. Second, the reduced scale of the image helps bring about the creative tension between small and great: the little space that is available is not taken by one big figure, but by a string of minuscule comics characters, who are then seemingly blown away into outer space. Third, the idea of collapsing, of tumbling down, generates the opposite vision of falling down, as a kind of horizontal translation: the parade of comics characters that is blasted away by the donkey on the left (a sardonic hybridization of the Democrat donkey, the symbol of one of the two leading parties in the United States, and an Arab-looking figure that stands for Osama Bin Laden[11]) does not fall downwards, but laterally. Fourth, instead of having one person falling (and how not to be reminded of the tragic icon of the fallen angel/falling man that has been used and reused countless times after 9/11?), Spiegelman's image displays a procession or parade in which each character represents one of the successive moments of one continuous movement; the effect of such a treatment tends to minimize the impact of the fall, since there is no character who really falls from the beginning till the end – an attenuation of the tragic events that the book will link partly to the healing aspects of the medium itself, namely the newspaper cartoons that constituted, if not created, a feeling of permanence and continuity in the wake of the terror attack.[12] Finally, the manipulation of the cover elements appears

also as an announcement of the material transformation that the inside
of the book will reveal to us: in order to read the second part of the book,
we will have to turn it, not upside down, but 90 degrees, and this "revolution" (in the etymological sense of the word) is the logical marker of
a world in which the difference between horizontality and verticality,
between walking and falling, is no longer assured. In all these ways the
layout of the cover encourages the reader to read the work through its
visual properties, the aesthetics taking on a narrative power.

Another example of productive page layout is given by *Nogegon*,[13]
the dystopian reflection on the perfect universe by François and Luc
Schuiten, the former the usual partner of writer Benoît Peeters,[14] the latter an eco-critical architect and occasional graphic novelist himself. The
word "Nogegon" is a palindrome, meaning that it can be read backwards
as well as forwards, and as such it is the perfect symbol of the planet
and the political system to which it refers: a world totally dominated
by the symmetry principle, with no room whatsoever for what disrupts
that kind of preestablished harmony (Illustrations 5.c and 5.d). *Nogegon*
is the story of someone who rebels against that rule, preferring surprise
and creativity to the cold and sterile beauty of absolute duplication. The
productive page layout of the book is in (instable) harmony with the
law of the universe that it foregrounds. Thus, each page is mirrored by
another symmetrical page, and the same applies to the drawings within
the frames. Since the layout is not decorative but productive, the content
of the book – that is, the actions, positions, attitudes, and gestures of the
characters as well as the visual characteristics of setting and backdrop –
are elaborated in such a way that they follow the general rule of symmetrical reflection: if, for instance, on a given page we find a character
descending a staircase, we will see the same character reappear on the
symmetrical page going up a similar staircase, and so on. However, the
repetition is never complete or mechanical, and it is in the small gaps
and mismatches between the repeated panels and pages that Luc and
François Schuiten suggest a visual equivalent of what happens at story
level, where the heroine of *Nogegon* decides one day to no longer embrace
the official ideal of the beautiful yet frightening symmetrical life.

The productive use is not the monopoly of avant-garde artists, although it cannot be denied that this mode seems to have, contrary to the rhetorical mode that dominates in classic visual storytelling, some family resemblance with a kind of storytelling that aims at questioning the stuck and uneventful domination of narrative and opening new ways of working with medium-specificity. Despite that, the productive use remains quite rare, at least in works that succeed in finding their way to a larger audience. The history of comics is strewn with examples of artists having used the medium in a tremendously productive way, without managing to survive in the market,[15] and to a certain extent the same might be true of the graphic novel, where examples of productive page layouts remain relatively rare – or rarely noticed – perhaps due to the concentration of this kind of layout in more avant-garde work such as Art Spiegelman's *Breakdowns* (see, for instance, the short story "A Day at the Races").

Peeters's article, first published in French in 1983 (the moment when comics theory had trouble in finding a second wind, after the first attempts to found a semiotically and very formally inspired scholarly theory of comics), gradually has become one of the most influential and important in the field. The author, who had always stressed the necessity of using his system in an open and nondoctrinarian way, has updated and nuanced it in many ways (it is the latest version that is now available in English), and it may be useful to remember some of Peeters's own caveats. First, it should be noted that the four categories are not always mutually exclusive: if, in most cases, it is clear whether a certain panel structure belongs to one of the four modes, in other cases, it is perfectly possible that it obeys or illustrates more than just one. A good example is *Watchmen*, more specifically the famous chapter V ("Fearful Symmetries"), which ought to be read in at least two perspectives. On the one hand, Gibbons and Moore stretch to its limits the classic conventional or regular use of the page; on the other hand, this chapter, which is based on the multiplication of mirror effects made possible by the checkerboard use of the 3 x 3 basic grid of the page as well as by the mirror effects between the left and right page (and, at an even larger level, between the various pages of the chapter), is also an example of the

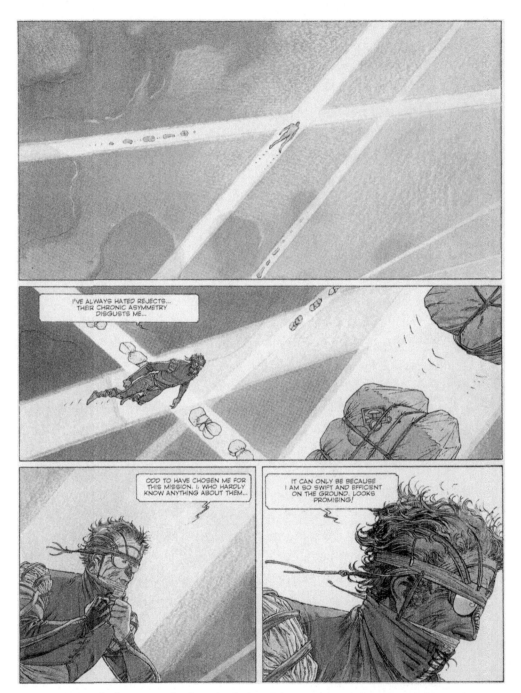

5.c and 5.d. An example of visual palindrome: the opening and closing pages of Luc and François Schuiten, *Nogegon* (London: Humanoïdes Publ., 2001; original French publication 1990). Used by kind permission of the artists.

5.c and 5.d. (*continued*)

productive use of panel division and page organization, since in many cases the narrative content is unmistakably the diegetic interpretation of the underlying formal grid.[16]

It is also noteworthy that Peeters refuses any reading of his system in terms of value judgment. For him, the conventional use of the page layout is no less valuable than the apparently more exciting cases of productive use. The latter can degenerate into a formula as well, whereas the former is perfectly capable of being a springboard for hugely original and daring experiments, as the *Watchmen* example again shows, as do many other cases from the graphic novel domain. Just as it is not possible to link panel structure and page layout to specific forms of the host medium (one finds examples of all types in newspaper strips, Sunday strips, and albums or books) or to a certain period of the medium's history (as shown by the presence of all Peeters's types since the early years of comics, as well as since the emergence of the graphic novel), it is not advisable to interpret the modes of the taxonomy in terms of inherent virtues or shortcomings. Peeters also admits that in several cases it is not always easy to distinguish between certain uses. For example, regular grids may have a productive utilization, as in Peeters's own graphic novel *Fever in Urbicand* (1985), where the central motif of the cube and the subsequent storyline on modern urbanism are clearly derived from the 3 x 2 grid layout. Obviously, the borderlines between rhetorical and productive works can be blurred and open to multiple interpretations.

Moreover, Peeters has not ceased repeating that his method, although universal for all works that have clearly marked panel structures, does not cover the whole field of possible relationships between narrative and composition. Thus he has acknowledged the specific, yet not therefore exceptional, position of authors and works that tend to avoid clearly defined or clearly edged panels, which leads them to do away with the borders between their frames. In certain cases, such a decision may add to the efficiency of a certain type (and this is how Peeters tends to read Will Eisner's use of the borderless panels in many of his graphic novels).[17] In other cases, it may blur the boundaries between types and produce a stronger reader involvement in the deciphering of the type or types used by the artist, clearing the ground for a polyphonic reading of the page layout (this is probably what happens in more experimental, if not abstract, graphic novels in which the reader does have to find his or her own way, as parodied in some of Art Spiegelman's *Breakdowns*, where the use of arrows to indicate the reading path to be followed from one panel to another is clearly in mock conflict with the necessity of combining various reading paths within the same page). Moreover, Peeters underscores as well the growing importance of the "third dimension" in layout questions. With the transition from comics to graphic novels, the importance of the book as a host medium and the systematic and innovative occupation of both its paratext[18] as well as the transformation of the work into a sculpted object (i.e., no longer as the gluing or stitching together of pages, but as a 3-D object with its own density and characteristics) are features that have come strongly to the fore, most exemplarily in the work of Chris Ware, to whom Peeters has devoted various essays and a book.[19]

Finally, it should be repeated that Peeters does not pay particular attention to an issue that is a "must" in most other page layout theories, but whose significance may be a little overstressed: the gaps between images and the transitions from one panel to another. A lot has been written on the role of the gutter (in more technical terms, the "intericonic space" between panels), and the exceptional place that the gutter occupies in graphic novel theory and criticism is symptomatic of an aspect of the medium's specificity.[20] Of course, the very fact that so many authors devote so much space to the gutter in their discussions of the graphic novel's visual language cannot be set aside as a detail. At the same time however, its importance may also have been inflated. Don't forget that most gutters go completely unnoticed, their role and meaning being no more significant than the (true or "invisible") white space or gap between two successive sentences in a literary text. Our position in this book is more cautious. On the one hand, it is necessary to stipulate that the diegetic function of the gutter can vary widely: in certain cases, it may be utterly unremarkable (in the two meanings of the words: *unnoticed* and also *not worth noticing*); in other cases, its role can be paramount (and of course, the same remark applies to the visual, pictorial function of the gutter, which is by all means a key aspect of page composition). It would be a mistake, however, to infer from this primary distinction that only "remarkable" gutters are structurally meaningful. It should be the concrete work, the concrete page, the concrete panel transition that signifies whether a certain treatment of the gutter fits best the needs of the sequence, the page, and the work as a whole. It is, on the one hand, not necessary at all that an essential event always takes place within two panels or that the space of the gutter is actively exploited as the virtual off-space of what is shown in the panels themselves. On the other hand, it is indeed advisable that the gutter does not merely copy or duplicate the shift that occurs between the images (or that, on the contrary, does not occur at all, if the panel's sequence presents the succession of the images as a non-event, a standstill, an eternal repetition, or a faux framing dividing a single image). If the sequence is merely a spelling out of the successive phases or moments of an action that can be foreseen easily by the logical structure or dynamism of each previous part, and if the gutter does in no sense provide some added value to such a quasi-mechanical conjugating of a given set whose elements are enumerated one after another, then the neutralization of the gutter's possibly disruptive or complicating possibilities may be seen as a real flaw (but the flaw here is that of the storytelling, not that of the gutter, whose weak use is just a symptom of weak storytelling).

A powerful example of this phenomenon can be found in Hergé's *The Secret of the Unicorn*, well known today to North American readers thanks to the Jackson-Spielberg adaptation.[21] If the first two-thirds of the volume manage to use the dialectical relationship of transition and interruption, of panel dynamism and gutter, in an outstandingly fluent and efficient way, its last third falls prey to a more mechanical use of this basic mechanism. Instead of having each time new panels that help the action move forward and gutters that stress the dynamic shift from one panel to another, the last pages of the book have various sequences that offer nothing more than successive variations on one single action or one single event (for instance, the scene of Tintin being chased by the guard dog), whereas none of the gutters even remotely suggests that something important may happen or be seen in the space between or outside the frame.

In *System of Comics*, Thierry Groensteen, while paying a well-deserved tribute to Peeters's taxonomy, appeals to some practical interpretive difficulties raised by his system and proposes an alternative model for analyzing the layout (see pp. 97–102). He begins by asking two questions: (1) Is the layout *regular* or *irregular*? (2) Is it *discrete*[22] or *ostentatious*? He then demonstrates that both alternatives cannot be reduced to one another, since regular layouts can be quite ostentatious (as, for instance, in the checkerboard effects produced by the intertwining of chromatic series in *Watchmen*, again the usual suspect for this kind of analysis) or vice versa (given, for instance, the erosion, in terms of readerly impact, of amazing or astonishing page layouts; one can get accustomed to, say, the unusual pages of many underground comix artists or, to take a more contemporary case, an author like Lynda Barry, and the layout effects of their graphic novels may become paradoxically discrete, at least to readers self-trained in the specific poetics of these authors).

Alison Bechdel's *Fun Home* offers a good testing ground for Groensteen's proposals. This graphic novel is based throughout on an elementary page grid containing three tiers that may be reduced to two layers each time the visual rhetoric of the book makes this suitable. In that case the page layout features larger images by either gathering two tiers into one large image preceded or followed by a two-panel tier or dividing this larger image vertically, still in combination with a two-panel tier. In all cases, the necessities of the content explain why the "average" panel has to be blown up (to more or less two-thirds of the image) or split in two vertical panels. Examples are abundant and can be found on almost any page of *Fun Home*, even if there is a definite shift from more-regular to less-regular layouts as one progresses through the story (yet this decreasing regularity does not imply that the use of the page layout ceases to be rhetorical). Decorative pages (227 and 230 are good examples) and strictly conventional pages (the double spread 220–221 is the exception that confirms the rule) are quasi-unknown (Illustration 5.e). As far as the productive page layout is concerned, this category does not seem directly relevant.

Overleaf: **5.e.** An example of "conventional" regular gridlike page layout. Pages 220–221 from Alison Bechdel, *Fun Home* (New York: Houghton Mifflin Harcourt, 2006), a division of Random House LLC. All rights reserved.

The book can thus be described in Peeters's taxonomy, but it is also a good example of what Groensteen has in mind when he insists on the double notion of (ir)regularity and discreteness/ostentation. Certain page layouts may be a little difficult to interpret (can't we think, for instance, that page 208 is, despite everything, an example of a productive page layout?), but this shouldn't be a problem. More worrying may be the fact that the overall rhetorical interpretation of the page layout does not really do justice to the permanent ingeniousness of *Fun Home* in this regard. In order to see what happens in the book, one should go beyond the mere labeling of the layout types and see how they are used and varied page after page. Here Groensteen's viewpoint proves very useful. On the one hand, the feature of discreteness or lack of it brings easily to the fore that the relative discreteness of the layout in *Fun Home* is dramatically disrupted each time something crucial takes place in the story. Bechdel always displays a radical shift from regular to less-regular page layout each time she wants to stress a plot turn (this does not diminish the overall rhetorical use of the layout but demonstrates how the analysis of the rhetoric can be fine-tuned with elements that leave more room for reader response). On the other hand, the feature of regularity proves to be even more prominent when *Fun Home* introduces pivotal changes in its plot structure.

The best example of this mechanism is the double page 220–221 (the failed "encounter" of father and daughter, who do not manage to acknowledge and accept their shared homosexuality). We see the two characters driving to the movie theater. During the ride, Alison's father is on the verge of making his great confession, but eventually he runs off in silence. This very poignant scene is represented with the help of an exceptional, and exceptionally conventional, gridlike page layout, with four tiers of three identical panels that directly underscore the exceptional status of this moment that will never come back. However, what is crucial as well in the twenty-four minipanels of the spread is that all of them are framed by a large black strip occupying more than the upper third of each image. At first sight, this representation is realistic: the two characters are shown during their ride to the theatre, and the black strip corresponds with the roof of the car. A more structural reading, however, gives a more profound and meaningful interpretation. When we turn the page, we are inside the theater watching a wide-screen film, *Coal Miner's Daughter*. Yet what matters here is not only the theme of the film ("The movie was good. It was about how Loretta Lynn makes it out of Appalachia to become a big country-western star," says Alison, the narrator, in the caption) and the lines the fictional characters of *Coal Miner's Daughter* are pronouncing: Father: "I ain't never gonna see you again." Daughter: "Yes you will, daddy."). The essential feature is the large black strip around the picture that Alison and her father, and the rest of the audience, is watching; it is the black of the unlit wall that surrounds the screen, and the reader is invited to compare the scene inside the movie theater with the scene inside the car on the previous page, where the similar black strip was rounding off the image of the characters. In retrospect, this relationship confers a touch of fictionality to the conversation between Alison and her father: the two "real" characters talking during the drive are shown the same way as the fictional characters of the film, and this similarity makes the reader no longer sure whether the conversation in the car is real or invented.

As already said, the most appealing aspect of Groensteen's discussion of Peeters is his strong insistence on the position and activity of the reader and, symmetrically, of the author. The former is crucial since the concrete interpretation of the characteristics of a given layout cannot be severed from "the subjective appreciation of the reader" (p. 101). The latter is important as well, since the reader will gear his or her interpretation to the supposed artistic decision of the author, which functions as "the motivation that is susceptible to justify the option retained by its correlation with the iconic and narrative contents" (p. 101). In other words, what Groensteen is pleading for is an approach that, although fundamentally based on the narrative/composition distinction introduced by Peeters, makes room for the interpretive input of the reader as well as for the underlying strategy of the artist. His own readings of page layout techniques and examples will therefore logically stress the heuristic virtues of a given layout (in the case of *Watchmen*, for instance, the symmetry principle of chapter V is defined as "the category, in sum, that allows us to think through the major themes" of the book [p. 100]), and the practice of this kind of reading is very analogous to what we have developed with some layouts and panels from *Fun Home*.

Charles Hatfield's *Alternative Comics: An Emerging Literature* is a third, both complementary and different, major contribution to our subject. The book frames the debate in more general terms, emphasizing appropriately the position of the reader, taking as its starting point the way in which the reader makes his or her way through a work. Hatfield makes a distinction between "single image" and "image-in-series," by which he refers to the tension between "breakdown" (dividing a narrative into single images; this is what is done by the author and then proposed to the reader) and "closure" (a term coined by Scott McCloud; the reverse process of reading through such images and inferring connections between them). As Hatfield summarizes: "In fact, 'breakdown' and 'closure' are complementary terms, both describing the relationship between sequence and series: the author's task is to evoke an imagined sequence by breaking a visual series (a breakdown), whereas the reader's task is to translate the given series into a narrative sequence by achieving closure" (p. 41). After having discussed the issue of closure, in a more medium-specific way than proposed by Scott McCloud in his well-known typology of panel-to-panel transitions,[23] Hatfield then proceeds to his own description of the question, which both integrates the basic elements of Peeters's and Groensteen's insights (although not their taxonomies nor their terminology) and rethinks them in a more overtly readerly way, always keeping an eye on the possibility of reading through the work image by image (an option that is not really taken into consideration by Peeters and Groensteen, who seem to think more in terms of composition than Hatfield, whose main concern is narrative):

Each surface organizes the images into a constellation of discrete units, or "panels." A single image within such a cluster typically functions in two ways at once: as a "moment" in an imagined sequence of events, and as a graphic element in an atemporal design. Some comic creators consciously play with this design aspect, commonly called page layout, while others remain more conscious of the individual image-as-moment. Most long-form comics maintain a tug-of-war between these different functions, encouraging a near-simultaneous apprehension of the single image as both moment-in-sequence and design element.[24]

If Hatfield holds back from advocating new, detailed proposals for the formal analysis of panel structure and page layout, his way of reading is paramount for two reasons. First, it establishes the foundational position of the reader, while not forsaking the technical analysis of the graphic novel's medium-specificity. Second, just like Peeters's and Groensteen's texts, it pays well-deserved attention to the materiality of the book, a crucial element in the analysis of the graphic novel that sets it apart from the world of comics.[25]

Both Peeters's and Groensteen's taxonomies as well as Hatfield's (and others') decision to frame the question of page layout into the wider dialectics of sequence and surface are attempts to counter formalist tendencies that frequently pop up in this context (and that may have an empirical basis in the production-line technique of the comics industry, where graphic artists only fill in the empty frames of a pre-existing page layout with their drawings). In Peeters's approach, the page layout is considered in relationship with the dynamic and shifting tension between *sequentiality*, which insists on guiding the eye from one panel to the next (the dominating element here is the *story*), and *tabularity*, which reorients the moving eye to a more global approach of the page as a visual whole (the dominating element here is the *tableau*). For Groensteen, Peeters's basic opposition between story and tableau should be nuanced by elements referring also to the *readers' response*, less in the case of the opposition between regularity and irregularity, which is rather easy to describe in purely formalist terms, than in the case of the opposition between ostentation and discreteness, which inevitably entails an assessment by the reader, as well as to the overall "artistic project" (p. 99) (which, after all, is also what has to be evaluated by the reader). Hatfield, who widens the aforementioned taxonomies, helps keep a strong focus on the activity of the reader and his or her trajectory through the text, a useful correction to the slightly more design-oriented reading of both Peeters and Groensteen.

Inside the panels

It should be possible to make further steps in the direction of a more global, integrated reading of the page layout that stresses the interaction with as many other aspects of the work as possible. In addition to their link with story logic and readers' expectations and reactions, one should try to include as well the *visual content* of the panels, which may warrant a more adequate appraisal of what is actually taking place on the page. In this regard, we propose not another model as a substitute for the analyses offered by Peeters and Groensteen but a supple and very simple set of complementary instructions aiming to establish what really matters: the revelation and critical evaluation of concrete works. In this regard, a first useful layer may be the degree of correspondence between the variations of the page layout and those of the panel content. The basic opposition here is that of permanence, stability, and repetition versus change, alteration, and transformation, but the most important feature is the dynamic character of the distinction. A given layout can be extremely "irregular" (in the terminology of Groensteen), but remain very "stable," if, for instance, the work tries to offer a new layout in each new page. In a way, this is part of Alison Bechdel's approach. Conversely, a layout can be extremely "regular," yet nonpermanent, if, for instance, the work shifts from one regular page layout to another one. A good example here is the mosaic-like composition of Daniel Clowes's *Ice Haven*, in which the transition from one character to another results in a greater or lesser change in page layout style, each style being, however, very regular and therefore immediately recognizable. The same remark applies to the panel content, which can be based on the systematic repetition of a given representation (for instance, two talking heads, repeated with minimal variations in the successive panels[26]) or rely instead on the maximization of visual differences (for instance, when the leap from one panel to another involves changes in as many aspects as possible: characters, setting, time, color, angle, distance, etc.; perhaps the most astute champion of such a style was the comics pioneer Herriman).

The combination of the axis stability versus instability with the distinction between page layout and panel content provides us with the following taxonomy, which can be added to the systems of Peeters and Groensteen:

- *Stable page layout + unstable panel content.* Many short stories by Ivan Brunetti represent the minimalist side of this composition; the maximalist side is well represented by Julie Doucet in *My New York Diary*. Between both, several intermediary solutions can be imagined.
- *Stable page layout + stable panel content.* This option corresponds with the "average" type in mainstream graphic novels, where regular and discrete layouts are combined with characters that are repeated panel after panel, although it cannot be denied that too systematic a repetition of the characters and the setting, as well as the theme, may generate quite uncanny effects.
- *Unstable page layout + stable panel content.* It is difficult to distinguish in absolute terms between this type and the previous ones, for how can one tell the difference between stable and unstable? Suffice it to state that there *is* a difference, and that it is up to the readers to judge whether the shifts from stability to instability that they may discover are relevant to their reading or not.
- *Unstable page layout + unstable panel content.* Examples here will be found more typically in avant-garde graphic novels, although not necessarily in the subtype of abstract graphic novels (often amazingly stable in layout terms). Some of Spiegelman's *Breakdowns* may fit into this category.

However, piling up reading grids and descriptive models should never be an aim in itself. It must have a critical and interpretive added value, helping the reader to identify, on the one hand, the relative position of a certain work (what is it doing in comparison with others?) and, on the other hand, its specific features (what is it doing by itself?). In other words, models are useful to the extent that they can become tools for reading and interpreting (and perhaps later on for evaluating, but this is always a very tricky matter). Also thinking through the above models with reference to a creator's entire oeuvre is important, because over time these models create expectations and norms that in later works are either replicated (for reader ease) or modified (for whatever narrative purpose, yet also to disturb a preestablished page look/content formula). Moreover, as discussed earlier in this book, artists historically are conscious of the tropes of their famous predecessors and enjoy playing with established modes, including page layout/content relationships.

The importance of a page layout taxonomy is not how it helps classify and pigeonhole certain forms and procedures, although such an operation is always instructive of the position that a certain work occupies in the field. Its major advantage, when combined with analysis of other elements of the story, is to orient the reader's attention. In that sense, its role is radically rhetorical: all page layouts make a crucial contribution to the building of story world as well as to the managing of the reading process, which is always also a reading for the plot. In short, provided we read layout and panel design in combination with the storyline and the visual representations inside (and sometimes outside) the panels, a page layout is paramount in the treatment of three basic effects: (1) foregrounding versus backgrounding: a good page layout helps distinguish between primary and secondary information, or in a mystery blurs the two by providing odd distractions or subversions; (2) establishing links beyond the mechanisms of mere panel-to-panel transition: a good page layout helps disclose the functional relationship between panels or elements that are not contiguous; and (3) speeding up or slowing down: a good page layout helps readers to strike a good balance between interest in the story (which pushes them to leap to the next panel, to turn the page, to try to finish the book as soon as possible in order to find the answer to the story's enigma) and interest in the images and the tableau (which invites them to abandon the narrative thread and to lose themselves in contemplation of the work).

Conclusion

In conclusion, let us stress once again some essential aspects of the layout analysis that we propose. A strictly formalist approach is insufficient. Following Meir Sternberg's "Proteus principle,"[27] we subscribe to the view that a form can have different functions and that a function can be realized through different forms. The very different uses and modes of the grid, the most rigid and least supple panel arrangement, have shown that even the most simple and elementary forms can prove extremely sophisticated. It is also paramount to emphasize the importance of the context, both internally (if one analyzes a page, for instance, one has to take into account the rest of the work as well) and externally (what are the norms, models, and constraints that are accepted in a given context?). Both elements help foreground an analysis in terms of figure/ground: the relationship image/strip/page/book is a kind of "figure" that can only appear on a contextual "ground." Simultaneously, it is crucial to underline the importance of close-reading individual works that have to be seized also in the dynamics of the reading process. Panel structure and page layout are no rigid phenomena that can be described as autonomous forms. Their appreciation emerges – and changes! – while we are reading. Finally, the analysis of panel/page layout organization should never be a goal in itself, but a means to better read the work as a whole. Criticisms of forms, patterns, and changes of panel and layout structures are intellectual devices, among others, to explore the specifics of a work, without regard to which any reading would very rapidly lose its *raison d'être*.

6 Drawing and Style, Word and Image

_____

Having discussed panel and page layout in the preceding chapter, we next turn to matters of style and the issues that graphic novels present because of their hybrid nature of combing words and images. One needs new critical tools to better understand graphic novels, and this book offers a series of summations to assist students theorize works that, at present, most of them read without reference to an explicit mode or method.

From style to graphiation

Drawing and style is an obvious, although sometimes neglected, facet of all graphic novels. Moreover, style is, in whatever context one studies it, a very complex notion. First, even if one reduces, for simplicity's sake, style to visual style – or more specifically to drawing style, leaving aside narrative style, for instance – the number of questions remains very high. For example, when introducing the *McSweeney's* issue on graphic narratives, Chris Ware writes:

> The possible vocabulary of comics is, by definition, unlimited, the tactility of an experience told in pictures outside the boundaries of words, and the rhythm of how these drawings "feel" when read is where the real art resides.

> All cartoonists have a signature "style" that exists beyond the look of their
> art or the quality of their writing – a sense of experience, a feeling of how
> they see the world – as expressed in how their characters move, how time
> is sculpted. Comics are an art of pure composition, carefully constructed like
> music, but constructed into a whole architecture, a page-by-page pattern,
> brought to life and "performed" by the reader – a colorful piece of sheet
> music waiting to be read.[1]

It is no doubt complex, too, because style is also often assimilated to one single aspect: the almost biological expression of the author, whose body is made manifest through his or her personal style.[2]

Furthermore, understanding what style means for the graphic novel supposes that one remembers how it worked (and to a certain extent still works) in the comics studio system. Here, style tends to be controlled as much as possible, in order to enable a smooth functioning of the production line: the artists who make the drawings (and it is important to stress that they normally translate into images a story already prepared by somebody else, namely the scriptwriter) are supposed to do it in the style of the work of the series (draftsmen are interchangeable in the system: at any moment, at least in theory, anyone should be able to replace anyone else) and the comic book, magazine, or publishing company, which has to distinguish itself from other players in the market. The stylistic possibilities of drawing are therefore both underemployed and disconnected from the individual artist.

In that sense, drawing a graphic novel is not the same as drawing for comics, which serves as a kind of anti-model. It is part of the graphic novelist self-construction as a serious author to oppose the industrial principles underlying the production of comics. More specifically the graphic novel rejects, once again at least in theory, the two basic principles of style in the comics' industrial production line: the dissociation of storytelling and drawing, and the disconnection of style from the individual artist. In the graphic novel, artists tend to be "complete authors," that is, authors who combine the two functions of scriptwriting and storytelling and drawing. It is a medium where personal and individual expression becomes a main goal, both at the level of graphic style and at the content level. The common emphasis on autobiography and reportage adding to this picture of pronounced individualism. The case of Harvey Pekar, whose extremely intimate graphic novels are drawn by others, is a fascinating counterexample, although the relationship between Pekar and, for instance, Crumb can by no means be compared with the pseudo-collaboration that often defined the encounter between storyteller and graphic artist in the studio system.

In short, drawing style becomes an absolutely central notion in the structure of any graphic novel. It is supposed to be one of the signatures or trademarks of the author, and one can easily observe that personality and individuality really matter in the field. Most authors want to draw "personally," rather than to draw "well," and perhaps the frequent fictionalizations of their nightmarish experiences in art school, where individual style is allegedly sacred but where cartooning is systematically and stubbornly rejected as silly and childish, may be a symptom of their struggle to achieve an individual style that does not have to comply with the constraints of what the art system considers good drawing.[3]

Indeed, it has become a common trope for graphic novelists to look back in anger (and for the reader's greater amusement, of course) on their formative years in art school. Two main themes systematically recur in their memories: first, the a priori rejection of comics and graphic novels as a form of "serious" drawing; and second, the hyperbolic amazement to have survived an inferno characterized by an explosive cocktail of utmost stupidity (of teachers, students, managers, and others) and a hilarious sense of (either unself-conscious or very cunning) self-admiration and snootiness. Julie Doucet's experiences at the Collège du Vieux-Montréal[4] and Daniel Clowes's studies at the Pratt Institute have been the source of great sarcastic work, which Clowes sardonically summarized as follows: "Remember, the only piece of paper less valuable than one of your paintings is a B.F.A. degree." This caption appears on top of a panel showing a former art school student preparing hot dogs in the local junk food joint.[5]

To describe the drawing style of the graphic novel, the notion of *graphiation* has proven both useful and very influential.[6] This concept, which can be read as a neologism for "visual enunciation" or "graphic expression," refers to the fact that the hand and the body – as well as the whole personality of an artist – is visible in the way he or she gives a visual representation of a certain object, character, setting, or event. It allows for a wide range of possible styles, which can be placed on a sliding scale between two extreme positions: the highly subjective style in which the personal expression of the author takes all priority over the representation itself (what matters at the subjective pole is the personal way something is drawn, not the object of the representation), and the decidedly objective style (in which the object of the representation is the highest priority, at the expense of the personal expression of the author who wants to stay as neutral and invisible as possible).

Graphiation is a powerful tool to examine in detail the varying degrees of visual presence of an author in his or her work, and in that sense it should be used in all serious analysis of drawing style in the graphic novel. Yet, if it is able to point to the differences in personal style between specific graphic novels and specific authors, graphiation per se can never give a sufficient understanding of the broader field. For how can one understand that, instead of opting for a subjective style, certain graphic novelists are eager not only to accept but also to highlight a very objective, seemingly nonpersonal – if not anti-personal style? An example of this is Jason, who sticks to the almost minimalist clear line drawing style that he was capable of fine-tuning after his initial attempts. And how can one understand, the other way around, why so many graphic novelists seem unable or unwilling to embrace "their" own style, as happens in the case of all those artists who draw, on purpose or not, in the style of a certain school, sometimes in the style of another author? Here, other considerations come into play that have less to do with the ambition to find one's voice and more to do with positioning oneself within a certain field. Jason definitely sees his "impersonal" style as an efficient way of distinguishing himself from the rest of the profession, whereas many followers are more impatient to be associated with a certain (admired) artist than to take the risk to leap into the unknown. We will see soon, however, that certain highly original and individual artists succeed in playing in a very self-conscious and sophisticated manner with the shifting frontiers between what is proper and individual and what is collective and borrowed (see also Chapters 4 and 9 herein, for further on the intertexuality and selective recycling of existing comics history).

One of the most striking features of drawing style is its incredible impact on the reader's perception and judgment of a graphic novel. Drawing style is an overall signature, immediately recognizable, even in the smallest fragment (as the voice of a singer, which is also instantaneously identified, but contrary to the sentence of a writer, for instance). The flipside of this mutual assimilation of artist and style, however, seems to be the difficulty to change style. It is a well-known cliché, often examined by graphic novel scholars, that authors who have found their style – or, if one prefers, their "voice" – apply it everywhere and always, independent of the specific content, and perhaps the specific constraints, of their story. It is generally accepted that authors can see their style evolve throughout their career. This is sometimes involuntary, as when, for instance, they lose their creative drive, and sometimes done in a highly conscious and willing manner, such as Alberto Breccia, who often discussed by U.S. scholars but unfortunately totally neglected by publishers, did by trying to adopt a completely different style in each of his book projects.

Before presenting some examples of changes in style, let us try to understand why these changes are so challenging. Drawing is an extremely labor-intensive, repetitive, virtually boring, exasperating, and desperately disheartening activity that can lead many artists to extreme states of depression that are not dissimilar to the despair evoked by Eisner in his depiction of a young artist as a slave of the comics industry in the graphic novel *The Dreamer*. Drawing is not always a source of joyful self-expression and successful communication. It happens also to be a mechanical, painful, and dull activity, whose repetitive dimensions (for often before getting "it" on the page, one has to restart over and over again) are mentioned by a great number of graphic novelists, to the extent that one of them, the French artist Lewis Trondheim, developed a theory on the intricate relationship between drawing and depression.[7] An ironic testimony is that of Chris Ware, as again given in the editorial introduction to *McSweeney's* 13: "Simply put, drawing comics demands an incredible amount of time and devotion from the creator, a willingness to put up with being not only misunderstood, but also possibly disregarded – not to mention an understanding of so many different disciplines – that it ends up not being a terribly inviting or rewarding field" (11).

Given the difficulties associated with drawing, as well as the time an artist needs to discover his or her own style, it should not come as a surprise that most styles do not vary very much.[8] However, changes exist, and they are not just a characteristic of very recent graphic novels.[9] There are countless examples of style shifts that are made *invisible* through diegetic motivation. In *Watchmen* the story within the story, namely the pirate horror comics *Tales of the Black Freighter* that a secondary character is reading inside the fictional world and during the whole book, is drawn in a style that is quite different from that of the overall narrative except for its chromatic features, which share the same palette, but since the differences between the two styles coincide with the distinction between embedded story and embedding story, they are unlikely to be decoded by the readers in terms of stylistic variation, since they look like separate works. *En passant*, the opposite mechanism of internal neutralization of stylistic differences between embedding and embedded level can be seen in Gilbert Hernandez's *Luba*, particularly in the section "The New Adventures of Venus," where the "True Love" romance comics of the 1950s are redrawn in the *Love and Rockets* style (black and white, highly stylized and stereotyped, enlarged female body-shapes). A similar and perhaps even stronger example is the intrusion of color in *The Tower*, one of the black-and-white volumes of François Schuiten and Benoît Peeters's series *The Dark Cities*:[10] the sudden surfacing of color is not perceived as a stylistic rupture but as a quotation, as a reproduction of an embedded element that is the marker of a shift from one diegetic zone to another. The burst of color produced by the discovery of a nineteenth-century painting also opens a door to a totally different fictional universe.

In general, graphic novelists apply one of the three following techniques when they want to modulate their graphic style. In all cases, however, there is a chance that these stylistic ruptures and transformations will pass more or less under the radar in cases where they are narratively or diegetically motivated.

The first technique is internal variations within their "own" style, such as in as David Mazzucchelli's *Asterios Polyp* (2009). In this graphic novel, differences in the chromatic code (shifts from black and white to color, the use of different colors for different characters) and differences in drawing techniques (shifts from hard-edged, angular forms to soft, curbed forms in the figuration of, respectively, male and female" characters and moods) did shake up the conviction that in the graphic novel style is something fixed and rigid between the two covers. As such it was received as the happy and highly praised exception to a dull rule.[11]

The second technique is the combination of various styles (within singular volumes), as done by Daniel Clowes in *Twentieth-Century Eightball* and, even more exemplarily, *Ice Haven*, where each character in this small-town chronicle is drawn in a specific style evocative of existing work or well-known cartoon animations. However, his experiments with shifting drawing techniques have not always been read in this stylistic perspective, perhaps due to the apparently less serious content of his work (humor and sarcasm are not always the best pathway to cultural recognition). The case of technical media changes is a comparable strategy. In the graphic novel, there is a discrete but irrefutable tendency to include photographic material next to drawn images. Let us recall that Spiegelman does it in *Maus*, albeit in very discrete ways, introducing photographs in the preface to the second volume, and then later almost as a coda in the final pages of the same work, as well as including some drawn images that are explicitly reconstructions of resistance photographs, notably of Auschwitz. Other graphic novels go much further: *The Photographer* (by Emmanuel Guibert and Didier Lefèvre, French original 2003–2006), for instance, is a cross-medial three-volume graphic novel on humanitarian action in Soviet-occupied Afghanistan that strives for a quantitatively comparable presentation of both media. Or they offer radically experimental hybrid forms that exceed the traditional boundaries of genre and media, such as Dave McKean and Neil Gaiman's *The Tragical Comedy or Comical Tragedy of Mr. Punch*.[12]

The final technique is the most interesting, as many graphic novelists do not see any contradiction between the reuse of an existing style and their own search for new forms of drawing and storytelling. Famous instances of this are Matt Madden's *99 Ways to Tell a Story: Exercises in Style* (2007), and the work by Seth, together with Chester Brown and Joe Matt, one of the major representatives of the (semi-)autobiographical Toronto school. Working in a graphic style that borrows much of its features from the culture of the 1950s that plays such a part in his personal and artistic universe,[13] Seth is not looking for a "signature style" in the superficial meaning of this word: rather than inventing his own style, his aspiration is to a style recognizable as "typically Seth," yet simultaneously based on the distinctive illustrations style of the magazines of the 1950s. And, as we discussed in Part I, this tendency for appropriation and meta-mixing is very commonplace.

The title of Matt Madden's work is a reference to *Exercices de style* (1947) by Raymond Queneau, the French cofounder of Oulipo, a literary group experimenting with techniques of "constrained writing."[14] The principle of the book is that the same (very simple) story is told in ninety-nine ways, each of them playing with a particular rhetorical figure or genre convention. As could be expected from an original and skilled artist, Madden explicitly craves for medium-specific constraints. Instead of mechanically adapting Queneau's verbal constraints, he invents new visual ones, a shift that becomes very clear in the way he plays with intertextual models. Whereas Queneau rewrites his story by using, for instance, the "free verse" model, Madden retells his story using, for example, the model of George Herriman's *Krazy Kat*. *99 Ways to Tell a Story* also stresses the complex and hybrid character of a comic, drawing attention to its genetic particularities – as in the "storyboard" variation, which is very different from a "literary draft" version – and even to the possibilities of ascertaining a purely textual comics, as in the "calligram" variation, a model with no image and only text (but text presented as visible speech). Madden also refuses to indulge in any form of aestheticism, with his very "basic," straightforward, efficient style that is immediately recognizable so that the reader can easily follow the transformations from one variation to another, without being distracted from the ongoing demonstration. The rather minimalist take of most variations obeys a structural logic: the drawings need to remain a little conceptual, stylistically speaking, in order to enhance the idea that the author is shaping on the page. Let's take for instance the case of Tintin, symptomatically called the "clear line" (and not "Hergé" or "Tintin") variation (Illustration 6.a). Following very closely the style and page layout of the opening variation of the book, the "clear line" plate offers the reader as much as it denies him. The page is an example of what the clear line drawing style means, yet it is not, despite the identifiable presence of Tintin, an example of what it means to draw like Hergé (those readers who might have expected a kind of pastiche will be disappointed). It is clear that the relative absence of Hergé is not a question of Madden's skills. Other variations in *99 Ways to Tell a Story* amply demonstrate the outstanding technique of Matt Madden. Here as well, the reason the artist does not try to "copy" Hergé underlines the overall strategy of the book. Madden does not want us to admire his capacity to compete with the maker of Tintin; he wants us to judge the way in which he manages to implement the set of constraints that he is applying to the basic story. Madden's stance is here perfectly in line with what he is doing elsewhere in his book. Just as he refrains from "thickening" his story, he refrains from "aestheticizing" his style, while keeping this style as recognizably "Madden" as possible, and this as well is in perfect accordance with the contemporary graphic novel field, where authors are less keen to make "nice" or "smooth" drawings than to enforce their own personal style.

A similarly fascinating experience can be found in the work of British artist Simon Grennan, who pushes the dialectics of personal and impersonal style beyond the limits we find in Seth or Madden.[15] Grennan does not use an existing style or feel from a given era in order to shape his own personal stories. Nor does he copy a wide range of existing styles in "his" way, more or less pastiche-like. What he does is redraw a given work in the style of another artist, but in such a way that it might have been produced by the imitated-artist herself or himself – and this is why his artistic strategy has nothing to do with pastiche. When redrawing, for instance, a page of Spiegelman's *Maus* in the style of J. Medway, or a page of Mike Mignola in the style of Chris Ware,[16] he not only adopts the drawing style, but also rethinks the page layout in order to better fit the specific narrative rhythm, feel, and touch of the graphic novelists he is copying (Illustrations 6.c and 6.d). Copying, however, is then a very complex and ambivalent notion, since the most meticulous graphic imitation is also the most original building of a new story world in an existing style.

One understands why it is easier said than done for graphic novelists to change styles within a given work: drawing is a painstakingly hard job, it takes a lot of time and energy to achieve a personal signature, and the use of a drawing style as an individual trademark is crucial for the recognition of a work and an author within the graphic novel market. In that sense, changing style goes against the grain of what graphic novel drawing is all about. Therefore, most artists will prefer a different method if the internal necessities of the work need such a visual change: they will make transformations at other levels or in other dimensions of the work, such as the way they work with page layout (discussed in Chapter 5) or their relationship to the hybrid nature of the medium.

Word/Image Hybridity

The hybrid quality of the graphic novel introduces a split at the level of the dispatching of information, which is presented through the visual as well as the verbal channel. What one needs to understand is that the story is provided not just by the images but also by the text (balloons or captions or otherwise integrated textual material), and much scholarship has been devoted to the meticulous scrutiny of any parameter that can display either a convergence or a divergence between the verbal and the visual.[17] For instance, text and image can meet or depart at

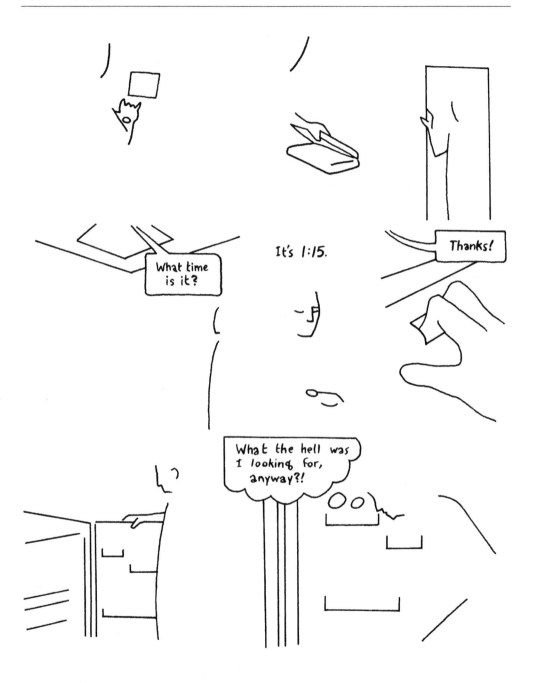

6.a and 6.b. An illustration of the limits (or nonlimits) of stretching one's style: two pages from Matt Madden's *99 Ways to Tell a Story* (New York: Chamberlain, 2006). Used by kind permission of the artist.

6.a and 6.b. (*continued*)

6.c and 6.d. Two unpublished pages (n.d.) by Simon Grennan: a redrawing of Mike Mignola in the style of Chris Ware. Used by kind permission of the artist.

temporal level (we see before we read, or vice versa), or they can overlap or contradict each other (we do not see what we read, we see something completely different, we don't see anything, and, in all three cases, vice versa). Or there can be a shift between the instance that utters the text (the narrator, or the embedded narrator if a second-level narrative is developed) and the instance that sees or filters the image (the focalizer), an extremely complex instance that can be very multilayered, since just like in matters of narrative voice, the structure of focalization – that is, of who is seeing what – is open to embedded structures. An image seen through the eyes of a character is not just an internally focalized image; it is also an internally focalized image embedded in a broader framework that is always already focalized by an external focalizer.

6.c and 6.d. (*continued*)

If images are never reduced to mere "illustrations," their role is to complete the text in a very specific sense, either by giving information that the text does not offer, or by giving an often-ironic counterpoint to what is said. In a certain sense, this was already the double mechanism of "anchorage/relay" coined by Roland Barthes in his seminal article on the word and image relations in publicity in 1964.[18] However, whereas Barthes took as his starting point the priority of the image and the communicative problems raised by it, graphic novelists work the other way around. Here it is not the meaning of the image that must be domesticated or completed by the use of words, but the meaning of the text that must be anchored or relayed. Often, the supplementary meaning created is one of subversion or pithy irony: the image contradicts the text, not just by showing something completely different, but by emphasizing some nuances that help us understand that the narrative voice is, willingly or unwillingly, deceptive.

Contemporary graphic novels may contain a lot of text, certainly in comparison with the tendency toward wordlessness in more avant-garde European works. Yet this quantitative element should not be overstressed. These graphic novels are not "wordy," and perhaps it would be more correct to state that the presence of words in text balloons or captions can be described as steady, stable, and regular. The narrative voice – be it that of the first-level narrator or that of the embedded narrators – is there from the very beginning and continues in most of the panels, its absence being generally a rhetorical device used to stress the emotional intensity of a given plate, as in Tomine's "Lunch Break,"[19] where the strangeness of the apparently insignificant anecdote – a lonely old lady goes out at noon in order to eat in an old car the sandwich she had prepared in the opening panels of the story – is dramatically increased by the complete silence of the scene that contrasts with the happiness and vivacity of the flashback given in the next page, where we rediscover the same car now hosting a lovers' noon rendezvous many years ago.

Simultaneously, wordlessness may represent another answer to some of the most frequently made reproaches against comics: first, that they use a rude, simplistic, heavily cliché-loaded, sometimes overtly racist and sexist language for semi-illiterate readers; second, that the no-less-stigmatizing existence of a minor subgenre, the literary adaptation (most blatantly and stubbornly exemplified by the *Classics Illustrated* series) produced an equally rigid and crippling use of language. Thus, the difficulty of using "correct" language has been a burden for the comics medium. In addition, one of the institutional responses given to this problem, namely the policing of the language via the Comics Code,[20] was immediately felt to be a form of censorship.

But, then, how do graphic novels escape from that encumbering tradition of perceiving the language of comics as either too rude or too bloodless? For the graphic novelists working out of the comix movement, still very alive today, crude realism presents an answer. Their struggle for the linguistic liberation of the medium has been essential, but it would be an exaggeration to believe that it solves all problems. "Liberated" language can be quite boring, and it never means good or efficient writing in itself. The underground tradition has rightly explored the necessary link between a certain type of language and a certain type of audience-building: targeting an adult readership, underground comics often contain quite a lot of text (children were supposed to be reluctant readers), and this text is in many respects much more complex than what text in comics was considered able to produce. In fact, the best example of this trend is not the inclination of the underground toward sexual matters, but the efforts of some creators to tackle historical taboos and offer comic book version of unwritten or censored pages of local or national history (see our discussion of Green, Jaxon, and Eisner in Chapter 3 and Art Spiegelman in Chapters 3 and 4). But underground authors did not only write "more" or on "different subjects;" they also wrote "better," and one of their great innovations consisted in transferring the care for language from the field of vocabulary and syntax to that of storytelling itself. They experimented with types and levels of narrators, introducing not just irony but also unreliable storytelling, multiple storytelling, and self-reflectivity.[21] In short, they started to question the unproblematic relationship between the verbal and the visual.

Thus, language in the graphic novel is always just half of the story: good language and good drawing are never enough; it is the interplay between words and images that has to work. For example, we think of the smart use of censorship in a distressing fragment of Chester Brown's *Louis Riel*. In these pages (68–80), which tell in a minimalist and deadpan style of the execution of a certain Thomas Scott, the blasphemous language of this character, who does not cease cursing while he is imprisoned, is replaced by endless lines of small crosses, an effect that is incomparably much stronger than would have been produced by the explicit reproduction of the cursing.

The quite unsatisfying results of the *Classics Illustrated* series, which never managed to play a role other than that of the model to be avoided at all costs, did not discourage graphic novelists from tackling this very logical dimension of graphic storytelling. Not surprisingly, this was the way Will Eisner defended the birthright of the graphic novel as a new medium, as a low-profile alternative for literary reading for a period when the public no longer had time to read. Yet the problem of this reshaping of literary comics adaptation as the independent new graphic novel was that many critics accused it of doing nothing other than adding images to texts and thereby failing to meet the standards of what a post-comics graphic novel was supposed to be: not an illustration of a script, but the making of an autonomous story world built by the creative interaction of words and images. In this connection, two important remarks have to be made.

First, there is a special attraction exerted by wordless adaptations. Two examples stand out, even if they are rather different from each other. The goal of Milt Gross's one-page wordless adaptation of William Faulkner's *The Wild Palms* (an adaptation disguised as a "review" of 47 panels, titled "I Won't Say a Word About") undoubtedly has some ironic undertones,[22] but it is a wonderful exemplar of what can be achieved. The highly acclaimed visual reinterpretations of Edgar Allan Poe's *Fantastic Tales* by the South-American graphic novelist Alberto Breccia[23] are a more serious endeavor: they have more classic ambitions, closer to the tradition of creative adaptation in film.

Second, and more astonishing, there is a relative absence of the literary adaptation in the graphic novel field. Contrary to in Europe, where the graphic novel has been increasingly drawn to the domain of the literary adaptation, most graphic novels in the United States and Canada are still dominated by the modes of reportage and (semi-)autobiography or reflexive and sophisticated genre work with adult readership codification.[24] We can add that the graphic novel established its literariness through other means: repackaging, editorial inclusion in text-based anthologies, adaptation from graphic narrative to standard fiction, critical appreciation through paratexts such as prefaces and afterwords written by "writers," novelizations, and fiction writers using comics for source material. We return to this in Chapter 8, when discussing more general exchanges between literary culture and graphic novels; for now, let us underline that there is an increased literariness about graphic novels, but not because of standard adaptation from famous literary works.

In an era of "convergence culture"[25] in which all works have now systematic tie-ins and in which cross-media translations of story material have become the rule, such a scarcity remains a mystery. The most reasonable explanation of this phenomenon may be the necessity to conquer supplementary cultural prestige: the tie-in craze and the cross-medial exploitation have now taken in the world of comics, and the graphic novel's resistance can be seen as the expression of a strong sense of medium-specificity and proud singularity. This is what can be seen in the limited number of examples of graphic novel adaptations themselves, which all try to replace the illustrative function of the image in the literary adaptation with a creative one. A good case in point is the self-conscious transposition of Paul Auster's *City of Glass* by David Mazzucchelli. It experiments with a very original quantitative constraint: each page of the graphic novel, which makes a very scarce use of words, corresponds with a comparable amount of text in the original novel. This is also what happens in the graphic rewriting of famous novels, such as in Posy Simmond's witty transposition of *Madame Bovary* to contemporary France,[26] which very cleverly translates the social class differences theme of Flaubert's novel in intercultural terms (the new Madame Bovary, whom Simmonds calls "Gemma Bovery" in order to put some distance between her and the original source, is a British divorcee who fled to Normandy). This is finally also what happens in graphic novels being written by novelists, for example, Audrey Niffenegger or Jonathan Lethem: these authors do much more than adapt their own stories to the language of the graphic novel; instead they explore the graphic novel as a medium with its own rights and privileges, which is an approach that one can argue was set up through the attention Alan Moore and Neil Gaiman gained as writers of graphic novels in the 1980s and 1990s, and not only as comic writers.

Before turning to the literal depiction of words as images, it is also worth repeating that wordlessness has been a relatively popular option for avoiding all of the issues posed above. For historian David Beronå, the wordless woodcut novels of the 1930s and 1940s by Frans Masereel, Lynd Ward, Otto Nuckel, and many others represent an important stepping-stone in the transformation of the medium. In recent decades, the rediscovery of textlessness has become a point of particular interest in graphic novels, and not only in the subfield of the abstract works.[27] The number of completely mute graphic novels may remain rather low, but the number of graphic novels including large wordless sections and sequences is steadily increasing. Chris Ware's *Jimmy Corrigan* is the most acute and astute example of it, but earlier in the graphic novel's rise there was Moebius' silent *Arzach*, a comic book brought out by Marvel that rapidly became a point of reference for later graphic novelists.

Given the medium's history and the long-time preference given in comics to the script at the expense of the drawings, it is the fear of creating an imbalance between word and image that pushes many graphic novelists, who tend to combine drawing and scriptwriting, toward forms of storytelling that maximize the role of the image. Skipping the text is then the most elementary answer to this apprehension. But even within those works that combine text and image, there is always the ambition to avoid the traditional reduction of the image to a role of (mere) illustration.

Finally, one of the most salient characteristics of text and words in the graphic novel is the fact that they are *drawn* as well as the fact that they appear on a specific *place* on the page, in the panel, in the speech balloon, and so on. Let us give some brief details on how to analyze these two aspects of visualized speech in the graphic novel. In the graphic novel words are not only meant to be read, but they must also be looked at, both in themselves and in relation to the place they occupy in the work. This is first of all because language in its written form unavoidably displays a strong tendency towards *grammatextuality*, a concept coined by the French theoretician Jean-Gérard Lapacherie (1984) and recently introduced in new media research by Terry Harpold:

I draw here on a terminology introduced by Jean-Gérard Lapacherie, who has stressed the need for a critical vocabulary for describing aspects of written and printed texts that are autonomous with regard to the reproduction of speech. In texts in which this autonomy is in evidence, he observes, the "graphic substance" of the letter, line, and page, are foregrounded or are otherwise independent of the "phonic substance" and discursive structures they may also represent.[28]

Grammatextuality (the graphic equivalent of Roman Jakobson's better-known "literariness" or "poetic function") is commonly associated with the typographic plays or excesses of some literary genres, but its role in the graphic novel is no less crucial. The form of the lettering, the configuration of the words in the speech balloons and the insertions of these balloons in the panels, the presence of letters and other written symbols within the fictional world, the presence of the typical onomatopoeias ("wham," "whoosh," "whap"), the visual dialogue between words and images on the page – all these elements underscore the importance of the visual form of the words in the graphic novel. A brief consideration of the translation of graphic novels makes this palpable: besides "proper" translation issues, translators have to take into account the space of the panel and the structure of the page; letterers cannot harmlessly change the writing style of the original version, for example.

An interesting example is Eddie Campbell and Daren White *The Playwright*, which proposes in almost each of its pages delicate variations on a basic model (the book has an oblong format featuring one tier per page, normally of three panels accompanied by an ironical narrator's text presented in handwritten captions generally placed on top of each panel), whose apparent simplicity is falsely reassuring (Illustration 6.e). Although the style of the book remains overall more or less the same, both in the images as in the texts, the slight changes in graphiation from one panel to another smartly reinforce the already-mentioned unstable relationships between words and images: one time words and image coincide, another time they don't, and at the end the suspicious reader may think they never really do while at the same time they also perfectly stick together.

Before giving further analysis of what grammatextuality can mean in the graphic novel, one should specify once again the importance of the

6.e. Sliding and unstable relationships between words and images in a graphic novel on the theme of the writer's block. Eddie Campbell and Daren White, *The Playwright* (Marietta, GA: Top Shelf, 2010), 158.

material publication form of the medium, which inevitably produces a split between two zones: the work itself and its surroundings. As already stated, the graphic novel can appear in different print formats (e.g., magazine serialization, comic book format, hard-cover album format, something very like a traditional paperback novel, etc.). Nonetheless, in all these cases, there is a very important *paratext* – that is, the set of elements that enclose and accompany a given work – when it is offered to the public in print form and whose function is both to identify the work and to control its reception by the reader (and, of course, the very fact of identifying and thus classifying a work is already a first step toward such control).

A helpful example of an image that perfectly seizes the imperatives and possibilities is a good cover illustration (Illustration 6.f and 6.g). Let us look at the cover illustration of the first edition of Daniel Clowes's *Ice Haven* as an exemplary paratext. It suggests (1) a clear distinction between (individualized, recognizable) people and (anonymous, interchangeable) places, a snapshot of small town America; (2) a network of relationships between characters; (3) a network of power relations (and the – deceiving – insinuation that the larger character in the foreground is the mastermind of the small town's intrigues and dramas that will be told in the book; (4) a dialogue between the verbal and the visual: as in Spiegelman's *In the Shadow of No Towers*, the line-up of the characters can be read as the successive words, sentences, and chapters of the coming book, whereas the visual design of the title words immediately suggests the kind of lettering one finds on postcards with "greetings from X" (whereby the letters occupy the whole available space, the visual representation of the place appearing inside them); and finally, (5) an example of good drawing that enables the image to function in a narrative/pictorial sequence, for it fills the image with an internal dynamism, a narrative twist, without fixing the reader's attention to its own attractiveness.

The paratext is an embellishment: especially in the case of graphic novels, it would be hazardous to thoughtlessly discard the strictly aesthetic dimension. However, the paratext is also very functional, which for the case of the cover elements could be summed up as:

- classification and identification of the textual object,
- presentation and summary of the contents,
- promotion of a work intended for sale,
- suggested instructions on the text,
- material occupation of the cover space, and
- safeguard of hierarchy between text and paratext.

This list is far from exhaustive, and it goes without saying that the functions mentioned therein overlap with and intensify one another in practice. As far as the graphic novel is concerned, the visual dimension of the paratext – not just the images it entails but also the iconic form that words are taking – are dramatically foregrounded. The most striking difference between an average novel and a graphic novel is the (visual) continuity between paratext and text, which both can easily share the same content (often the cover illustration quotes a panel or redraws a certain scene or character) as well as the same grammatextual features (the way in which words and letters are visually represented can follow similar paths on both sides of the line dividing text and paratext).

6.f and 6.g. One image, multiple stories: the sequence within the single panel. From Eddie Campbell and Daren White, *The Playwright* (Marietta, GA: Top Shelf, 2010), cover, and from *Ice Haven* by Daniel Clowes. Published by Jonathan Cape. Reprinted by permission of the Random House Group Limited.

Chris Ware's *Jimmy Corrigan: The Smartest Kid on Earth* (2000) is undoubtedly one graphic novel that displays most conspicuously the many possibilities of the play with paratext and grammatext (Illustration 6.h). Almost any page of the book is a paradise for all those who are in search of new ways of doing things with words, both visually and spatially. However, the first thing to do when one wants to understand the singularities of the many innovations explored by Chris Ware is to have an overall idea of the paratextual and grammatextual logic of the graphic novel system itself. For such a system exists, and it is possible to enumerate its four principal rules (and all four of them are "rhetorical," in the sense that we discussed in our analysis of page layout).

1. The graphic aspect obeys the principle of "functional differentiation," meaning that all differences in text type or category coincide with a difference in place, and vice versa. The major types or categories – the paratextual information, the narrator's voice, the dialogues between characters, and the verbal elements within the fictional diegetic world – occupy different places – respectively, in the margins of the book, in the margins of the panel, within the speech balloons, and inside the story world. Elementary if not totally self-evident as this may seem, it is the very basis on which the rest of the system relies.

2. The spatial distinction of functional categories is further marked by a system of formal, visual features that underscore and highlight these very differences. In other words, the visual design of the four groups (paratextual information, narrator's voice, dialogues between characters, and other verbal elements) will not be the same, and these material differences are supposed to be unambiguous enough so that the average reader can recognize almost instantaneously the kind of function or category to which it belongs. If, for instance, a panel proposes a mix of narrator's text and characters' speech, the very visual form of the letters and words will help distinguish between the words of the narrator and those of the characters, even

if there is no special framing or spatial distinction of captions and speech balloons.

3. Within each group or type or category, grammatextual differentiations will introduce new specifications, mainly in order to establish an internal hierarchy between words, letters, syntagms, and sentences. The most basic example here is the shift from normal to bold (or from lowercase to capitals, from black to color, from small to big, and so on) each time the text wants to underline certain elements. Of course the opposite choice, that of downsizing essential elements (for instance a title on the cover, as in Rutu Modan's *Exit Wounds*)[29] or of neutralizing the difference between essential and anecdotal information (for instance in the deadpan verbal style of many Chester Brown stories), is a possibility as well, but in no way does this inversion break the general rhetorical spirit of the grammatextual manipulations. Moreover, it should be noted that these manipulations also tend to vary according to the place where they occur. At the paratextual level, it is not unusual to observe that the visual play with the form of words and letters tends to convert these verbal elements into something figurative (systematic examples can be found in the introductory panels of Will Eisner's *The Spirit*, a series hovering between comics and graphic novel, where the very form of the letters "S-P-I-R-I-T" often tend to sculpt figuratively a meaningful element of the story, such as a typical building of the Spirit's fictional universe). At the textual level, this kind of back-and-forth movement between letter and icon is much less frequent.

4. Finally – and this dovetails nicely with the idea, problematic as it may be, of an essential stylistic permanence and stability inside the graphic novel – the above mentioned rules do not really change throughout the work. From the very first, it is normally clear how the graphic novel in question will apply the set of grammatextual possibilities at its disposal, and it is only in exceptional cases that it will diverge from its own rules – this is, after all, a submanifestation of style/graphiation; we are talking about drawing letters and words. Chris Ware, of course, may be such an exception.

6.h. How to shape and lay out the visual form of words and letters: an excerpt from Chris Ware, *Jimmy Corrigan, The Smartest Kid on Earth* (New York: Pantheon, 2000), n.p.

To turn to our example, the book version of *Jimmy Corrigan*[30] not only is a gold mine of grammatextual imagination and clever questioning of the borders between text and paratext, but is also a work that rethinks the graphic novel system in this regard (and many others as well) in a very methodical way, producing thus very new and surprising effects. Ware dares to transgress the most elementary rules that organize the visual and spatial form of the graphic novel's textual components. In many pages of *Jimmy Corrigan*, the major categories are mixed or blended: paratextual elements appear inside the text, or vice versa; the narrative voice manifests itself in places where one expects characters' speech, or the opposite; and it is no longer clear whether verbal inscriptions that seem to be part of the fictional universe do not belong also to other spheres, and perhaps the other way round as well. In addition, he questions the three other principles that we identified above, most notably the formal underlining of functional differences. That is to say that in Ware's world, these material transformations can migrate from one zone to another, and each zone may host a large set of visual procedures. The relationship between specific types and specific transformations (in principle, any formal procedure can appear anywhere), as well as the stability of the chosen procedures, is fluid. It is true that one of the constraints of *Jimmy Corrigan* seems to be that each page should be different from all of the others.

The overall effect of these mechanisms, of which most pages of *Jimmy Corrigan* offer examples, is twofold. On the one hand, it redefines in a fundamental way the rhetorical "unconscious" of the graphic novel's treatment of paratext and grammatext. Contrary to what graphic novelists usually do, Chris Ware does not comply with the basic rule that formal choices and changes have to serve the double cause of immediate readability and instant differentiation between more important and less important material. It is up to the reader to decide what the materiality of the text means and why it changes permanently in this or that sense. On the other hand, the dizzying diversity and multiplicity of Ware's paratextual and grammatextual interventions does not produce visual turmoil. In contrast, it stresses the extreme sobriety and painstaking meticulousness of his work, and it is the mutual enrichment of both that has to be further questioned, for here the very specificity of Chris Ware's contribution to the graphic novel can be shown very neatly.

First of all, it appears that there is a structural, necessary link between form and content. *Jimmy Corrigan* is often called, by those who do not particularly appreciate Ware's style, "boring," by which they mean that "nothing happens" (at the narrative level) and that the drawings are "flat," "shallow," and lacking emotion as well as rhythm, action, and movement. In fact, this kind of boredom (which we will further comment on in Chapter 7) is more than just a misunderstanding. It is a blatant case of misreading because the visual style and narrative are completely disconnected from the rest of what happens on any page of *Jimmy Corrigan*, which explains why Ware refuses to make "dynamic" drawings and to tell "thrilling" stories. What is dynamic and thrilling in Ware is the work itself, but this work can only exist if the *estrangement*[31] produced by the numerous experiments of the author is compensated by a great sense of symmetry, balance, order, stylization, and quietness at other levels (more specifically that of the drawing style and that of the storyline). Without an extreme sense of narrative and visual control, even mastery, *Jimmy Corrigan* would simply fall into pure chaos. Seen from this angle, Ware's work can be interpreted as utterly productive (once again in the sense discussed in Chapter 5): the formal priorities of his treatment of paratextual and grammatextual elements force the author to make his drawings and to tell his story the way he does. The very fact that the rules of *Jimmy Corrigan* and Chris Ware's way of working change throughout the book is a further argument in favor of such an interpretation: the author discovers progressively the possibilities of the kind of work that he is trying to materialize, and the progressive results feed back into the ceaseless refinement and alteration of his own artistic practice and policy.

To conclude, the classic notions of drawing and style, which are often mentioned but rarely analyzed in graphic novel studies, are an important key to a better understanding of the medium. One has to approach them in an open way and link to them fundamental issues of page composition (see Chapter 5) and storytelling (see Chapter 7). To draw is a medium-specific form of storytelling, and style is more than just a reflection of the author's personality. It is instead one of the many parameters that the narrative can transform in order to present a story world. The same medium-specific approach should apply to word and image relationships as well. As we have just discussed, words, no less than images, are drawn and so play a role in the overall structuring of panel and page and contribute to the narrative complexity and depth of a work.

7 The Graphic Novel as a Specific Form of Storytelling

There exist as many theories on storytelling as there are ideas about the novel itself. And the (rhetorical) definition of narrative by James Phelan as "someone telling someone else on some occasion and for some purpose that something happened"[1] remains, in all its abstract generality, one of the soundest statements ever on what storytelling actually means. However, in this chapter we will not go into a complex discussion of what words such as "narrative" or "novel" signify, but emphasize instead medium-specific aspects of storytelling in the graphic novel. In other words, this chapter focuses on what is particular about the graphic novel as a storytelling device and what makes it different from a novel or from a film, even if in some regards one may recognize some similarities.

It would be absurd indeed to deny that stories are everywhere. Nobody has ever doubted Roland Barthes's claim: "There are countless forms of narrative in the world.... Moreover, in this infinite variety of forms, it is present at all times, in all places, in all societies."[2] But we maintain that a story in graphic novel format is more than just a story told in graphic novel format: the choice of the medium induces a set of possibilities as well as impossibilities, of obstacles as well as chances, that are not found in other media, even if it remains always possible to retell or remake a given story in a different medium. The recent love affair between Hollywood and superhero comics[3] and the growing number of experiments in retelling graphic novels across media – as, for instance, in the film versions of *American Splendor* (2003, Shari Springer Berman and Robert Pulcini) and *Ghost World* (2001, Terry Zwigoff) or the animated cartoon version of *Persepolis* (2007, Marjane Satrapi and Vincent Paronnaud) – display some of the opportunities and dangers that characterize these kinds of adaptation. And, of course, the process can go the other way around as well: comics and graphic novels can adapt stories that have already been told in other media, such as *City of Glass*, David Mazzucchelli's 1994 reinterpretation of Paul Auster's 1985 novel; *Waltz with Bashir*, Ari Folman's (and David Polonsky, 2009) graphic novel version of his own 2008 movie; and the *Escapist* series, built in 2004 as an homage to the character invented by Michael Chabon in his novel *The Amazing Adventures of Kavalier and Clay* (2000). However, rapid comparisons with narrative devices and problems in other media have tended to become less popular than medium-specific approaches, as demonstrated by the relative decline of studies that blur the boundaries between comics and film, once a staple theme in popular comics surveys.

Inevitably, many aspects of narratology apply to the graphic novel, and it would be absurd not to benefit from the existing narratological research on storytelling, both in its general, abstract form and in its manifold concrete examples. Just as in narrative studies in general, the study of narrative in the graphic novel cannot do without questions such as the difference between story and plot (and their countless combinations) or the status of the narrator (is he reliable or not? what about third-person narration? does he pretend to be omniscient? and so on). At the same time however, narratology is also being redefined by graphic novel studies.[4] First of all, the graphic novel helps take a stance in the classic debate between general and medium-specific narratologies. Is narrative a universal mechanism that can be studied independent of the concrete medium that actualizes it, or is it on the contrary something that takes different forms, raises different stakes and different issues according to the medium under scrutiny? To this question comics studies in general, and consideration of graphic novels in particular, give a clear answer: storytelling cannot be separated from its inherent materiality; the form is critical. Second, the graphic novel reintroduces certain aspects of story analysis such as world-making, space, and characterization that had been neglected if not simply discarded as inessential by the formal-ist methodologies that have dominated narrative analysis so strongly for long parts of the second half of the twentieth century. Logically speak-ing, a methodology more aware of medium-specific issues cannot but highlight these features. For clarity's sake, we will limit our analysis to storytelling in the graphic novel itself, more particularly to the features that may distinguish it from storytelling in other media, but always in the open, nonessentializing spirit of this book.

Drawing the line, creating a space

In the previous chapter, we discussed the differences between drawing in general and drawing in and for the graphic novel. The specifically nar-rative dimension of graphic novel drawing, though, goes far beyond the characteristics we have already underlined, so much so that it is impos-sible to tackle that issue with the methods associated with reading fine art. What is essential in the graphic novel is that drawing is less a tech-nique that is used to shape a given story than a creative operation that produces the images and the very stories themselves.

A seminal contribution to the discussion on the role of drawing, and more specifically on what he calls the "line," has been made by Jared Gardner in the article "Storylines."[5] Gardner's perspective is not sim-ply stylistic or reduced to medium-technical debates but is linked to the storytelling, more concretely to the *history* of storytelling, as suggested by Walter Benjamin in his much-quoted essay on Nikolai Leskov.[6] As Gardner argues, comics and graphic novels are probably the medium that best matches Benjamin's craving for the storyteller's actual physi-cal connection to the artisanship of storytelling, which has been lost by the progressive spread of machines overtaking the role and place of the actual storyteller (we no longer hear the storyteller, we read his or her text, and this text, which is no longer handwritten, no longer bears any physical relationship with the body of its maker). Gardner states:

> In fact, alone of all of the narrative arts born at the end of the nineteenth century, the sequential comic has not effaced the line of the artist, the handprint of the storyteller. This fact is central to what makes the comic form unique, and also to what makes the line, the mark of the individual upon the page, such a unique challenge for narrative theory. We simply have no language – because we have no parallel in any other narrative form – for describing its narrative work. In comics alone the promise of Benjamin's looked-for "moving script" continued to develop throughout the twentieth century. Here the act of inscription remains always visible, and the story of its making remains central to the narrative work.[7]

The fact that the story is less told or shown than drawn is what defines the difference between comics and graphic novels and storytelling in other media. Lines may not tell other stories than those narrated in novels or movies, but they tell them differently. Lines display a story world in which the act of drawing cannot be separated from the drawn result. And lines, whether functioning as figures or contours or not, do inevitably manifest themselves as narrative agents and vehicles of storytelling. To an extent, one does not have to study anything other than the line to see how a world is constructed, a story told, a character sketched. And behind or beyond each line emerges the source of any storytelling whatsoever: the narrator. The very singularities of the line can teach us a lot about the actual presence of the storyteller, his or her involvement in the fictional world, and his or her moral stance toward it. By linking the materiality of the line to the hand and the mind producing it, and that we reproduce in our reading, we better understand which kind of narrator is doing the telling and how we are supposed to make meaning of the narrative act.

Charles Hatfield adds a second crucial contribution to the discussion of the line. As he repeatedly puts it in his study of Jack Kirby, a comic books artist whose creative involvement is as personal and deeply committed as that of any auteur-like graphic novelist, it is not possible to isolate the drawing from the story told. Hatfield's perspective completes the debate on the indexical link between drawing and artist with new viewpoints on the link between drawing and the actual production of a story world in panels that are sequentially organized on the page while crafting also an internal temporal dynamics:

> [T]he overwhelming evidence shows that Kirby wrote and drew many of his stories directly to the boards. So storytelling, composition, and rendering, and in many cases the brainstorming and development of ideas as well, were part of a seamless graphic process: narrative drawing.[8]

Commenting upon a spread from the first issue of *The Demon* (1971), which he considers typical of Kirby's endeavor to impose a narrative force on 2-D panels, Hatfield observes:

> This spread ... is not a snapshot in the strict sense but a montage. Here is a bald-faced violation of that dictum most famously handed-down by Lessing in his seminal *Laocoön* (1766) and since reinforced ad infinitum: that, whereas writing and storytelling are arts of time, unfolding in sequence, painting and drawing are arts of space, to be apprehended all at once and thus necessarily separate from writing. Kirby always ignored this distinction. That's what comic artists do, and Kirby did it especially well. The power of drawings like this one ... stems from the tension between reading the image as a single moment and reading it as a synchronous compression of an extended length of time – in short, a tug-of-war between an iconic reading, assuming semblance, and a symbolic one based on convention.[9]

But what are the consequences of such a thesis for the work that is being produced, and how can the reader observe the specific features of a story told in words (and here as well it should be noted that "words" are not a passive and post-factum device, but a medium that invents the story grammatextually in ways that would be unthinkable elsewhere) and images, a story told by a graphic novelist?

To begin to answer this question, perhaps the most visible medium-specific feature is the importance given to space (as a dimension of world-making), a notably undervalued aspect in traditional narratology. Classic analyses of narrative and storytelling have been inclined to foreground action and plot naturally, at the expense of (visual and other) representations of space. These spatial aspects are definitely more important in the graphic novel than in narrative in general. It is possible, of course, to skip the spatial representation of the setting (for instance, in stories that use a silhouette style or that do not make the setting very explicit) or to use only undefined characters (for instance, abstract, allegorical figures), but this is certainly not the most common situation.[10] The reasons for this foregrounding of space are twofold. First, drawing a character often implies also drawing the setting in which that character will evolve. Second, and more importantly, the sheet of paper or the computer screen on which the artist is working is always a space itself, whose characteristics cannot be wiped out at the moment of publication, as is normally the case in modern verbal narratives, where the final format of the book does not censor only the hand of the author but also the spatial and visual specificities of the surface on which the work literally has been written.

Moreover, in the graphic novel the importance of characterization and spatialization is also increased by the difficulty of finding efficient and supple ways of visualizing temporal relationships, as imagined, for instance, by characters. As long as time can be represented through space, however, the power of the medium can be dramatically high. For example, the graphic novel has no problem in representing a phenomenon such as aging, which can be shown by the comparison of a "before" and an "after," just as it is extremely efficient in condensing slow, long-term changes, as exemplarily demonstrated by Robert Crumb's stunning "A Short History of America," which shows in twelve identically framed panoramic views, followed by three utopian or counter-utopian ones, the industrial destruction of Eden and the inexorable penetration of the "machine" in the "garden," to quote Leo Marx's classic book on the tradition of pastoral literature in the United States (1964).[11] Crumb's rise and fall of U.S. civilization and environment is definitely about people, but their presence, actions, and impact are shown via the metamorphoses of a given landscape.

The dramatic importance of space can also be inferred from the large amount of graphic novels whose protagonist, so to speak, is a place, a spatial environment. Chris Ware's *Jimmy Corrigan* is as much about the transformations of Jimmy's family house and the construction of the Chicago World Fair and other neighborhoods as it is about the hero himself, typically an antihero whose life is largely defined by nonevents, emptiness, and boredom. Other projects by Ware make the transformation of the place or setting into a character totally explicit, such as his *Building Stories*. Daniel Clowes' *Ice Haven* is certainly not a book in which nothing happens. It is, on the contrary, filled to bursting point with small and big events, although always on the small town scale. It is also a book that contains a tremendous amount of characters. Yet the main agency is clearly that of the place: if people do what they do, behave as they do, and talk as they do, it is because of their living in a particular place that makes them into what they are – small town losers. For American readers, it must be easy as well to recognize the cultural subtext that lies underneath Clowes's debunking: the nostalgia of lost communities, as expressed by the lasting success of the all-American classic *Our Town* (Thornton Wilder, 1938) and the unease provoked by the rootlessness of a nation of people always on the move.

And where would *American Splendor* be without Cleveland? *Love and Rockets* without Palomar? *Maus* without the maps that feature on its back cover illustration? Where is the substance of Eisner or Katchor's work without the New York tenements or the Catskill Mountains? Not to mention the incomplete graphic novel *Big Numbers* that evoked Alan Moore's hometown, Northampton, in the East Midlands of the United Kingdom.

Space, however, is not only more or less about a fictionalized setting for a story. It is also a material given, that of the board (or the screen) on which the artist is drawing and eventually that of the page (or the screen) on which the story will be published and whose impact on the fictional world is tremendous. For the artist invents by filling in that preexisting space in one way or another: page design, graphiation, and grammatextual envisioning of text.

Notably, there are myriad examples that create a literal overlap between, on the one hand, the implicitly layered and segmented structure of the graphic novel page, which is never totally "empty" even if it is totally blank at the beginning, and, on the other hand, the cross-section of a fictional building, with the floors representing the various tiers of the page and the rooms representing the successive panels of each tier.[12] Rather than referring one more time to the usual suspect – the work by Chris Ware – one might take a look here at the work of comic and post-comix artist Kim Deitch, whose psychedelically tinged fictions have never achieved the same status as the work of his two great contemporaries, Robert Crumb and Art Spiegelman. Deitch clearly takes the page as the springboard for his imagination, trying always to find new techniques of filling the page's initial void as completely but also as dynamically as possible, converting the horizontal and vertical tiling of the average page with imaginary constructions that offer a fictionalized counterpart of the grid: office, hospital, home, or entertainment places (re)structured and (dis)organized by windows, bars, and all kind of spaces within spaces, places inspired by the imaginary prisons à la Piranesi, but in which the columns of the mutually encroaching galleries are replaced by bottles, places, in short, torn between unity and fragmentation,[13] putting upside down the logical rationality of the hierarchy of page, tier, and panel (Illustration 7.a). Deitch translates the abstract 2-D structure of the grid into unique but paradoxical and Escherian architectures in which space turns into time, for these kinds of constructions cannot be seen or watched; they can only be crossed in various directions, and in this process the reader is as lost as the characters.

Martin Vaughn-James's *The Cage*[14] is a paradigmatic example of the overwhelming importance of place and space at the expense of character and character-bound action.[15] The book immediately became famous for offering a story breaking all the written and unwritten laws of the medium: each page contains only one panel (the format of which does not stop varying); there are no speech balloons but instead captions

7.a. This example from Deitch's work offers further exemplification of how the page provides a space for the imagination. Reprinted with kind permission of the publisher, Fantagraphics, Seattle.

(although certain pages remain totally wordless); its length of some 180 pages is quite unusual; and, most strikingly, it is a story with no characters, containing only images of objects and places. In addition, its graphic black and white style is astonishingly "cool," if not "cold." *The Cage* is, in short, light-years away from the expressionist transformations of traditional drawing techniques that can be found in many innovative works of the post-*comix* period. Yet Vaughn-James's book is anything but a "dead" object, a specimen of those descriptive graphic novels that cash in on the *genius loci* of their settings, replacing action by mood. On the contrary, *The Cage* is an extremely dynamic example of a place that becomes a character and testifies to its agency, while at the same time displaying a wonderful example of the creative interaction between fictional space and material space, between the world invented by the storyteller and the material aspects of the tools used by the artist at the moment of the drawing.

The Cage brings to the fore a homogeneous world, with an apparent continuity in all its graphic dimensions: dot, line, angle, grid, cube – all of them traced with the same pencil. In addition, one easily observes how each of these abstract geometrical units or components is translated into thematic and fictional forms that naturalize its material basis. The clouds in the sky, for instance, with their dotted contour lines, the absolute rectilinear form of their bottom lines, and the regularity of their dispersion over the implicit lines of the page, are so stylized that one "feels" the mechanism that has uploaded the form (ink, lines, pages) with meaning (clouds above the horizon line, sand and pebbles below). Moreover, there is an almost perfect symmetry between these clouds and the rows of pebbles in the desert, among many other comparables items, so that one can almost immediately decipher these iconic figures as equivalent to letters and words on the page (Illustrations 7.b and 7.c). Each fictional object present within the dehumanized world of *The Cage* can be explained this way and turned back into its abstract components. The cage itself, a quadrangular fence surrounding a wide set of smaller buildings or constructions, refers to both the book as a container (in the case one reads the fictional world as a transfer of written signs into a visual world) and the white cube of the exhibition space (in case one focalizes on the iconic dimension of the work). Words become things, pages become walls, covers become cages, and vice versa.

Yet this oscillation between abstract forms and their figurative translations is never mechanical. In this regard, it is certainly not by chance that behind the fence one finds a power station, the very symbol of the shift from (static) *form* to (mobile) *force*. The generative force of the power station – a symbol that represents, among other things, the work of the author – is less the locus of a single sudden burst than it is the repetitive and virtually endless site of production, including of ruptures and gaps. It is true that starting from a line one can draw, as Vaughn-James does, a grid and then a hospital room and eventually a full-fledged city

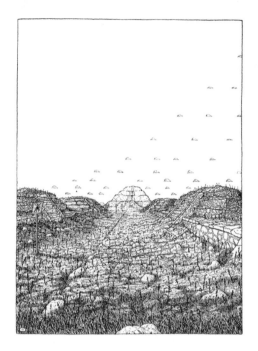

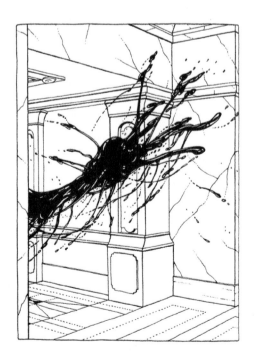

(although still a city with no inhabitants, no traffic, no noise), but this generative dynamic is at the same time jeopardized from the very beginning by the appearance of cracks.

Once again, none of these stories or none of these structures is absolutely typical of the graphic novel as such. Even in the apparently radical case of Vaughn-James's book, it suffices to think of experiments with characterless storytelling in the first years of the French new novel. Verbal narratives can rely as well on the importance and influence of places; they can find their formal and compositional inspiration in the particularities of a given place, just as they can make a place the main agent of a story. After all, Mark Z. Danielewski's cult novel *House of Leaves* (2000) is also an illustration of all of these aspects. But what is typical of the graphic novel is the regular foregrounding of these elements, which often changes the rest of the story and the very spirit of storytelling.

Alison Bechdel's *Fun Home* is once again a helpful example. In this family memoir that tells the double story of a father and a daughter's discovery of and dealing with sexual difference – unsuccessfully in the former case, successfully in the latter one – the key motif is that of Ithaca, the mythical place of home to which Ulysses will only be able to return after ten years of rambling and suffering after the end of the Trojan War. In *Fun Home*, the Ithaca motif is no longer another name for the archetypically temporal structure of the journey and of storytelling as journey, but an alternative, mainly visual, spatial, and architectural version of it. The characters know where Ithaca is (in the book: Beech Creek, a small community in rural Pennsylvania), they either live there or know how to get there, but they all desperately feel that they are not really *at home*. Hence the attempt of the father to rebuild the family home, restoring the original style of their old Victorian house but as a matter of fact transforming it into what the mother calls a "whorehouse"

Opposite page: 7.b and 7.c. A fictional world in permanent metamorphosis: excerpts from Martin Vaughn-James, *The Cage* (qtd. after the latest French edition, published with Les Impressions Nouvelles, Brussels, 2006), n.p. Reprinted with kind permission of the publisher.

(and what the children experience as a museum that prevents them from being really fully alive). Hence also the attempt of the daughter to construct a new Ithaca elsewhere, before realizing that the real Ithaca is at home and can be reached only through reconciliation with her father, which eventually only happens in an imaginary way. During their last meeting, they cannot say the words that should be uttered,[16] and it is only after the father's death that full forgiveness and mutual understanding can occur. Such a move from the temporal to the spatial (visual, architectural) aspects of the journey motif is very typical of the graphic novel, which cannot do without spatialization of its main narrative structures.

A neglected dimension: the character

Analogous remarks to that of spatialization apply to another aspect of storytelling that narrative studies have until recently also often overlooked: characterization. Analyses like that of E. M. Forster, putting forward the difference of treatment between "flat" and "round" characters, were abruptly cut down with the arrival of structural readings of narrative in the 1960s. Characters became roles, actors, agents in abstract structural diagrams. Their physical appearance and psychological depth or shallowness proved superfluous details located at the most superficial level of a story's algorithm. In the graphic novel, however, which (not unlike other visual media) may have a difficult job in communicating thoughts and feelings, the situation is completely different. Basically, what we are confronted with from the very first until the very last panel is not the character's *thinking* (although it is of course possible to suggest inner life through images, captions, dialogues, voice-overs, and so on), but the character's *body*, more specifically the character's *face*. Even in the case of autobiographic telling, the narrator tends to display not just his or her thoughts, but his or her bodily appearance – a considerable difference from the autobiographical mode in verbal storytelling, where the person who says "I" can keep out of sight throughout the whole book.

The critical feedback from the graphic novel on narrative theory and methods of narrative reading finds precisely here a very clear further outlet. Thanks to our better understanding of the graphic novel, it is now possible to disapprove of much narrative speculation as excessively disembodied. This rediscovery of the body in cultural theory is far from being an isolated phenomenon: the flight into pure and virtualized bodies is a permanent temptation in a culture characterized by the split between body and mind, and the example of the graphic novel, which roots the story in stubborn materiality of characterization, is a modest but useful way of backing the efforts of those who, like N. Katherine Hayles, resist the "disembodying" effects of certain strands of posthumanist thinking.[17] The graphic novel brings us healthily back upon our feet, confronting us with characters (that are something other than narrative elements) that we see before our eyes (and this as well is something other than characters behaving mainly at a cognitive level). The overwhelming presence of the protagonists' bodies is another sign of the times where the graphic novel corresponds with and adds to contemporary thought. (Here we should note that *Maus* is a complex example, since its use of drawings of animals for people achieves a wonderful ambiguity: it is autobiography, but it is a distanced and muted approach because of the metaphor.)

The emphasis on the body not only has not a strong impact on the audience's interaction with the medium but also affects the analysis of the graphic novel itself. In the graphic novel, the verbal/textual accompaniments of the panels tend to transform the character's body and to produce a shift from the body in action to the portrait, as demonstrated in Dave McKean's groundbreaking graphic novel *Cages* (1998) and its almost Cassavetes-like use of talking heads in close-up. The aesthetics of a film such as Cassavetes's *Faces* is felt throughout *Cages* (once again a title that hints to the agency of place!). The multiple-character story of a London apartment building, *Cages* is a book that tells numerous deeply moving stories, but at the same time it often freezes the action at the level of its visual representation. Rather than showing the (sometimes violent) action, McKean shows us the faces of the persons telling their (or others') stories in order not to distract the reader's attention from the emotional consequences of the action on the mirror of their minds: their bodies, their faces, their eyes. In addition, the foregrounding of the graphic novel's basic grid – most pages respecting the recurrent pattern of nine similar panels often containing only a close-up of the same face – reinforces dramatically the all-determining influence of the medium's own material space, that of the board and the page.

It is therefore a persistent misunderstanding to believe that the visual string of a graphic novel shows the successive parts of an action unfolding in time, as if the graphic novel was offering a selection of shots from a sequence of a virtual movie. The visual logic of the graphic novel is often less syntagmatic than paradigmatic (or if one prefers, less narrative than illustrative). What it shows is in the first place a series of variations on the face. Even if graphic novels do tell stories, their first concern is not infrequently the portrait of the characters and the multiperspectival representation of their bodies.[18]

But what is it about, finally?

Storytelling, however, is not only about space and characterization and how their integration into the virtually segmented structure of the page is being achieved. It refers also to the specific content. Recent critical contributions to literary theory, such as the work by Jacques Rancière on the democratizing significance of the staging of nonelite themes and characters, have demonstrated the importance of subject matter in the permanent reshaping of "the distribution of the sensible."[19] The graphic novel plays a key role in this process, for it has shown a growing thematic diversity, not only in contrast with the narrowing down of subject matter in superhero comic books, but also in comparison with literary production in general, which is also much more streamlined and victim of hypes and fashions than one often imagines.

Our representation of the Holocaust is nowadays more marked by Spiegelman's *Maus* than by Spielberg's *Schindler's List*, what we think of Generation X is as much indebted to what we have seen in *Ghost*

World as what we have read in Douglas Coupland, and modern boredom, ennui, spleen, and melancholy can no longer be seriously envisaged without direct references to the universe of Chris Ware. Nevertheless, the thematic scope and breadth of the graphic novel, which in the United States is mainly invested in semiautobiography and documentary fiction and faction, does not pass without problems. There is an often-made remark that certain topics resist their treatment within the graphic novel while other themes are definitely overrepresented (see Chapter 4 for discussion of the recent trends and Chapters 8 and 9 for further current debates and dispositions). Just like the newspaper comic, condemned to specialize in humor, or the superhero comic books, forced to extreme escapism, the graphic novel seems to have an elective affinity with stories of the self, the self in crisis because of history or trauma, maybe because, as Gardner's thesis on drawing suggests, the self is harder to remove when a work is drawn as well as narrated. A further good overview of what the graphic novel manages to represent efficiently and what it still fails to cover satisfactorily is given in the concluding remarks of "Not Funnies," a significant article by Charles McGrath on the social and artistic position of the graphic novel as a possible substitute for the dying novel:

> How good are graphic novels, really? Are these truly what our great-grand-children will be reading, instead of books without pictures? Hard to say. Some of them are much better than others, obviously, but this is true of books of any kind. And the form is better-suited to certain themes and kinds of expression than others. One thing the graphic novel can do particularly well, for example, is depict the passage of time, slow or fast or both at once – something the traditional novel can approximate only with empty space. The graphic novel can make the familiar look new. The autobiographical hero of Craig Thompson's "Blankets," a guilt-ridden teenager falling in love for the first time, would be insufferably predictable in a prose narrative; here, he has an innocent sweetness.
>
> The graphic novel is also good at depicting blankness and anomie. This is a strength of Daniel Clowes's and also of … Adrian Tomine, who may,

incidentally, be the best prose writer of the bunch.... His young people, falling in and out of relationships, paralyzed by shyness and self-consciousness, might be unendurable if depicted in prose alone. Why would we care? But in Tomine's precisely rendered drawings ... they take on a certain dignity and individuality.

The graphic novel is great for stories of spookiness and paranoia, as in David Mazzucchelli's graphic adaptation of Paul Auster's novella, "City of Glass," where the panels themselves become confining and claustrophobic, or in Charles Burns's creepy "Black Hole," a story about a plague spread by sexually active teenagers .... And of course, drawing as it does on the long tradition of comic and satiric art, the graphic novel can be very funny.

In fact, the genre's greatest strength and greatest weakness is that no matter how far the graphic novel verges toward realism, its basic idiom is always a little, well, cartoonish. Sacco's example notwithstanding, this is a medium probably not well suited to lyricism or strong emotion, and (again, Sacco excepted) the very best graphic novels don't take themselves entirely seriously. They appeal to that childish part of ourselves that delights in caricature, and they rely on the magic, familiar but always a little startling, that reliably turns some lines, dots and squiggles into a face or a figure. It's a trick of sorts, but one that never wears out.[20]

McGrath's nod to the graphic novel's craving for more realism and his stressing of old, exhausted themes made new can be read in relationship with Rancière's plea for art as a socially and politically founded attempt to reshape our ways of world-making. The graphic novel, in that sense, proves capable of continuing the novel, which seems no longer capable of speaking seriously of certain themes without boring or exasperating the modern reader. At the same time, its very earnestness is limited by its enduring relationships with caricature and cartoon art.[21] But McGrath represents the positive side of the story. Relying on the current quasi-monopolization of the graphic novel by autobiographical or semi-autobiographical productions, other observers accuse the graphic novel of astonishing thematic shallowness and irksome sentimentality – a feature that McGrath already diagnoses. In a review of a Harvey Pekar anthology, Sam Leith writes: "[W]e're now at the point when depressed men doing nothing are as much a comic-book cliché as superheroes."[22] And in a somewhat harsh introduction to a bittersweet review of Craig Thompson's *Blankets* (2003), one of the most commercially successful graphic novels ever, Douglas Wolk observes:

> Two ideas that have poisoned a cross section of contemporary writing in general have also seeped into comics a little bit. One is the sentimental memoir – the first-person story that explains why the author is in the right and why the author's pain and sadness are more sad and painful than yours. The other is the toxic maxim "write what you know": the idea that, even in fiction, an author's imagination has to be directly limited by his or her personal experience. The rise of autobiographical or semiautobiographical comic books brought those ideas into play in comics and opened up the question of how cartoonists might best represent their own experience.[23]

It is true that graphic novels seem more willing to tell some stories rather than others (and some scholars suggest that the strange overrepresentation of autobiographical or semiautobiographical narratives is not totally fortuitous, given the medium's obsession to distinguish itself from the previous comic books model). However, it would be an overstatement to believe that the current specialization of the graphic novel in this or that form of narrative is an essential feature of the medium. The supposed restriction of its content to things such as violent action (at least in that part of the production that has evolved from the thematic and ideological upgrade of the superhero comics), risqué humor (itself a continuation of the underground comix tradition of the late 1960s and early 1970s), semiautobiography, history and the documentary (either of which having also direct links with the comix), and, of course, boredom (as an easy wink to postmodern *Weltanschauung*) is itself approaching a critical cliché. Perhaps graphic novels are more appropriate to tell this or that kind of story, and to do it this way rather than that way, but it is important to avoid any overgeneralization beyond our contextual discussions offered earlier herein that situate graphic novels as self-conscious inheritors of existing comics and comix formats, now very much swimming in the same cultural waters as literature.

What is definitely totally new in the field of storytelling is the redefinition of the relationship between narration and description. In verbal storytelling, these two modes are generally presented as mutually exclusive: either one narrates or one describes. An infamous example of this antagonism is the campaign against description conducted by the French surrealist André Breton, who in his first *Manifesto* advocated the replacement of all descriptions (tedious, boring, superfluous) by photographic documents (that would no longer be skipped by the reader, as was the case, according to Breton at least, with verbal descriptions). In the graphic novel – and the foregrounding of characterization and space have already hinted at this – both aspects coincide: it is not possible to narrate without describing, and conversely all descriptions will be deciphered immediately in relationship with their contribution to the story. This yin-yang connection between narration and description explains a certain number of thematic and semantic particularities of the graphic novel, which make it a more-than-welcome remediation of traditional (verbal) storytelling: first the spread of new forms of "actionless" graphic novels; second the rise of the so-called abstract graphic novels. In either case, the graphic novel brings us to new visions of storytelling that are no longer monopolized by plot and action.

From an intertextual point of view, lack of action is perfectly understandable in the American context. For the graphic novel, it is a logical choice to accentuate the differences with what is its antimodel (and part progenitor): the superhero comics. In the work of Chris Ware, probably the most prominent representative of this fascination with lack of action, the avoidance of plot-driven, high-speed storytelling can be seen as the inversion of traditional super-heroic forms. To give the reader a clue as to what he is doing in *Jimmy Corrigan*, Ware downgrades the character of Superman to the figure of the pathetic loser. He does not jump into the sky and fly like a bird or a plane, but is rather associated with the theme of suicide. Uneventfulness and boredom are omnipresent in work by

Daniel Clowes (one of his books is called *David Boring*). This inversion is not limited to the mere absence of thrilling or pseudo-thrilling attractions; it spreads also to the mockery of comics culture itself. For example, Clowes's *The Death-Ray* (2004, as issue 23 of the author's own serial *Eightball*; separate publication as a graphic novel in 2011) is a cruel parody of the myth of the superhero. The young suburban hero of the story discovers that he possesses special superpowers, but contrary to Clark Kent (the one and only real and original Superman) and all the like, he does not use them to fight crime or to make the world a better place. Instead he makes bad use of them, just for fun, just because he's bored and not a good character at all. The same themes are recurrent across the creator's oeuvre: for example Clowes's *David Boring* offers another good example of ambivalence towards comics (see also Chapter 9).

Similar critiques extend to the whole sociology of comics reading, more particularly the incapacity of grown-up readers to supersede the culture of their childhood and youth. One of the longer short stories by Adrian Tomine in *Sleepwalk*, "Dylan & Donovan,"[24] offers a powerful critique of comics/comix culture. "Dylan and Donovan" is the story of two twin sisters who consider themselves the unwilling heirs of the 1960s. First it is that whole period associated with comix that is critiqued through humor, in remarks such as: "Before you can even ask, let me just say that, yes, those *are* our real names, why would I make that up? Our parents were hippies.... They were probably high on grass or something when they named us." Second, the comics culture and the subculture of the comics convention is mocked. Dylan and Donovan's father offers them a trip to a big comics convention, where old comics and old counterculture seamlessly meet. One of the sisters remarks: "Can you believe that? That's his idea of a 'family experience.' I mean, I guess it's cooler than going on some outdoors-y camping trip or taking us to a baseball game or some crap like that, but it just seems so weird."

Plot reduction and lack of action (as a formal device) and boredom (as one of its possible thematic consequences) should not only be read in a negative mode, as a strategy to criticize the excesses of both superhero comics and underground comix. In light of the interweaving of narration and description, it can be argued that the graphic novel is also a medium in which other forms of storytelling, no longer based on plot and action but on the narrative potential of drawing itself, become possible. The action is now "in" the drawing, both in the drawing as a process creating a world that is open to narrative interpretation and in the drawing as panel and sequence in which the very treatment of the images makes room for temporal, chronological, and narrative relationships. In the graphic novel, the creation and eventual transformation of a space suffices to create a story, and the staging of the characters' boredom and inactivity should not divert us from that essential lesson. In a certain sense, one might even say that the explicit presence of boredom at the level of the characters functions as a signpost pointing at the passionate and fascinating discoveries to be made when shifting the focus from plot-driven action to the adventures of the drawings on the page. Yes, in many pages and sequences of *Jimmy Corrigan* "nothing" happens. But as soon as one accepts that the real "action" is taking place elsewhere, in the way Chris Ware constructs a universe that is simultaneously a fictional world and a world shaped by the figures on the page, both inside and outside the panels, his book becomes the starting point of a limitless number of unending stories.

The fast-growing field of "abstract" comics can be approached along comparable lines.[25] Rather than labeling this form of nonfigurative graphic novel as antinarrative or nonnarrative, it is possible to understand in its recent success the sign of a greater awareness of the storytelling capacities of works that are no longer based on the representation of human or humanized characters and action-driven plots. Abstract comics have a long-standing tradition (the notion of abstract graphic novel is not yet in use), but they have only been projected into mainstream culture thanks to successful anthologies such as Andrei Molotiu's *Abstract Comics*.[26] In the context of narrative analysis, the notion of abstraction is tricky. First of all, there may be some confusion in pitting abstraction against narrative, for both notions actually belong to different domains. Abstraction has to do with the problem of representation and mimesis, and is part of the analysis of images, not of stories. At the level of images, the basic distinction is that of abstract versus figurative. At the narrative level, such a distinction is not directly relevant, since the main dichotomy is between narrative and nonnarrative. It may, of course, be true that abstract images do often appear in sequences whose narrative status remains open or unclear, but the link between abstraction and nonnarrative is less automatic than is usually presumed. Moreover, as already said before, the very specificity of storytelling in the graphic novel, with its coincidence of action and description and the possibility of downsizing action in favor of a more descriptive mode of storytelling, makes the idea of "abstract storytelling" (i.e., of storytelling with the help of abstract panels) more than just a wisecracking thought-experiment. It should not come as a surprise that Andrei Molotiu, the major theoretician of abstract comics, underlines the temporal and therefore narrative possibilities of abstraction, provided the latter is combined with sequentiality. Abstract images may be completely nonnarrative. However, sequences of abstract images can produce perfectly coherent narrative strings:

> [The term "abstract comics"] applies to the lack of a narrative excuse to string panels together, in favor of an increased emphasis on the formal elements of comics that, even in the absence of a (verbal) story, can create a feeling of sequential drive, the sheer rhythm of narrative or the rise and fall of a story arc.[27]

Second, the concept of abstract comics is *in practice* a much smaller challenge to the doxa of comics and graphic novel as a basically sequential – and therefore narrative – art than its promoters like to suggest.[28] The reason is simple: it is the reader. Comics connoisseur Douglas Wolk, already quoted for his critical remarks on the graphic novel's romance with schmaltzy semiautobiography, reminds us also of the hard fact that when processing abstract comics or graphic novels, readers actually rely on their knowledge of the narrative potentialities of the medium to make sense of a genre that challenges many of their expectations:

> The artists assembled by Andrei Molotiu for his anthology *Abstract Comics* ... push "cartooning" to its limits.... It's a fascinating book to stare at, and as with other kinds of abstract art, half the fun is observing your own reactions:

anyone who's used to reading more conventional sorts of comics is likely to reflexively impose narrative on these abstractions, to figure out just what each panel has to do with the next.[29]

It is difficult to put with more clarity what reading narratively apparently nonnarative material means: it has to do with readers' decisions (to "impose"), with the capacity of retrieving cognitively stored information (readers are "used to" this or that, they react "reflexively"), and with the emphasis on sequentiality as the basic feature of narrativity ("what each panel has to do with the next"). Although Wolk's claims require additional nuancing – it is one thing to decide to read nonnarative material narratively, and another thing to bring off such a reading successfully – the idea behind his argument is clear: the reading habits of the average comics reader will push that reader minimally to suppose that a narrative is hidden below or behind the surface of an abstract sequence. The practical success of such an experiment can never be guaranteed; some readers simply are better than others at making narrative sense of abstract images, and some abstract material is more open to narrative reappropriation than other material of this sort is. But Wolk is right when claiming that the transition from abstract sequences to narrative deciphering is almost unavoidable.

Another conclusion drawn by Andrei Molotiu in his defense of abstract comics can also find its place in the broader framework of the blurring of boundaries between narration and description: "Though for much of its history, comics' connection to popular culture negated the possibility of overt experimentation with abstract forms, abstract play and the sequencing of formal events often snuck in, whether consciously intended by the artists or not."[30] With compelling examples borrowed from Winsor McCay and Steve Ditko, he shows how even mainstream, commercial comics can give rise to abstraction within narrative thanks, for instance, to the importance taken by the setting and the visualization of the action.

Molotiu's idea that the current interest in abstract comics not only helps rediscover forgotten or censored examples of nonnarative works but also allows for a fresh reading of abstract elements in publications whose narrative status had been unchallenged until now, supports the general thesis that graphic novels are not necessarily action-driven. Many works do contain nonnarrative aspects, while some others impose more radical forms of lack of action or plotlessness. Yet it is the case that none of this prevents the reader from interpreting them in temporal and narrative terms.

The field of nonnarrative aspects should moreover not be restricted to that of abstraction. If it is true that abstraction is an issue (but, in our eyes, more an opportunity than a threat) at the level of the representative status of the image, the question remains how to give a more concrete meaning and content to the nonnarrative pole of the narrative level. According to recent cultural theorists such as Lev Manovich, the structure that opposes narrative most directly is the database, whose spatial logic exceeds the opposition of linearity and nonlinearity. The list, which is the basic structuring principle of the database, becomes a kind of textual reservoir capable of being activated permanently in new forms and combinations. As Manovich puts it:

> After the novel, and subsequently cinema, privileged narrative as the key form of cultural expression of the modern age, the computer age introduces its correlate – the database. Many new media objects do not tell stories; they do not have a beginning or end; in fact, they do not have any development, thematically, formally, or otherwise that would organize their elements into a sequence. Instead, they are collections of individual items, with every item possessing the same significance as any other.[31]

Therefore, nonnarrative or antinarrative ways of structuring a graphic novel can be found not only in "abstract comics;" they are also characteristic of "database comics." As far as we know, the notion of database comics has not yet gained critical street-credibility,[32] but the graphic novelists' practice is, as often, ahead of their theory. Quite some graphic novels, whether using abstract panels and abstract representations or not, have started exploring the uncharted territory of the database, converting their pages into lists and displaying stories that look like more or less random selections of the units of these databases. Once again, work by Chris Ware offers several examples of this technique.[33] Yet here again, it is less antagonism than complementarity that is the name of the game. As argued by N. Katherine Hayles, the splitting of these two principles of sequencing – the nonlinear logic of the database and the linear logic of narrative – can be overcome: "Because database can construct relational juxtapositions but is helpless to interpret or explain them, it needs narrative to make its results meaningful. Narrative, for its part, needs database in the computationally intensive culture of the new millennium to enhance its cultural authority and test the generality of its insights."[34]

The graphic novels that take advantage of nonlinear sequencing of forms and objects also provide us with many good illustrations of the simultaneous combination of the list or database principle, on the one hand, and story logic, on the other.

Conclusion

As already frequently claimed in this book, it makes sense to conclude storytelling in the graphic novel in medium-specific terms. Seen from that point of view, the activity of the storyteller appears to be as much about the shaping of space as about the telling or showing of events, to the extent that some graphic novels are focusing more on places than on people. This does not mean, however, that characters are not important. In a graphic novel, characters are never disembodied, and this emphasis on the body and, more specifically, on the face, produces new forms of storytelling in which the story told is that of a body or face in action. In addition, it is important to stress the thematic breadth of the graphic novel, which is capable of presenting new subject matter (see, for instance, its fascination with presentations of boredom) yet struggles with a perhaps facile tendency to limit itself to "very serious" or semiautobiographical subject matter. Abstract comics, a new move in the graphic novel, may be one of the possible answers to this narrowing down of the medium to a tool of life storytelling. Finally, one should notice as well how different a graphic storyteller is from the narrator of a novel (and also from the author and implied author). In a graphic novel, the words of the narrator are visually present, for example, and this overt presence of his or her speech act creates new possibilities of rethinking the relationships among author, implied author, and narrator.

PART THREE

THEMES

8 The Graphic Novel and Literary Fiction:
Exchanges, Interplays, and Fusions

The final two chapters of this work address some important thematic ways of exploring contemporary graphic novels. In Chapter 9 we discuss the theme of nostalgia, while in this chapter we analyze the interplays between graphic novels and literary fiction that have occurred over the past decade or so.

In 2005, British novelist, writer, and journalist Iain Sinclair published a new work titled *Edge of the Orison*. It is an exploration of the poet John Clare's walk from London to Northborough. Sinclair follows in Clare's footsteps, musing on themes of memory, space, past times, and present conditions. This is what critics call psycho-geography, the sounding out of places for their forgotten historical meanings, discussing echoes of past stories woven into the everyday environment. When Sinclair reaches Northampton, extended passages of his work feature his meeting Alan Moore. For example, of Northampton, Sinclair writes: "A market square as generously proportioned, commercially sound, as a Flemish town. Such solidity of purpose demands its Bosch, its painter of demons; its Alan Moore."[1] Maybe one should not be surprised at the attention Sinclair pays to Moore here. In fact, their agendas and interests have criss-crossed for several years now. In particular, Alan Moore and Eddie Campbell's *From Hell* overlaps with Sinclair's own fascination with London, its dark corners, and its occult traces. In any case, after Sinclair featured him in *Edge of the Orison*, Moore repaid the compliment when in *The League of Extraordinary Gentlemen* series he invents his interpretation of Iain Sinclair, the character Andrew Norton. These quick snapshots of dialogues between literary writers and graphic novelists are far from isolated incidences, not just lone sightings in the small world of English life and letters. In America, France, and Belgium too, there has been a significant warp and weave occurring between literary fiction and the graphic novel, and vice versa. Students researching the graphic novel as part of their studies on literature courses would be missing out greatly if they did not start to piece together the many connections that have developed between the two forms. This chapter aims to assist in that venture and to point out some of the most relevant material. The structure proposed is (1) an analytical description of where fiction writers are exploring linkages and connections to graphic novels; (2) a discussion of the complimentary pull of the tide, when graphic novelists have approached literature; and (3) analytical suggestions for where this leaves the contemporary graphic novel.

How the literary milieu courted and recuperated comics and graphic novels

Over the last decade, literary culture has been changing to become more receptive and open to graphic narratives and visual culture, per se. Jim Collins writing in *Bring on the Books for Everybody* explains that through the 2000s literary publishing has been significantly affected by cinema and the rise of the text-image forms of digital culture.[2] He explains that this has meant that novelists and publishers are no longer in a privileged position, their status and the status of the word has evolved to accommodate an increasingly visually oriented public-commercial sphere.[3] Collins explains that major film adaptations (often produced by Miramax) have created hit literary novel bestsellers, while television shows and their associated book clubs (such as Oprah's Book Club) have had similar effects on publishing. Online reviewing, especially at Amazon.com, has also meant that literary works gain status through an association with the visual arts/digital culture. To generalize, one can say that this means that traditional writers and publishers are far less secure in their cultural status and increasingly building bridges to the visual world. This is because it seems that cultural status of a work of literary fiction is no longer generated by words alone, but is situated in a more complex economy of words and images (cinema, television, online reviews). Interestingly for a writer such as the aforementioned Iain Sinclair, this has been a journey from conventional literary fiction to writings grounded in history, localized cultural practices, psycho-geography.

It is in these conditions that some (but, of course, far from all) literary novelists have been drawn to address visual and popular culture in their writings, including comics and comics retrospectively described as graphic novels. The outstandingly successful example is Michael Chabon's novel *The Amazing Adventures of Kavalier and Clay*.[4] Herein Chabon mined the history of comics to tell a fictional tale about themes of American history. Perhaps inspired by *Maus* and also wanting to write "The Great American Novel," Chabon melds the history of popular culture (he invents the story of a comic – *The Escapist* – which echoes Will Eisner's *The Spirit*) with treatment of Nazism, adding for good measure a critique of homophobia. Lauded by critics, it was awarded a Pulitzer Prize for Literature and has subsequently inspired a spin-off graphic narrative, *The Escapist*. That work features further writing from Chabon and employs major artists from adult comics, including Howard Chaykin and Chris Ware (for cover design work). It offers the reader the fictional comic strip that *Kavalier and Clay* first invented only in words. It adds to the counter-factual history of comics already narrated in the original novel.

However, *Kavalier and Clay* is just the best known and most successful of many other similar works. For example, in 1990, Jon Stephen Fink produced his tale of a superhero radio play character, The Green Ray, in his novel *Further Adventures* (1990). Cultural commentator and literary historian Jonathan Lethem has also written fiction inspired by his love of comics, notably *The Fortress of Solitude*. Lethem, like Chabon, is also a perceptive writer of essays and criticism. In arguably his best work, *The Disappointment Artist*, comics are reinterpreted as serious art, graphic novels.[5] Tom De Haven's oeuvre is similarly important evidence of literary fiction encountering our subject. As well as recently writing a Yale University Press published discussion *Superman: The History of a National Icon*, he has written novelizations about the eponymous hero. In a different vein in the 1990s and early 2000s, he authored the "Derby Dugan" trilogy. Therein De Haven plunges the reader into a fictional history of American comic strips through the stories of the men responsible for various incarnations of an imaginary strip *Derby Dugan*. Beginning in the 1920s, the series culminates with *Dugan Under Ground* (2001) that explores how young artists in the 1960s take forward the comics medium and change it into something more experimental and autobiographical. De Haven's descriptions here represent imaginary histories of the comic and the graphic novel. His fictional artists are shown wrestling to create existential meaning from the childish strip that so fascinates them, a process that drives them insane. Of special note is the second part of the trilogy. Here Art Spiegelman provided a cover illustration and an imaginary one page of a *Dugan* strip (attributed to De Haven's fictional cartoonist Walter Geebus).

There were earlier adopters of using fiction to reimagine comics and to thereby instill a popular cultural form with the intellectual prestige of literary fiction. Robert Mayer's *Superfolks* is a satirical reinterpretation of the worlds of DC and Marvel. Filled with in-jokes and intertextual references, it pokes fun at the improbable fantasy world of the superhero. The British writer-artist Grant Morrison – whose noir rethinking of Batman, with Dave McKean, *Arkham Asylum*, was a bestseller in the early 1990s – describes it as "some of the aboriginal roots nourishing the '80s 'adult' superhero comic boom."[6] Hergé's Tintin too was being systematically reinterpreted in the mid- to late-1970s. This occurred through a series of short stories published in leading literary and fine art periodicals by the avant-garde novelist Frederic Tuten. Here he blurred together the stereotypes from the Francophone comic books with situations and references to Thomas Mann's *The Magic Mountain*.[7] When Tuten's completed novel, *Tintin in the New World*, was published in 1993, it was further intellectualized with inclusion of cover art and a frontispiece illustration from Roy Lichtenstein (fine art elevating pop culture). Nonetheless, the works that gained the most critical attention before *Kavalier and Clay* are Jay Cantor's *Krazy Kat: A Novel in Five Panels* and Rick Moody's *The Ice Storm*.[8] As with Tuten's experiment, much of the point of Cantor's work was to play with the universe of the inter-war Herriman strip. Moody was different, with the world of comics being one part of his critique and celebration of 1970s middle-class New England. What Moody predicted and announced in his work was the potential for comics to become popular with readers of fiction looking to reconnect with their memories of youth and the immediate-but-now-fading past. Ang Lee's brilliant interpretation of the novel for cinema (1997) only added to its success and influence. Probably the most celebratory of American comics history through the form of the novel is Umberto Eco's contribution. Though he was well known for his essays on popular culture and comics, the epitome of this strand in his work is his novel *The Mysterious Flame Queen of Loana: An Illustrated Novel*.[9] Extensively illustrated with reproductions of comics from the 1930s and 1940s, Eco narrates how a dying man's memories and thoughts turn to his love of the American import comic books. It is there that he learns a vision of democracy that counters the negative popular culture he has ingested from Italian fascism.

So, a subfield of literary fiction has developed that focuses on superhero mythology and the wider world of the history of comics. These fictions have been highly successful, gaining sales and prestigious awards. Chabon's work is especially praised and has generated a small academic literature of its own. In 2006 *Time Magazine* (Canada) touted him and Jonathan Lethem alongside David Foster Wallace and Jonathan Franzen as the "voice of the generation," though reporter Lev Grossman subsequently moderated the claim. Nonetheless, in the same essay Bret Easton Ellis identified *Kavalier and Clay* and *The Fortress of Solitude* as "the best novels of my generation."[10] For what it's worth, writing elsewhere Ellis has noted that in his youth he read the EC horror comics, and they surely inspired his own imagination. Talking to an interviewer while driving his BMW through the Hollywood Hills, in a passage that would make Fredric Wertham twist and turn in his grave (pun intended with apologies), he commented on how EC horror comics inspired the bloody details from his infamously violent-pornographic novel *American Psycho*: "When I wrote about those scenes I was thinking about a lot of things – the EC comics of my youth, like *Tales from the Crypt* and *The Vault of Horror*, and various slasher movies I saw as a kid and a lot of horror fiction I'd read."[11]

Besides writing fiction, Jonathan Lethem and Michael Chabon publish regularly on aspects of pop culture, including contemporary graphic novels and the history of comic books. This is a substantial critical and intellectual endeavour that is supported by publishers and periodicals. *The New Yorker*, *BookForum*, *London Review of Books*, and others have featured their criticism, which so often seeks to encourage more reverence for pop culture and cult authors, and the books and comics once relegated to the margins are to now be accepted and seen as valuable. Stylish writing – combining analysis, praise, and personal recollection – pulls the reader into the Chabon-Lethem universe. The best exemplary critical essay from Chabon is his extended discussion of the modern short story wherein a persuasive case is made for authors and their works that are like "Trickster" situated in-between at intersections in genre and style, neither fully popular and nor elite, but somewhere in the exciting borderlines. So, Chabon comments: "Trickster goes where the action is, and the action is in the borders between things."[12] Lethem too has been incredibly persuasive and erudite in numerous clever pieces: one recommended companion to the Chabon essay is his "Against 'Pop' Culture," wherein he delineates how labels such as "pop" shut down readings and were not helpful, remarking: "Couldn't we just say *culture*?"[13]

Literary fiction in the 1990s and 2000s playfully blurred borders of traditional notions of high and low culture and readily indulged in using comics and graphic novels as a basis for work or helpful backdrop. Literature and preexisting fan cultures were oddly merging, and the novels evoking comics played their part. Probably influential on the works just cited was the huge commercial and critical success of Nick Hornby's novels on similar issues of fandom, *Fever Pitch* (soccer) and *High Fidelity* (music).[14] These two books introduce and use a literary voice to investigate subcultures of entertainment, sports, and music. Lethem himself explained the phenomenon by saying that "Now a lot of writing has a very natural degree of engagement with vernacular culture,"[15] and clearly his work and that of several other mainly white, male, younger novelists has developed in this direction, following Hornby but, instead of soccer, taking on memories of comics. We return to this issue of nostalgia in Chapter 9, as it is so often coming up in our considerations.

What conclusions can we draw? First, the literary world's interest in comics and graphic novels further legitimates both fields as being part of the wider literary realm; it is no coincidence that Chabon has stated that the novel and graphic novel "are in the same boat" of good culture. Here, one of the original motives for the graphic novel has been met, the aspiration to be taken seriously and to be rated as comparable to the novel. Ironically, this does now mean that the term is not so strategically significant as it used to be. Second, as a result of the above encounter, new graphic novels have been created and novelists have been recruited to provide scripts and commissioned to collaborate on original graphic novels. Chabon has worked on *The Escapist* scripts, while Lethem scripted a remake superhero title, *Omega the Unknown*. There has been an intensification of production out of which the graphic novel has gained renewed attention. Third, it has tended to be nationally recognized, vernacular comics that have featured most commonly in literature. Krazy Kat, Marvel, Superman, and Tintin are used because they are popular and speak to the history of comics and of comic reading in specific times and places. This does mean that more "literary" graphic novels and less well-known titles that are quite avant-garde do not get noticed in this way. For example, the work of a fine artist such as Andrzej Klimowski, who is published by literary house Faber and Faber, will probably never figure in a novel by an upcoming writer or in a title by a now-recognized talent such as Chabon or Lethem.

Before discussing how graphic novelists use and rethink the literary world, let us pause to give time to two important figures who sit between the two spheres we are discussing. Literary culture is a small world, and one can map on to it quite clearly how significant individuals have played a part in raising the profile of the graphic novel in the last two decades. In fact, no serious discussion of the graphic novel should ignore the contributions of Chip Kidd and Dave Eggers, who have both done more than most to reach out to interact with the graphic novel and shape its very production. Both in their own way, and sometimes working in collaboration, have done much to integrate an appreciation of graphic art, *grosso modo*, and graphic novels more specifically into the wider literary culture. They have worked tirelessly for its recognition among nontraditional comic readers and reviewers. Their work has been central to attaching graphic novels to literary culture and making literary culture appreciate the graphic novel.

The influence of Kidd and Eggers is too frequently overlooked in discussions of the graphic novel. For instance, they are hardly noted in recent work such as the Modern Language Association' s *Teaching the Graphic Novel* and the scholarly collection *The Rise of the American Comics Artist*.[16] So let us begin to fill the lacunae. Chip Kidd is a graphic designer who is best known for his original dust jacket designs. As well as providing "the look" for numerous major works of contemporary literature, Kidd has been highly influential in the promotion of the graphic novel in the 2000s. Kidd narrates his role as graphic novel editor at Pantheon:

> In 1997 editor Dan Frank contacted me about a manuscript that had caught his eye by someone named Ben Katchor – did I know anything about him? What I knew from his weekly strip *Julius Knipl, Real Estate Photographer* was that Ben was a genius and I was a fan. Yes, please, let's do publish him, I said. The result was *The Jew of New York*, which I designed with Pantheon in-house staff member Misha Beletsky. Then I asked Dan, "Is Pantheon going to start doing this again, publishing comics?" to which he replied, "Should we? Who else is there?" And I told him: Chris Ware, Dan Clowes, Kim Deitch, Mark Beyer, Charles Burns, – all of whom had works in the pipeline. So one by one we published them, and the "Graphic Novel Phenomenon" has steadily emerged as one of the few publishing success stories post -9/11.... Dan

handles the business end of it and I act as editor and in some cases designer, depending on the artist's needs.[17]

The collaboration has been quite remarkable. Following Ben Katchor's work, Kidd and Pantheon brought out Chris Ware's *Jimmy Corrigan: The Smartest Kid on Earth*. Kidd was an admirer of Ware from long before his name was well known to the public. He has recalled that in 1991 he was already a great supporter, passing copies of Ware's unsigned contribution to *RAW* magazine to students in the class he was teaching at the New York School of Visual Arts. The men then had subsequently worked together, with Kidd commissioning Ware to provide an invitation for a talk he was delivering on book jacket design to the Director's Club in New York. Further design collaborations followed, including Ware working with Kidd on dust jackets such as Haruki Murakami, *The Wind-Up Bird Chronicle* (1997). Kidd has described Ware as a genius, and in turn Ware has noted that Chip is "one of his best friends … and I doubt very much if I could still be drawing comics if it wasn't for his efforts on my behalf, starting in 1995 up until now … he's the greatest living designer."[18]

Besides promoting graphic novelists through his editorial role at Pantheon, Kidd's passion for comics, pre-graphic novels, has also been much evidenced. In particular, he has played an important curatorial role in the history of comics by bringing out glossy, high production value coffee table books devoted to DC superheroes. In addition, Kidd collaborated with Art Spiegelman in publishing a book-length edition of the former's essay on Jack Cole. Kidd's love of Charles Schulz's *Peanuts* led him to work on a similarly reverential art book, *Peanuts: The Art of Charles M. Schulz*. Kidd is a huge supporter of many different comics and graphic novels, and his design work has assisted far more artists than work by any other creator of his type. Kidd's taste is truly eclectic when it comes to publishing and graphic design for graphic narrative: it ranges from Ware's *Jimmy Corrigan* to work on Frank Miller's *Sin City* and reissues of Miller and David Mazzucchelli's *Batman Year One*. His thinking for dust jackets for numerous graphic novels or related publication crosses over so many different types of work that it makes him one of the preeminent inventors of the form, certainly as a saleable book commodity that looks good on a bookstore shelf or on an adult's desk or side table.

Two further comments are important to add. First, Kidd's embracing of new graphic novels and curatorial reissuing of books about superhero art provide a bridge between these two types of otherwise distinct publications. Kidd is at the center of this new world that pulls graphic novels and comics close together in publishing, linking Spiegelman to Miller, Ware to Batman, and many other points in between. This has raised the profile of DC-style superhero material for intelligent adult book buyers, and partly it has also grounded graphic novels close to their roots in comic strips and dailies. Second, Kidd's meticulous attention to designing literary books (jackets and layouts) has made a generation of novelists more aware of the look of their work and hence visual culture in general. His treatments have added to the blurring of the literary space with the visual. Indeed, this blurring effect has only been exaggerated by Kidd's recent projects. In the late 2000s, he shifted from designer to writer, offering two novels (one on teaching design at university and one on the ad-design profession of the early 1960s) and a script for a new Batman graphic novel. Though Kidd instigated these creations, their final look was created with help from his graphic novelist colleagues, notably Charles Burns (cover to the novel *The Learners*) and Ware (design features to the novel *The Cheese Monkeys*).[19]

Whereas to some extent Kidd has worked inside existing publishing houses (Knopf, Pantheon, cooperating with DC), Dave Eggers has almost singlehandedly invented his own publishing machine, the periodical *McSweeney's Quarterly Concern* and the magazine *The Believer*. Launched in 2000, the *McSweeney's* "world" was created as a new space for innovative creative writing. Like Kidd, Eggers wanted his publication to look and feel appropriate, concentrating greatly on the look of his periodical. Over the life span of the journal it has also included and embraced the work of graphic novelists, including several of the prestige names Kidd "made" at Pantheon. Thus *McSweeney's* number 13 is entirely devoted to the theme of comics and graphic novels and is edited by Chris Ware. Later publications have echoed this, including a faux-comics supplement to the *McSweeney*'s issue on San Francisco and publication of prints of Spiegelman's drawings. The hip choice of using graphic novelists in the magazine for new fiction lent it lustre. And of course, the same process worked in the other direction, bringing graphic novelists and their works to the attention of the creative writing literati.

Eggers's own background no doubt prompted this process: he had worked as a cartoonist and in the 1980s was a style magazine editor. There are many links one could tease out in fact. For example, certainly Eggers's literary work shares the common autobiographical theme to be found in many graphic novels.[20] Moreover, besides editing, he has also worked on major film adaptations that have celebrated the world of illustration. Thus he worked on the film script to the Hollywood adaptation of Maurice Sendak's famous *Where the Wild Things Are* (Spike Jonze, 2009) and along with that wrote up the excellent novelization for younger readers (of all ages) titled *The Wild Things*. In short, if one were looking for a real-life exemplar of what Michael Chabon called "the Trickster," equally at home on the frontiers and borderlands of different cultural spaces and forms, he would look just like Eggers.

When graphic novelists encounter literature

Communication is normally a two-way process and just as members of the literary milieu have courted comics and graphic novels, so too have graphic novelists been drawn to address literary themes and make literature a subject of their storytelling and creativity. In fact, the exchange working in this direction has been very productive, with some graphic novelists becoming novelists (e.g., Alan Moore, Neil Gaiman, and Warren Ellis); many treating the world of literature as a major theme in their graphic novels; and others contributing graphic novel work to collections of conventional writing.

Literary adaptations have always been part of comics culture. As all new media in search of cultural respectability, comics have tried to cash in on the prestige of the literary (national and world) heritage, and series such as *Classics Illustrated* have attempted for decades to transfer this literary material to the world of visual storytelling. In that sense, comics are not really different from, for instance, movies, which have often adopted similar strategies. It would be an error, however, to believe that in their confrontation with canonized culture, all new (popular, commercial, reputedly low- or middle-brow) media behave the same way. As cleverly observed by Martin Barker and Roger Sabin in their study on adaptations, in *The Lasting of the Mohicans*, there is a striking contrast between the "freedom" of the movie adaptations and the (relative) timidity of the comics adaptations, and here it is necessary to take into account the social status of the adapting medium. Sabin and Barker explain:

> Comic book versions raise quite different issues from the films. . . . [T]he history of comics in both Britain and America is a history of nervousness about their cultural position. When, therefore, a comics publisher decides to do a version of a classic book, there has almost always been a hint of genuflection to "serious culture." Comics have thought of themselves as second-class citizens, and their treatment of books, especially classics like *Mohicans*, is essentially reverential. Therefore the comics rarely, if ever, change the main elements of the plot or the sequence of events. Particular moments may be eliminated . . . and the special "grammar" of comic books means that in complicated ways they can shift our understanding of characters' motivation. But the fear of offending means that, with the American and British comic versions at least, the book rules.[21]

It should be noted that the didactic and reverential attitude toward the literary masterpiece and the big book is still there, as can be seen in the frequently made adaptations of classic books, although in renewed forms and with the help of up-to-date technology: in France, the graphic novel adaptation of Proust's *Remembrance of Things Past*[22] is a real bestseller, and in the Anglo-Saxon world an appealing example is *Ulysses "Seen"*:

> *Ulysses "Seen"* is a web based comic adaptation of Joyce's masterpiece, developed with the aim of reinvigorating an appreciation for a work which

has established a reputation for inaccessibility. The project offers itself as a unique companion piece to the novel, transposing the subtlety and humour of the book into a comic narrative form which will be familiar to 21st Century readers.[23]

Yet if, as this book argues throughout, there is a real difference between comics and graphic novel and if, as we believe, this difference is cultural rather than narrowly formal or visual, it should not come as a surprise that graphic novelists today do encounter literature in different ways to comics.

This difference can be analyzed at two levels. First of all, it should be noted that the graphic novel itself, regardless of whether it adapts previously existing literary material or not, claims now to be literature, and this was always an implicit element of the term, including, as it does, the word "novel." A watershed moment in this shift was the creation of the French magazine *(A Suivre)*, whose doctrine touched the American public through *RAW* and *Heavy Metal*, the two strongly European-oriented publications that featured authors working in the *(A Suivre)* spirit such as Jacques Tardi (see Chapter 4). Typical of the monthly magazine and of the zeitgeist that it represented was the awareness that the graphic *novel*[24] could be an example not just of popular genre fiction, but of literature tout court. *(A Suivre)* defended in very explicit terms a literary conception of the graphic novel, and even an unabashedly traditional and almost romantic one, strongly influenced by, on the one hand, *auteur*'s theory (the model of the author being here the writer, and not the film director), and, on the other hand, adventure narrative (for example, Hugo Pratt's highly praised *Corto Maltese* implied strong references to nineteenth-century adventure novels *à la* Stevenson).[25] So *(A Suivre)* not only offered the technical and, thanks to serialization and prepublication, financial opportunities for making graphic novels as long as real novels (for size mattered!). It also created a new vision of BD that could now be framed as "literature" or, more specifically, as "graphic novel." In addition, this new form of literature no longer had to rely on the amalgam concept of "literary adaptation," already well known in commercial BD, where it did not always have an excellent reputation. As a matter of fact, the recent fashion of literary adaptations is often seen in France as a vulgar attempt to milk the new literary prestige of the graphic novel itself. On the contrary, the craving for new, apparently "plotless" or less action-driven, more visually challenging forms of storytelling was put on top of the creative agenda. How confidently self-conscious the graphic novel has become can be seen very neatly in Jason's *Left Bank Gang* (2008), which retells the story of the great American writers exiled in Paris during the Roaring Twenties, as if these writers, F. Scott Fitzgerald, Ernest Hemingway, Ezra Pound, and James Joyce, had all been graphic novelists (Illustration 8.a).

Second, the difference between comics and graphic novel is displayed also at the level of the adaptations themselves. Contrary to the reverential attitude observed by Barker and Sabin, graphic novels are not afraid of taking liberties with the material they adapt, and here as well French models and influences may have played a historic role. For example, among the experiments that have paved the road to cultural recognition for the graphic novel was the "visual reinterpretation" of Raymond Queneau's *Zazie in the Metro*[26] by French typographer Jacques Carelman (1965). This work – a mix of comics, illustration, and traditional book and album publication[27] – astutely plays with different existing models such as the French bowdlerizing habit to insert comics summaries in books for adolescents (the French version of *Classics Illustrated*, if you want). The worldwide success of Louis Malle's 1960 film adaptation as well as the prestige of Carelman's typographical experiments, which also circulated widely, have drawn a lot of attention to this adaptation, which opened new ways of thinking for visual adaptations of literary texts. (See Illustration 8.b.)

It is certainly in the spirit of creative adaptation that Simon Grennan is working on Anthony Trollope's *John Caldigate*. At present this is a work in progress, but as the sample pages included elsewhere in this book finely illustrate, it will show how a contemporary artist can respect a classic but also remake it to create a new piece. Noticeable already is how Grennan uses perspective and turning points of view, suggestive of nineteenth-century dance, to create a rhythm in the graphic novel that is not possible in the original work. (See Illustration 8.c.)

8.a. Here, Jason's work brings the literary imagination into the graphic novel. Reprinted with kind permission of Fantagraphics, Seattle.

Après tout, disait le type, c'est peut-être vott dame qui me l'a fauché, mon pacson. Elle a peut-être envie de porter des bloudjinnzes elle aussi, vott dame. Ça sûrement non, disait Gabriel, sûrement pas. Qu'est-ce que vous en savez? répliquait le type, l'idée peut lui a être venue avec un mari qui a des façons d'hormosessuel.

— Qu'est-ce que c'est un hormosessuel? demanda Zazie. — C'est un homme qui met des bloudjinnzes, dit doucement Marceline. — Tu me racontes des blagues, dit Zazie. — Gabriel devrait le mettre à la porte, dit doucement Marceline. — Ça c'est une riche idée, Zazie dit. Puis méfiante : Il serait chiche de le faire? — Tu vas

oir. — Attends, je vais entrer la première. Elle ouvrit la porte et, d'une voix forte et claire, prononça les mots suivants : — Alors, tonton Gabriel, comment trouves-tu mes bloudjinnzes? — Veux-tu vite enlever ça, s'écria Gabriel épouvanté, et les rendre au meussieu tout de uite. — Les rendre mon cul, déclara Zazie. Y a pas de raisons. Ils sont à moi. — J'en suis as bien sûr, dit Gabriel embêté. — Oui, dit le type, enlève ça et au trot. — Fous-le donc à a porte, dit Zazie à Gabriel. — T'en as de bonnes, dit Gabriel. Tu me préviens que c'est un ic et ensuite tu voudrais que je tape dessus. — C'est pas parce qu'il est un flic qu'i faut n avoir peur, dit Zazie avec grandiloquence.

C'est un dégueulasse qui m'a fait des propositions sales, alors on ira devant les juges tout flic qu'il est, et les juges, je les connais moi, ils aiment les petites filles, alors le flic dégueulasse, il sera condamné à mort et guillotiné et moi j'irai chercher sa tête dans le panier de son et je lui cracherai sur sa sale gueule, na.

Gabriel fermit les yeux en frémissant à l'évocation de ces atrocités. Il se tournit vers le type : — Vous entendez, qu'il lui dit. Vous avez ien réfléchi? C'est terrible, vous savez les gosses. — Tonton Gabriel, 'écria Zazie, je te jure que c'est hà moi les bloujinnzes. Faut mdéfen-lre, tonton Gabriel. Faut mdéfendre. Qu'est-ce qu'elle dira ma noman si elle apprenait que tu me laisses insulter par un galapiat, un gougnafier et peut-être même un conducteur du dimanche...

Merde, ajouta-t-elle pour son compte avec sa petite voix intérieure, chsuis aussi bonne que Michèle Morgan dans La Dame aux camélias. Effectivement touché par le pathétique de cette invocation, Gabriel manifesta son embarras en ces termes mesurés qu'il prononça médza votché et pour ainsi dire quasiment in petto : — c'est tout de même embêtant de se mettre à dos un bourin. Le type ricane. Ce que vous pouvez avoir l'esprit mal tourné, dit Gabriel en rougissant.

8.b. Between illustrated novel and graphic novel: excerpt from Carelman, *Zazie dans le métro* (Paris: Gallimard, 1965). © Éditions Gallimard.

Art Spiegelman's work in the years immediately following *Maus* repeated much of the *(A Suivre)* attack on literary ground, as well as, of course, its visual inventiveness. Again it is a new and distinct approach from the old reverential tone of earlier adaptation strategies. His own initial post-*Maus* publications were clearly original interventions pushing toward the world of literature. First he worked on illustrating and republishing a 1920s extended poem, Joseph Moncure March's *The Wild Party*.[28] In addition he cooperated with the Neon Lit publishing house to try to promote highly original graphic novel adaptations of existing, well-received literary texts. Spiegelman and Françoise Mouly were the force behind significant literary achievements in the early 1990s. This was when David Mazzucchelli and Paul Karasik worked together with Spiegelman and novelist Paul Auster to create the adaptation *City of Glass*. Today it is considered something of a classic and in some ways is far less dated than the original fiction, which was very much late 1980s post-modern experimentalism. In parallel, the RAW house also managed to create a graphic reworking of David Gifford's novel *Perdita Durango*, and Spiegelman is said to have encouraged Spain Rodriguez's work on an interpretation of William Lindsay Gresham's *Nightmare Alley*. In addition, Spiegelman joined the staff of the *The New Yorker* magazine and was responsible for cover designs, including several controversial ones. Following 9/11, the same magazine turned to Mouly and Spiegelman for an image to capture the city's emotions, and it was here that his work toward the imagery of *In the Shadow of No Towers* began. We should also note here the so-often overlooked Spiegelman-related project *The Narrative Corpse*, for it is relevant too.[29] Published in 1995, it evokes experimental writing – here André Breton and not Raymond Queneau. Editors Spiegelman and R. Sikoryak pulled together sixty-nine artists to create a chain-written graphic novel, each creator making three panels and then passing the story on to the next contributor. The final coherence of the work is provided by consistent page size and a standard layout pattern, as well as black-and-white printing throughout. This is

a visual experiment, but it is also in the tradition of Parisian literary experimentation and game playing.

A new threshold is passed when graphic novelists, rather than adapting literary texts in their own way, with all the creative freedom endowed by the new prestige of their medium, start to compete with literary authors in their own field. A good example can be found in the work of the Matt Madden, U.S. correspondent of the international French Oulipo group. Specializing in so-called constrained (i.e., rule-generated) writing, Oulipo has extended its work to other than strictly literary fields, such as painting and also comics. In that domain it has created a subsection named Oubapo (OUvroir de BAnde dessinée POtentielle," or "workshop for potential comics"). Well-known in France, the Oubapo production, which significantly combines hands-on practice and theoretical research, has been successfully introduced in the United States by Madden, a teacher of comics at the School of Visual Arts and Yale University.[30] His already-mentioned book *99 Ways to Tell A Story: Exercises in Style* (2005) is a creative homage to *Exercises in Style* (1947) by Raymond Queneau, a founding work of the Oulipo movement in which the author retells the same simple story in ninety-nine different ways. What Madden does in his own book is transfer the variation principle from the field of literature to that of visual storytelling. The dialogue with the French model is here threefold: (1) the direct transposition of a work by Queneau, (2) the dialogue with the other techniques and achievements of the Oubapo network (which Madden both emulates and remediates), and (3) the integration in the Oulipo network whose influence in the United States has been rapidly increasing over last two decades (culturally speaking, Oulipo is now at the heart of the canon in contemporary French literature).

As borders between two existing fields become much closer, maybe for some a new common space is clearly in the making. Thus graphic

---

Opposite page: 8.c. An example of shifting perspective and point of view: excerpt from *Dispossession*, Simon Grennan's unpublished adaptation of A. Trollope's novel *John Caldigate*. Used by kind permission of the artist.

novelists have contributed work to be included in collections of short stories from leading younger fiction writers. A good example here is the Zadie Smith-edited collection *The Book of Other People*. Published by Penguin, the work gathers together short fiction from an impressive array of contemporary literary talent; besides Smith's own contribution, there are short pieces from Jonathan Safran Foer, David Mitchell, Colm Toibin, Dave Eggers, and Jonathan Lethem, among others. Alongside these contributions the collection also invited work from Daniel Clowes, Chris Ware, and Posy Simmonds working with Nick Hornby. What is important here is that the graphic novelists were included and published alongside the novelists. Clowes, Ware, and Simmonds and Hornby impressively fulfill the brief of the anthology to be "about character ... to make someone up."[31] Ware offers a bleak depiction of adolescence through the life story of Jonathan Wellington Lint to the age of thirteen. Simmonds and Hornby offer an invented literary life. The chapter from Clowes more directly acknowledges nonliterary pop culture: it narrates the story of an online film reviewer, Justin M. Damiano, a know-it-all character who is a legend in his own blogosphere. The Zadie Smith collection was not the first blending of work from graphic novelists and other writers in a predominantly literary context. Earlier examples include the Dave Eggers-edited *Best American Non-Required Reading* from 2002. In this first anthology (annually published, several have followed that include links to graphic novelists: for example, in 2009 it was again edited by Eggers but included an introduction from Marjane Satrapi) there is again a mix of traditional writing and an extract from a graphic novel, in this case, Adrian Tomine's work "Bomb Scare" that had been first published in his own series *Optic Nerve* and that is reprinted in *Platinum Blonde*.

Another comparable phenomenon is the creation of a further series: *The Best American Comics* (first printed in 2006, edited by Harvey Pekar, and then subsequently annually). What is important about this and *The Best American Non-Required Reading* is that when graphic narratives were edited in this format, readers started to see them as analogous to the publisher's other famous series, such as *The Best American Poems* and *The Best American Short Fiction*. Moreover in some bookshops, all this material is presented on the same tables, so there is further integration of text-image culture into the contemporary literary space. And, by the way, we do not even begin to account for author websites, interviews, blogs, and promotional blurbs for friends or colleagues that are all areas where graphic novelists use literary connections or find their work being viewed as if it were a novel.

In fact, through much of the 2000s, several graphic novelists have moonlighted from their day jobs as graphic narrators to produce book covers drawn in their own style and often with thematic links from their oeuvres. Importantly, the leading fiction house, Penguin, reissued numerous classics as Penguin Classic Deluxe editions and in order to brand them for new, younger readers, commissioned jacket designs from prominent graphic novelists. Among the titles that were produced by graphic novelists one discovers Charles Burns's work on Upton Sinclair's *The Jungle*; Chester Brown on D.H. Lawrence's *Lady Chatterley's Lover*; Daniel Clowes on Mary Wollstonecraft Shelley's *Frankenstein*; and Frank Miller on Thomas Pynchon's *Gravity's Rainbow*. What we wish to highlight with this specific trend is that these covers are telling because they make the published novel inside look as if it is going to be a graphic novel, and *not the original text*. Such confusion is likely because some novels were being adapted (notably Auster's *City of Glass* and Gifford's *Perdita Durango*), and graphic novel artists were becoming known for their individual trademark aesthetic look. The strategy at Penguin also seems to suggest that the way to sell classics is to appeal to people familiar with and presumably already purchasing graphic novels. Whereas the old *Classics Illustrated* covers tended to hide the fact that inside there was a comic book adaptation (using large single images conventional to fiction illustration and avoiding panels and speech bubbles), some of the Penguin covers to novels created by graphic novelists imply that the text is going to be a great adaptation, including grids, common comic aesthetic styles, and even speech bubbles.

Maybe inevitably, literature has become a recurrent and important subject matter in the graphic novels themselves. This has been notably the case in the series from Alan Moore and Kevin O'Neill, *The League of Extraordinary Gentlemen*. Now composed of some six graphic novels, the series provides a mock Victorian action-adventure narrative complete with heroes and villains. However, none of the characters are at all new, and each main part is an imaginative reinvention of a classic protagonist: H. Rider Haggard's Allan Quatermain, H. G. Wells's Invisible Man, Jules Verne's Captain Nemo, and so forth. Thus Moore and O'Neill have set about completely reimagining literary history and have pushed these protagonists into distinct adventures. As the series has shifted time zones, some relatively obscure literary characters have been added, including psycho-geographer Iain Sinclair. The work is multi-layered – very multi-layered – and provides a rich story world where the lines between history, science-fiction, and old and new literary constructs are repeatedly blurred together. The cross references are so fulsome that entire books and websites have been written to provide guidelines for readers without master's degrees in literature. Ultimately what this achieves is a twofold process: (1) it entwines Moore's and O'Neill's creativity as graphic novelists into the realm of the literary, and (2) it points to the sharp and significant lines that exist between late nineteenth-century popular fiction and the later world of comics, American superheroes, and the graphic novel. Moreover, the form of the graphic novel serialization is uniquely able to handle the detail and scope of material without becoming destroyed by its own weight. Drawing pastiche characters from fiction is quicker and more economical than rewriting them; choices of literary style, old or new, are also neatly avoided by the emphasis on visualizing the famous literary roll call. The box-after-box narration similarly keeps a close control on a fantastical and often circular narrative that could not be told in the same way through a standard form of writing. The dominant technique in *The League* is appropriation, turning adventure fiction into an ironic graphic novel, which is closer than one first thinks to the work of Warhol and Lichtenstein.

It is intriguing to note here the interesting parallels between Anglophone and Francophone developments. Thus, the aforementioned work from Moore and O'Neill was first published in 1999, precisely the point when graphic novel publishing was becoming very confident. In France, a very thematically similar work was published in the late 1970s, precisely when French BD culture was becoming more literary via *(A Suivre)*. Here, we refer to Floc'h and Rivière's wonderful *Rendez-vous à Sevenoaks* and many subsequent works. Floc'h and Rivière reinvented BD adventure series by pulling them directly into the world of English literature. Thus this first book includes a cameo from Agatha Christie, and over the course of the adventures a range of real-life writers have featured. Moreover, in a further breaking down of boundaries, the characters from the graphic novel feature in Rivière's detective novels, and he is also a biographer of writers Christie and Enid Blyton. It is also the case that the 1977 founding work, *Rendez-vous à Sevenoaks*, demonstrated that the trapped, circular, narrative use of time that was pioneered in the *nouveau roman* was very possible in a graphic novel. One might add that Hergé was pointing in this direction already in his groundbreaking experimentalism of *Les Bijoux de la Castafiore* (*The Castafiore Emerald*; serialized 1961–1962; published as book 1963), the Tintin adventure where nothing happens at all.

Today, perhaps the best example of how graphic novels are arguing for consideration close to the literary field is the literary-prize-winning autobiography by Mary Talbot and Bryan Talbot *Dotter of Her Father's Eye* (Illustration 8.d). The work provides a more subtle, slow, and serious approach to reflecting on the literary world, from the vantage point of the graphic novel, than Moore and O'Neill's work. Herein the Talbots, husband and wife, artist and writer, blend together two biographies, that of Mary's own youth growing up as the daughter of a strict and conservative teacher who is also writing and publishing on James Joyce, and the parallel, tragic life history of Joyce's own daughter, Lucia. The blurring of three different time periods into a single text – the present, Mary's childhood, and Lucia's tormented descent into mental illness – is a classic graphic novel technique. What is now new is that this is being used to explore the echoes and reverberations between the family life of the literary critic and her subject, Mary Talbot and Lucia Joyce, respectively. It is

very interesting that while artist Bryan Talbot is pictured in the work, his actual role in the plot or narrative economy (besides, of course, drawing it all) is negligible. This is uncannily appropriate for a work being awarded a prize as a literary biography and not a graphic novel. We do not have space to do the work full justice here. Suffice it to say that it marks the most recent example of how the graphic novel is moving into the terrain of literature, literary biography, and being recuperated by that field.

Conclusion

This chapter has highlighted how creative writers, novelists, and literary publishers have worked with and on graphic novels and history. They have made them the theme of their novels and edited and placed them in their periodicals. Clever theoretical commentaries have attempted to break down the borders between disciplines and more generally to question the notions of high or low culture, literature, pulp fiction, and comics. In reality graphic novelists have assisted in this process by themselves moving to develop work that has evoked "the literary," and this was partly implicit in the idea of the graphic novel itself. This has been through thematic tropes as well as through taking graphic novel material and including it in collections of literary writing. And certainly the circle is completed when graphic novelists become novelists; although the list is not that long, it already includes Alan Moore, Neil Gaiman, and Warren Ellis. What then does the push and pull between literary culture and comics and the graphic novel add up to as a totality? We have three modest beginnings to an answer. One, the processes analyzed in the two parts of this chapter are not antithetical but mainly complementary. In fact, the above processes are a new argument for the validity of the graphic novel label and concept, now capturing quite well where literature and adult comics are being merged together in multiple ways. We

---

Opposite page: 8.d. *Dotter of Her Father's Eyes*: where literary criticism and biography blur with the graphic novel. With the kind permission of the artist, Bryan Talbot.

add a new definitional inflection to our subject here. Two, a new space is being established by editors and publishers, where the frontiers between visual and literary culture are no longer present, and instead the two aspects conjoin to provide an attractive original offer to the public. And three, this leaves the old comics as a subject of quite great nostalgia for writers who use them to evoke a former lost time or place, to recall first reading experiences, or to ground a novel in a vernacular culture. As we will suggest, this can be a quite contradictory process: comics are celebrated, but it is because they are old and not the new graphic novels. This ambiguous turn is vital to further discuss in Chapter 9, which takes up nostalgia for its subject.

9   **Nostalgia and the Return of History**

It seems that wherever one looks in our contemporary culture, including to the world of graphic narratives, history and nostalgia are a common theme. After the post-modernism and the "end of history" of the early 1990s, the past has maybe never been as popular as it is today. Here we want to make a further contribution to the ongoing debate on the meaning of the dominance of the past in the present in the field of graphic narratives, and more specifically in the graphic novel. For us, when discussing the graphic novel, several aspects stand out and merit analysis and further consideration First, on the face of it, the rise of the graphic novel has reflected and contributed to the wider culture of nostalgia.[1] Graphic novelists are talented at generating sophisticated treatments on history, and many of the most prominent exponents have been drawn to this subject. Certainly, it is also the case that along with the appearance of "all of this history," underneath the real issue at stake is how selection processes work, the reorderings that bring some material back into fashion and leave other work behind. Second, nostalgia-inspired graphic novels can look formulaic. More importantly, reprinting or playing with old comics pose some creative problems as much as original solutions. Some of the old comics display value systems that are dated and inappropriate; putting works in museums poses difficult questions of how to display narrative sequence. Third and finally, the graphic novel can represent a pulling away from the conventional formulations and dilemmas associated with cultures of nostalgia. In this last chapter we explain how important and influential creators Spiegelman, Baker, Clowes, Backderf, Ware, and others provide a more complex and nuanced set of discourses on history. Their work is a sophisticated, and at times radical, treatment of the past when compared to other material from within the otherwise predictable fashion for anything vintage.

Nostalgia culture and graphic novels: the zeitgeist and some of its mechanisms

The Internet, YouTube, other database technologies, and new technical devices give us greater access at greater speed than ever before to examples of past cultural activity and practice. Moreover, this new ease of accessibility has coincided with ever-greater social anxiety about the present, running from the *fin de siècle* angst of the late 1990s, through the shock of 9/11 and the never-ending "war on terror," to the "double-dip" economic recession. This synchronicity means that not only are we able to hold past times closer to us than ever before but also there is seeming good reason to be nostalgic. Our society and economy appear threatening to us, but at the least one can today return to different times – in fact, to the greatest cultural forms from different times, chosen individually by us via the Internet.

Jared Gardner makes a clear case for how graphic novelists have added to this culture that is so disposed to history and nostalgia. In his study *Projections: Comics and the History of Twenty-First-Century Storytelling*, he explains that we are living in an age of "Archives and Collectors" that is exemplified by the work of Art Spiegelman, Ben Katchor, Seth, Chris Ware, and Kim Deitch.[2] The web/Internet format is labyrinthine and requires a reading style that does not look for linearity or detail but rather that encourages bricolage. As Gardner states very boldly: "[I]t is the structural affinities of the comics form with the 'database' aesthetic that has contributed to the increasing visibility and relevance of the comics form in the 21st Century."[3] And, in turn, by implication, the new graphic novels prime the reader for the new technology and also their ability to hold so much history, such as the history of popular culture, including the comics that preceded them.

Certainly, digital technology and new graphic novels and comics have exploited each other to achieve some remarkable archival results that further confirm much of Gardner's reading. In this vein one cannot fail but to be impressed by the recent remake of Spiegelman's *Maus* as *Meta-Maus*.[4] Therein the digital format has transformed the original graphic novels into a virtual Holocaust museum wherein each page of the original two books is now an interactive window into huge amounts of additional pertinent historical data, including the original sound recordings of Spiegelman's interviews with his father. It is a fascinating project and powerful educational tool of great importance. More recently the scale of *Meta-Maus* is matched only by the ambition of Chris Ware's *Building Stories*.[5] This work does not have a digital component, but it is comparable in scale and effect, as it is composed of some fourteen differently printed episodes of text-image narration and exposition. Here Ware appears to have used the Internet as a metaphor; its loops and crossovers literally are repackaged into the multiple publications (akin to separate Web pages or series of pages) that are in the box and are left free for readers to work through in a sequence of their own selection. Sold in the run up to Christmastime 2012, the work resembles a traditional-seasonal (Victorian) board game, even arriving in a box. It is a packaging that evokes bygone days, but it also chimes with the reading styles inspired by new technology that can so well capture so much history.

Adding further to Gardner's argument on graphic narratives and digital culture we can point out a steady rise in graphic novel-related works that use digital technology to combine images with sound effects to return us to past times. These are especially productive as nostalgia-works because they impact not only on sight but also on memories of music. Thus, in works such as a Tardi and Grange's *N'effacez pas nos traces*[6] and Robert Crumb's *Heroes of Blues, Jazz and Country*, the traditional book format is expanded to include an accompanying music CD that supports and adds to the standard text-image content. In the case of Crumb this is via a collection of original recordings from the 1920s and 1930s, whereas Dominique Grange recorded cover versions of historically accurate protest songs to accompany Tardi's images.

We should add next that these newer trends are built not only on similarities between comics and digital culture but also on some basic formal properties that make page layout/grid communication a convincing format for handling representations of time. As has been often pointed out by several others (Scott McCloud, Thierry Groensteen, Hillary Chute, Jared Gardner, et al.), the page and its mapping into panels allows a creator to trace passages of time through linear progression, which is also done through counterpointing images of one period with another[7] or using words from one time (speaking in the present) and pictures from another period (the remembered past). It is true that graphic narratives have a great ability to blend present and past together on single pages, while progressing narration through chapters. In addition, the fact that comics were once associated with youth and childhood further enhances their role in any society that is concerned with its own history.

The relative institutionalization of graphic narratives (comics, graphic novels, and the middle ground between) has certainly contributed further to all this historicism, above and beyond the technology. As artists and writers of graphic novels have become increasingly taught to students in colleges and universities, there has been a need for educators to map the traditions in which they can be understood and compared. This very publication is one small part of this process, and today it is true that more students in more universities know more about once-obscure visual-art-historical practices than perhaps ever before. Woodcuts, silent comics, and minor superhero writers and artists are all an important part in the study of comics and graphic novels. Publishers and academics have played a role in providing this material for students in texts that generally work with historical knowledge rather than abstraction or future speculation.

An important corollary of the above process has been the growth in reprinted collections of previously forgotten comic strips and their repackaging as complete graphic novels or art history-style illustrated catalogues. Throughout the 2000s, publishers (large and small) have adroitly repackaged their backlisted comics, hoping to demonstrate that the origins and traditions that preceded the graphic novel are relevant for the new adult readers. In some of the most famous examples (*Tintin*, *Peanuts*, and *Batman*), the multiplicity of formats of reprints has been exceptionally diverse. There is, however, a standard variety of formats, each of which works slightly differently with our sense of past time. They include exact replica editions that directly mimic an earlier print run. These works gain plausibility by seeming authentic, but in their sometimes old-fashioned style, they are less attractive than new contemporary graphic novels. British comics publishers have a disposition for this reusing of vintage formats, especially when repackaging genre comics (such as war stories) or children's annuals. Similarly, in Belgium, the Foundation Moulinsart has reprinted facsimiles of Tintin books from several different periods of publication (including the 1930s, 1940s, and 1960s), always trying to make them look accurate. Alternatively, cover and design features from the original publications are changed and adapted to offer a better or improved version than the historically accurate original comic. Here the comic from the past is reimagined as a more impressive and powerful medium than the original material conditions could realistically achieve. A good example is the presentation of a recent collection of 1950s Zombies horror comics, *The Chilling Archives of Horror Comics!: Zombie.* Its cover is more or less entirely new: it is too large and too bright to be anything else. And the comic pages inside are almost the inverse, being consistently small panels in nine panel page layouts, black and white or in dull matt color. Here the book designers have updated the old original material to make it more consumable (closer to looking like contemporary horror cinema than the original "archive" inside the covers). In addition, publishers develop their own reprint formats to assert their comics' status as being today's classics. This is the preference for major publishers such as DC or Marvel, or Titan in the UK. Here the most important label of historical importance is the brand itself and its well-established logo, rather than the content of the work, which is possibly not very well known as it is so old. Black is the color used in these "classic" formats. It is employed ubiquitously to sell (once again) Judge Dredd, Swamp Thing, "Essential Marvel" collections, and DC's Showcase range.

Contemporary graphic novelists have legitimated and contributed to the reprinting process and played their role in stimulating the fashion for nostalgia by becoming editors and informed historical commentators. For instance, Chris Ware has worked extensively on bringing new attention on Frank King's *Gasoline Alley*. His role as an authority on old comics means that new readers who have been drawn to Ware's oeuvre are likely to want to find its roots, guided by the author-artist himself. Spiegelman too has played a similar role, writing with Chip Kidd on Jack Cole and offering numerous prefaces and essays to historical anthologies. Indeed, Ware and Spiegelman more or less came together in their work as historians on Jerry Moriarty's *Jack Survives* reprint. In his acknowledgments Moriarty writes of his debt to Spiegelman, thanking him for his support by first publishing Moriarty in *RAW* and then offering him a RAW one-shot publication. Following these remarks, Chris Ware writes an introduction to the reprint explaining why Moriarty's work is so significant and merits the new collection.[8] Thus the second career of major graphic novelists has been to act as historians of the field, charting out its temporal boundaries and inventing their own definition of aesthetic traditions for readers to follow up on through the anthologies they have created or recommend. Besides reexamination of some star figures (notably Crumb), two tendencies seem to dominate: first, there has been a bias toward comics from the pre-1950s period, and second, there has been a greater emphasis on exhibiting important aesthetic visual content, rather than celebrating traditions of narrative style. Of course we know these aspects are interlinked (drawings tell stories, and words appear as images on a page); however, one does not read the reprinted anthologies of the Tijuana bibles for their narrative power, nor, for that matter, old genre works for their sophisticated plots. Instead, it is the look and the page designs that are being returned to in the present day for our approval and gratification. One might underline that this historical disposition for imagery runs counter to the earlier 1990s' emphasis on scriptwriters and their contributions, in particular to the rise of the British writing talent that was contracted to DC (discussed briefly in Chapter 4). It also means that some of the late 1980s breakthrough graphic novels are now forgotten and rarely reprinted. For example, few today have heard of Janwillem van de Wetering and Paul Kirchner's *Murder by Remote Control*, first published by Ballantine books in 1986 when it attracted a favorable review in *The New York Times*.[9] Similarly forgotten is the one-time best-selling business studies graphic novel from the same period, *Japan Inc.* It too received good press coverage during the late 1980s breakthrough period but has disappeared into cultural oblivion.[10] Some comparable forgetting has occurred with Jason Lutes's *Jar of Fools* and Jack Vance's *Kings in Disguise*.[11] This is not to mention titles such as *1941: The Illustrated Story*, drawn by the influential Stephen Bissette, of *Swamp Thing* fame. It was a film tie-in title like *Alien* (discussed in Chapter 3) and even included a preface by Steven Spielberg. Its current status is that of complete cultural oblivion, like the flop movie that inspired it.[12] Unlike the superhero comics or newspaper strips, these works were all one-shot-style exercises, and they have not achieved cult status or been perceived as vintage works. Also unlike with the comics, they did not generate what might be called a fan community but instead cultivated readers who were more likely to want to read new works rather than reprints. Similarly these works have not been rediscovered by curator figures such as Spiegelman or Ware, perhaps because they are too close to their own experiences and milieu. It is also the case that these apparently lost works do not seem to signal toward the present styles – such as clear-line drawing (Seth), reworked pop art (Clowes; Ware – to an extent), or highly elaborate page layout design (Spiegelman in *No Towers*, Ware et al.) – nor to the memory of the 1960s (Crumb, Deitch, and others). Ultimately, it is this churning over of graphic novel-like material, some for inclusion in the present market and some for excision, that is the real central mechanic of the current nostalgia industry. Of course, such processes are not new or original to our subject; much of the literary culture of the twentieth century is now forgotten, that is until a contemporary intellectual (writer, journalist, film director, graphic novelist) reactivates its significance.

One can add too that maybe there is a great longing today for the old comics and other vintage popular culture precisely because they are disappearing and being replaced with new graphic novels that are more original and arguably far better (adult content, complex design, synthetic graphics drawing on multiple art traditions). That teaches us two things: (1) a break was felt when graphic novel publishing developed and became the main new way of selling adult comics; and (2) selected examples of the old forms remain important as a way of preserving some sense of tradition, precisely while that very tradition is being revised, changed, and eroded.

Problems and possibilities posed by revisiting the past

The republication of old comics as historically significant new "classic" collections means too that outdated, stereotypical, and racist images from these earlier time periods are circulated anew in the present day. The list is long and too complex to discuss in full here, ranging from Hergé to Crumb to Frank King. Researching this subject one finds that the Internet does provide a space to discuss these matters, and that it is on fan sites and discussion lists (also part of the digital culture) where the scope of these issues is most clearly mapped out and debated.[13] There discussion over the political appropriateness of republications (which can be quite furious) often goes hand-in-hand with complaints about the retail price of the same archival republications. One can add that in some of the critical discussion of the politics of the older comics returning to view, there has been too-unmeasured criticism toward Jack Kirby. For example, Spiegelman and others have described Kirby's attraction to violent and larger-than-life physical body shapes in his action drawings as being fascistic. Speaking with Gary Groth for *The Comics Journal*, Spiegelman mused:

> Yes I was actually thinking of the word Fascist even though he was a great defender of Democracy. . . . But seriously, the triumph of the will, the celebration

of physicality of the human body at the expense of intellect, is very much an impulse in Fascist art. It has a lot to do with the motor for Kirby's work, even though I understand that his work [includes] characters who fought fascists.[14]

In hindsight, and even with the sensible qualifications that were made, it does seem a little unfair for an artist who served as a combatant GI in the liberation of Western Europe to have his later postwar superhero and sci-fi fantasy aesthetics discussed as fascistic works. We are not proposing to control the debate but just to point out that Kirby fought in the Second World War, and besides his superheroes and mythical fantasies (which are the texts seen as fascistic) produced classic strips set during the Second World War, for example, *Sgt. Fury and his Howling Commandos*. That same strip even inspired some neo-Nazi violent hate mail to the Marvel offices in the 1960s.[15] And the discussion does show again how recovering history is often about preference and selection, evaluation and reordering of material, and issues of value judgment and aesthetic preference rather than a smooth organic process.

The question of what, who, and how of commemoration processes has loomed large when major art galleries have mounted shows featuring comics and their history. This reveals that there are genuine difficulties of really fully agreeing on a "golden age," because that is a question of ideology and aesthetic choice. This type of tension has been especially marked when comics art has been invited into the space of the art gallery. Thus the two major shows, "High and Low" (1991, MOMA) and "Masters of American Comics" (2006, Hammer Museum and the Museum of Contemporary Art) were both subject to polemic and controversy. While on a superficial level nostalgia-culture appears an uncomplicated and rewarding reconstitution of the past, the making of this process is often about power, and to repeat about inclusion and exclusion, decisions of this kind create their own authorities and dissidents even amongst colleagues.

Let us note *en passant* that besides issues of selection, graphic narratives present their own difficulties when exhibited into museum spaces. Galleries and museums are not easy sites to use to exhibit the narrative power of the printed form; and the fact that the completed final work is often a small page in a magazine (comics) or book (graphic novel), as compared to a painting, makes for difficulties of achieving a good viewing environment. Probably the best results of museum-work have been where comics artists/graphic novelists have moved directly beyond their own field into something closer to installation art, performance happenings, or set designs/sculptures inspired by strips or that then go on to be retransformed back into graphic novels or adult comics. This area is increasingly proving of interest to Alan Moore, who has staged several performance events (theater happenings) in London and Newcastle. These events have provided scripts for artist Eddie Campbell to create two graphic novels, *The Birth Caul* and *Snakes and Ladders*, that have been subsequently brought out in a single volume, *A Disease of Language*.[16]

It is also the case that while some comic artists have literally become curators and historians, others have written about fictional characters or alter egos fulfilling that very same role. In the last decade there has been something of a rash of this kind of publication, led in the United States and Canada by Seth and Chris Ware, but also including work from Kim Deitch and Ben Katchor. Their works are praised and analyzed very successfully by Gardner in *Projections*, where he notes how they narrate stories about lost sites of popular culture and the difficult and complex nature of preserving and remembering. One can add that these narratives do not so much focus on the graphic novelists of the 1980s and 1990s who have disappeared under the sea of nostalgia reprints (see the above examples). Instead, in Seth and Deitch at least they are framed as quest narratives where the Holy Grail is an old (1930s–1950s) pop cultural item or icon. Indeed, these works tell readers it is hip to swim back to the past and pull out lost cultural items. With their selected reprints the publishing houses make this desire possible for even ignorant amateurs. In other words, thanks to the archive reprints from the major houses, we can all feel as knowledgeable as a Deitch or Seth. This whole mythology does therefore tend toward the accumulation of purchasable products, whose reprints are no doubt carefully managed. And as noted above, not all types of graphic narratives or periods are equally represented.

We can add here a brief discussion of another variation on these narrative themes that is captured in the new work by Chip Kidd and Dave Taylor, *Death by Design* (2012). This work combines a number of previously distinctive retro-narrative modes all in one strip. Firstly, it is an inter-textual superhero strip – a new Batman story – and in that regard it resembles how in the 1980s Frank Miller commemorated and changed the same tradition. Moreover, it is not a Batman set in the present or near future but rather one set in a past time described by Kidd as "Gotham City, during a glorious Golden Age." Finally, it is also a Batman story that is explicitly about preservation and heritage (and in that way comparable to a plot in a Seth or Deitch graphic novel). In his Preface Kidd explains his motivations: "The inspiration . . .: the demolition of the original Pennsylvania Station in 1963 and the fatal construction crane collapses in midtown Manhattan of 2008. What if, despite the years they were connected? And what if they happened in Gotham City."[17] In Kidd's story Batman's greatest achievement is the rebuilding along original architectural plans of the famous railway station that was in reality destroyed in 1963. Thus Kidd taps into a deep strand of American architectural preservation that dates from at least the 1970s.[18] It includes conversations between Bruce Wayne and Cyndia Syl, an urban preservationist who is campaigning to keep the old station design. Along with the Joker and the Penguin, the villains to be defeated include a postmodern architect (whose glass floors start to crack, ill-positioned as they are atop a skyscraper) and a corrupt trade union boss who deliberately constructs buildings badly because he wants to be hired to put up new ones. Batman is not only a symbol of the rich tradition of old comics; herein he is also literally a heritage champion. That is to say, he is the perfect hero for nostalgia-obsessed pop culture. Kidd, who has contributed to several reeditions and commemorative publications of historically significant older comic strips, is here inventing Batman in his own image as a cultural critic, designer, and historically informed citizen. The Batcave has not become a site for a collector's flea market but it is where the hero devises how best to save and rebuild New York's architectural heritage.

All this repetitious interest in the past can sometimes be almost too much. In any case, an important part of our present-day ordinary nostalgia is also that nagging sense that there is maybe something problematic or limiting about this whole fashion. For several years now there has been a consistent part of the wider heritage debate where commentators bemoan the excessive weight of history and the limitations of always looking backwards. Similar concerns can be expressed about how graphic novels have been a part of the wider retro culture. For example, the archival/database mode blends times and places with such sophistication that one can be left without a conventional sense of chronology at all. One sometimes sees this kind of confusion in otherwise fascinating academic works. Thus, the historian Jerome de Groot appears bamboozled when he describes how Jay Cantor's *Krazy Kat* was an influence on Spiegelman's *Maus*.[19] Of course this was not much the case, as *Maus* was in publication in serial form in *RAW* since 1980 (and earlier in preparatory short works) and the novel from Jay Kantor was published in 1987, though before the graphic novel *Maus* was fully completed.[20] One can add here that long before the digital age, the construction of time in *Maus* is subtly complex and is difficult to read with any full historical accuracy, even for a relatively experienced critic. For example, it is very possible to (wrongly) read *Maus* and assume that Artie's interviews with Vladek are occurring simultaneously with the drawing of the images on the page. This was not the case at all since Vladek Spiegelman died on August 18, 1980, and the final page of the work that so memorably inscribes this death scene into the public domain of the graphic novel was not completed in standard print form until 1991. In other words, much of *Maus* was written after Vladek's death, yet in the work this "real time" is almost completely suppressed and replaced with an imagined present where Vladek is alive. In reality Art Spiegelman was working on *Maus* while mourning his father, but this is never clearly represented on the page. Similarly the complexity of the American present is limited to the representation of the Spiegelman family drama and to some clever hints on the theme of contemporary racism. The politics of real-time America (the Vietnam War, the draft, Watergate, Reagan's presidency) never shows through in the work because it would have inevitably distracted from the key theme of the recounting of the interwar and Holocaust period (justifiably so, as ultimately it is an account of an oral history of Vladek's story and not Art Spiegelman's alone).

The huge volume of reprints and archival publications can also imply a false sense of the whole direction of history, making presentation far too teleological. The example of the old Zombie comics reprint collection mentioned earlier is an interesting case in point. From looking at this publication, one might conclude that the recent works of Robert Kirkman, Charlie Adlard, Tony Moore, and Cliff Rathburn on *The Walking Dead* are a continuation and an offshoot of those earlier strips. This is quite clearly not the case. It is because of the popularity of the new comics and the collected *Walking Dead* graphic novels that a publication about old Zombie comics finds any kind of current market place. It is because of the cultural present-day success of *The Walking Dead* that relevant sites from the past are reinvestigated and recommercialized, not the other way around. Moreover, the ambitions and subtexts to *The Walking Dead* are quite different to the works from the 1950s in the archival publication. There the zombies are depicted as generic elements in short story horror fiction, whereas in the contemporary publication the zombies offer a complex mirror on the politics and social dynamics of modern-day America. Indeed, Michael Chabon has sensed a similar issue of historical anachronism and raised it as a short warning note in his fascinating new novel, *Telegraph Avenue*. In it he recounts the adventures and misadventures of two couples living and working on the street of its title. The work is bathed in references to popular culture, especially cinema and music. Comic books and issues of time and teleology feature, and they are referenced most sharply in one powerful scene wherein the hero, Archy Stallings, meets Gibson Goode, the millionaire who is threatening the former's independent record shop. Chabon describes how Goode discourses on Archy's keen knowledge of comics, trying to flatter Archy into a partnership with his business plans. In one passage of the novel, Goode recalls them meeting once before as youths and sharing an appreciation of Marvel's *Luke Cage* strip. Goode recollects to Archy:

> This motherfucker was peeling off all these sophisticated interpretations. Inner-meanings. In *Luke Cage*. Talking about American penal system as portrayed in Marvel Comics. Referencing all kinds of heavy reading materials. Eleven, twelve years old, telling me what, like Frantz Fanon has to say about the possibility of black superheroes in a white structure and whatnot.

But this is not what Archy recalls:

> This claim was almost certainly 90 to 97 percent false. The shimmer of what Archy remembered from that afternoon at House of Wax was only an awkward mutual series of passwords exchanged, the chance encounter with a random nerd brother in an unexpected location. . . ."You have a better memory than I do," Archy suggested.

The passage reveals that Chabon possesses a great awareness of how comics culture has changed since the 1970s. His depiction of Goode's flattery is a neat example of how we think of graphic novels today and so reread comics quite wrongly. Chabon implies that in the 1970s, a youth could have read *Luke Cage* and Fanon but would have been unlikely to meld them together. It is only after the 1980s and the graphic novel that such a synthesis could make sense and actually be put together (as Chabon knows). One can add too that the passage reveals Chabon's awareness and reinterpretation of the theme Borges discusses in his famous short essay "Kafka and His Predecessors," which is that one must take care not to interpret the past by always thinking it drives toward a single definitive conclusion. And as we have explained throughout this book, the rise of the graphic novel was not like that at all, rather coming from patchwork of highly complex aesthetic traditions and still today reflecting a very wide range of works.

Turning to a different issue, a real casualty of all this history has been the science fiction genre. Even though science fiction graphic novels were an important part of how comics came to be taken more seriously in the 1970s and 1980s, the fashion for history is strangling this genre. Indeed, historical and heritage thematics now seemingly frame even the best sci-fi narratives, and this is becoming the far too-standard way of approaching imagining the future – that is, by situating it in the past. Thus, the anthology collection *Yesterday's Tomorrows* features strips that are drawn to look like old sci-fi works, including Grant Morrison's treatment of Dan Dare. Also, for example, Alan Moore and Kevin O'Neill's *League of Extraordinary Gentleman*, Volume Two, describes a Martian invasion of Earth set on the eve of the First World War, complete with major use and celebration of the writings of H. G. Wells. All this steam-punk genre material positions science fiction narratives back into Victorian or Edwardian settings, and it is proving an exceptionally popular retro mode in the United Kingdom, where there are reenactments and fairs as well as examples in cinema and literary fiction. Intriguingly even in the cinema sci-fi seems to need to connect to history, even if it is a very deep history. Thus, in the reemergence of the *Alien* series the film *Prometheus* (2012, Ridley Scott) is about a search for a past history as much as it is about new technology, different worlds, or alternative future social models. It is telling that the main heroes are now archaeologists, whereas originally in *Alien* (1979) Ripley (Sigourney Weaver) was an engineer and an astronaut. Here it is tempting to argue that when times are more optimistic and open, then the cultural sphere turns toward discussion and exposition on possible futures; this is often how sci-fi's popularity is accounted for in the 1960s. This is in contrast to times of less confidence and greater social anxiety – such as today, post-9/11 and post-economic crash – where there is a preference for glorifying past times, looking backwards in art and culture to find a sense of security and grounding, as one has found for much of the past fifteen years.

Finally, the new nostalgia in graphic narratives very quickly denies the fact that this is a longstanding aspect in comics' culture. Just as the recent Woody Allen film *Midnight in Paris* (2011) indicates, we need to appreciate that a fascination with the past is not unique to our own time. From the moment when the first generation of comics readers seemed too old to be buying new comics, a market emerged that was more interested in collecting, preservation, and commemoration: nostalgia. Relatively early on comics were being consumed not as original popular culture but rather as a way back to an earlier age (the prewar). The common marking point of the trend is Jules Feiffer's *The Great Comic Book Heroes* (1965). Therein Feiffer argued against Wertham's negative attacks on the comics. He suggested that for his generation they were worth rereading because what the old comics offered was far more charming and reassuring than the contemporary popular culture of the mid-1960s. Feiffer explains how the old junk (comics) is far superior to the new junk (modern life post 1965). He writes: "[W]e have staged a retreat to a better remembered brand of junk. A junk that knew its place was underground where it had no power and thus only titillated, rather than above ground where it truly has power – and thus, only depresses."[21]

In summary, graphic novels intersect with contemporary nostalgia culture in quite classic ways. They use and align with the digital archive culture that tends toward preservation and nonlinearity. They have tapped into the fashion for vintage and, in works by Seth and others, offer original narrative expositions on that theme. Likewise any review of this material will note that graphic novels have also suffered from some of the difficulties faced by all this type of material. The backward look to the past can seem limited and sometimes provoke more confusion than clarity. What we hope to show in this section is that there is always a selection process around what is being recovered from the past and that this is often about jostling for the future: one tends to recall and revive what seems to map forward to present needs and current fashions. This carving out to create a tradition is thankfully an unresolved process that is still in flux and that is a far preferable state of affairs to a frozen version of the past that is set up once and for all.[22] We underline too that the reprints and their reframing of old comics does in the end consign that material to the past and hence clears a space for different work in the future – that is, products that look more like graphic novels and less like comics. It is an efficient operation because it is nuanced and seems to celebrate the historical, yet simultaneously forgets many products and frames the others as "museum exhibits." However, as we explain in the next section, it would be silly to take all these examples around issues of retro-mania as parts representing a whole picture. The depiction of history in graphic novels is not tied to themes related to nostalgia and tradition-making. Several works offer productive, radical, and nuanced ways through which history is being drawn and narrated. History in graphic novels does not belong entirely to the collectors, curators, reprinters, and archivists, though as we have acknowledged, they have been very active.

The near nostalgia mode

As just stated, it is far too simplistic to discuss graphic novels as only exponents or victims of the digital era's retro-mania, to account for graphic novels exclusively around the twists and turns of what is recalled and forgotten, what past best lends itself to our present needs. If only in the slipstream of these processes, there are many different and more radical ways in which graphic novels relate to history (as a subject, and in their own terms). First, it is important to underline that the graphic novel does represent a significant break with the past and in its own roots was a radical and not nostalgic intervention. Looking back over the material from the mid-to-late 1980s, this is precisely how graphic novels were being presented and interpreted: that is, as innovation and a new literary experience. The emphasis in this fundamental period for the form was to see it as a new departure, as an original and avant-garde development away from the traditional comics culture. The graphic novel was defined by its originality and difference from past formats and its original narrative content. It was aimed and used explicitly to signal a break from perceptions of comics being for children or adolescents. It was there to challenge the idea that comics were not always funny or crude in the comix mode but instead capable of achieving the most impressive narrations about serious subjects. Similarly, at least in the eyes of some publishers, the graphic novel even looked to have a potential to take over from mainstream literary fiction; the zeitgeist was about the future of literary culture and how graphic novels would change reading habits and add to the decline of the book but also provide a new format that would assist in keeping up literacy rates.[23] In the 1980s heritage was, of course, commonplace, particularly in major works of cinema that were adapting classic novels. When compared to that set of developments (Lean's *A Passage to India* [1984], as well as the Merchant and Ivory adaptations of Henry James's *The Europeans* [1979] and *The Bostonians* [1984]), the treatments of history in *Maus* or *Watchmen* or in later works such as Kyle Baker's *Nat Turner* or Spiegelman's *In the Shadow of No Towers* stand out as anything but traditional or nostalgic. The heritage cinema used *mise en scène* (costume, make up, set design, lighting) to literally recreate history and literary source texts without any acknowledgment of the present day. That was a far more standard retro mode than the possibilities of the graphic novel. In particular, one can see very clearly one marked difference: the personal or autobiographical dimension to the storytelling process in the historically informed graphic novels. As we have underlined on several occasions in this book, this was a dynamic and original style, especially in a text-image work. More generally speaking, it provided a more human and seemingly more authentic form of reconstruction of the past than that which was being favored in the cinema. Blockbuster literary adaptations were very powerful and no doubt changed the world of creative writing to be more accommodating to the importance of visual culture.[24] However, the new graphic novels were offering a more underground and authentic encounter with historical reconstruction wherein the individual voices, memories, and experiences were so well captured. One might add that some thirty years after *Maus*, it is today common practice for major international museums (Holocaust Museum, Washington DC; Flanders Fields, Ypres) to use individual life stories of ordinary people from the past to get visitors to engage more directly with their collections. Though modestly and unintentionally, the autobiographical aspect of the graphic novel "turn" anticipated these future ideas of good practice.[25]

The content of some of the new graphic novels of the post-2000s is distinctive from the more typical nostalgia culture because these works have real political energy and bite. One thinks here of many works from Joe Sacco but also recent contributions from Derf Backderf and Kyle Baker.

Let us look briefly at Sacco's latest work, his collaboration with journalist Chris Hedges, *Days of Destruction, Days of Revolt*. Here Sacco has curtailed his sometimes excessively underground, Crumb-like drawing style and instead created a new and original set of political testimonies on poverty and social crisis in the United States. In a series of short strips and full-page illustrations he highlights his encounters with people living under huge social pressures and facing racist oppression and capitalist exploitation in contemporary America. The strips and Hedges' essays highlight the terrifying conditions of those without money or status. The historical context provided in the essays and the sequences of graphic narration from Sacco have not a single trace of the nostalgic about them. On the contrary, they track the harsh and exploitative conditions that have led to the present sense of agony. Here the point is for Sacco to relay personal stories of suffering and bravery and to show in detail how this suffering was perpetrated. This is campaigning material made to make readers take real notice of the social issues that are all around them. Moreover as noted above, the aesthetic that is developed by Sacco is carefully controlled to stop the form from triumphing over the content. Besides avoiding any obvious reference to earlier cartoon styles, the work offers page layouts that evoke personal scrapbook collections or drawn photographic stills. There is a powerful stillness to many of the images and layouts, and Sacco gives his all to capture the journalistic story, rather than construct an aesthetic that would distract.

Backderf's *My Friend Dahmer* offers an equally disturbing account of modern America. It is an autobiographical treatment of its creator's memories of growing up and attending high school with the future serial killer of its title. What is important to spotlight briefly here is that Backderf carefully pieces together not only the painful details of Dahmer's descent into madness but also the wider social context that seemed to ignore this trajectory and, if anything, push Dahmer toward violence. The past is not a place to be remembered fondly, and Backderf

HOW DID HE GET AWAY WITH BEING **STINKING DRUNK** DURING SCHOOL HOURS? IT **STILL** BLOWS MY MIND. **EVERY** KID KNEW WHAT DAHMER WAS DOING... BUT NOT A **SINGLE** TEACHER OR SCHOOL ADMINISTRATOR NOTICED A THING. NOT ONE.

WERE THEY **REALLY** THAT OBLIVIOUS? OR WAS IT THAT THEY JUST DIDN'T WANT TO BE **BOTHERED**?

HIGH SCHOOL IN THE SEVENTIES WAS **FAR** DIFFERENT THAN TODAY'S LOCKED-DOWN, ZERO-TOLERANCE INSTITUTIONS. THERE WERE **NO** SECURITY CAMERAS, **NO** STRIP SEARCHES. KIDS WERE **SMOKING WEED** IN THE BATHROOMS AND **CHUGGING BEER** IN VANS IN THE PARKING LOT.

EVEN **THE TEACHERS** PARTIED. THE YOUNGER ONES WERE STRAIGHT OUT OF **SIXTIES COUNTERCULTURE.** I RECALL **ONE** IN PARTICULAR, WHO ONCE BRAGGED TO ONE OF THE JOCKS...

I BET **I** CAN ROLL **A JOINT** FASTER THAN **YOU!**

BROTHER!

DAHMER KEPT QUIET AND DIDN'T MOUTH OFF. MAYBE HE WAS REGARDED AS JUST ANOTHER **HARMLESS STONER,** TO BE **IGNORED** AND **SHOVED ALONG.**

repeatedly emphasizes how he feels it was the social context of small town 1970s America that was partly responsible for Dahmer drifting to murderous insanity.

As with Sacco's recent work, there is also a very strong and effective correspondence between form and content in *My Friend Dahmer* (Illustration 9.a). Thus, Backderf develops an ugly, almost pastiche version of the bubbly-ugly-funny comix look. What is clever is that this clearly is not Crumb or the Furry Freak Brothers or television animations of the 1970s period, but it captures something of that feel and then makes it look even more disturbing. This aesthetic choice is not to make any excuses for the serial killer's later conduct or ignore the suffering of Dahmer's victims and their families. Instead the look deeply underlines Backderf's critical interpretation of history, exemplified in remarks such as this:

> High School in the Seventies was Far different than today's Locked-down, Zero-tolerance institutions.... Even the teachers partied.... Dahmer kept quiet and didn't mouth off. Maybe he was regarded as just another harmless stoner, to be ignored and shoved along.... "I can't say there were any signs he was different or strange," one of the School Guidance Counselors would later state.[26]

Clearly Kyle Baker's *Nat Turner* is a further good example of where graphic novels and history make an encounter without indulging in nostalgia (Illustration 9.b). Throughout *Nat Turner* Baker draws large and powerful images of the 1831 slave revolt and its eponymous leader running amok. Above these splash pages he includes what look like scanned but still original and authentic images of photographs of the slave owners' mansions. These deliberately photographic-looking pictures have the effect

Opposite page: 9.a. The past as nightmare: Backderf's memories of school days in his account of knowing the eponymous serial killer. Reprinted with kind permission of the publisher, Abrams, New York.

of evoking not only the past (drawn in the splash page illustration) but also the contemporary post-Civil War houses that remain a part of the Southern states to the present day. Baker uses this technique to suggest that although the memory of the slave revolt in Southampton County, Virginia, in 1831 is to some extent limited, the locations where it took place remain in the present day, offering a direct visual link on the page to this troubled heritage. Likewise, the realism of these images lends gravitas to the work, contrasting neatly with the occasionally more cartoonish drawing style (Kirbyesque tone) that blurs nineteenth-century illustration technique with the look of action hero comic book clichés. Moreover, the fact that often today these kinds of mansions are sites of museums and gardens open for visitors is important, too. Manicured lawns, beautiful settings, and rooms displaying antiques and pretty paintings should not conceal the system of oppression that facilitated such riches.[27] Baker's work questions this kind of exhibition approach to the history of slavery. In some respects it anticipates the similar political mode of Quentin Tarantino's *Django Unchained* (2013) and its subsequent graphic novel adaptation.

It is also important to stress that works that seemingly advocate a nostalgic love of comics are also quite ambivalent and nuanced. Spiegelman's *In the Shadow of No Towers* has been cited as being a nostalgia piece, but that would be something of a limited assessment. Certainly, Spiegelman is explicit about the role of the history of comics in *In the Shadow of No Towers*. For instance, he explains how the old comics books were his source of solace in the genuinely anxious days after 9/11. He writes:

> The only cultural artifacts that could get past ... my eyes and brain with something other than images of burning towers were old comic strips; vital, unpretentious ephemera from the optimistic dawn of the 20th century. That

---

Opposite page: 9.b. A rejection of nostalgia? Baker's interpretation of the Nat Turner rebellion (1831). Reprinted with kind permission of the publisher, Abrams, New York.

they were made with so much skill and verve but never intended to last past the day they appeared in the newspaper gave them poignancy; they were just right for the end of the world moment.[28]

Nevertheless, one must be careful because Spiegelman is far more sophisticated and discursive about the role of history than this much-quoted comment suggests. Thus the material that he includes from the 1900s in *In the Shadow of No Towers* is open to being read as marking out themes that are haunting him rather than reassuring him after 9/11. The comics are restored as problematic ephemera that are all apiece with Spiegelman's questioning and critique of 9/11 and the "war on terror." The historical comics are not silent museum pieces but rather open images that pose questions about American culture. Spiegelman knows they are reassuring, but he also selects them because they are disturbing and nightmarish too. Thus therein we find the Kind-der-Kids leaving New York; that is precisely the opposite journey of the traditional and more reassuring stereotype of the city functioning as a migrant's haven. This is followed by Plate 2, "The War Scene in *Hogan's Alley*," that looks as relevant a commentary on George W. Bush's war plans as any contemporary antiwar caricature. Thus, Spiegelman directly encourages the reader to return to the U.S. comics of the past not only for therapeutic reassurance but also as metaphorical and critical comment on the politics of the present. In an often-ignored part of the same center page essay, Spiegelman also notes how after 9/11 his much-loved Krazy Kat cartoons by Herriman are open to a disturbing new reading. He remarks: "[T]he ineffable beauty of *Krazy Kat* was that it was simply about a Kat getting Konked with a brick. It presented an open-ended metaphor that could contain all stories simultaneously; and after September 11, Ignatz started looking a lot like Osama Bin Laden to me!" This is a joke, yet it shows how Spiegelman was selecting old comics not just because of their historicity and comforting nostalgia but actually because they chimed with his very modern political fears and concerns. The images from the comics exhibition in part two of *In the Shadow of No Towers* are anything but outdated or simply decorative and reassuring. Their very content implicitly invites an analysis that is informed by 9/11 and the war on terror. The Kin-der-Kids, the Yellow Kid, and Krazy Kat are all part of post-9/11 America and are implicated in the politics of the present day, as much as they are left as museum exhibits or therapeutic devices. To put it another way, and very crudely, Spiegelman is too clever, too open to debate and ideas, discussion, criticism and evaluation, to work in a conventionally nostalgic style.

Conclusion

Citing Seth or Deitch as representatives of the modern historical graphic novel and its database style rather narrows down understanding of the field as a whole. Spiegelman, Baker, Sacco, and Backderf provide images and narratives that use history, but they do not chart obsessive stories of collection or recollection. Instead, they use the graphic novel to address major political questions and themes, recalling history to comment implicitly on contemporary society, as well as what and why we remember. That is not to say that there is a good or bad way to engage with the past; it is simply to note that there are trends distinctive from the world of nostalgia discussed earlier. One could propose that there are therefore two distinct narrative types: (1) the stories of collection, memorabilia, and personal reflection on obsessive collecting or history (as analyzed so well in Gardner's work); and (2) parallel works that focus on a more traditional understanding of a historical event as a political crisis, a revolution, an act of terror, or a social issue news story. The former works are more intimate and arguably poetic in tone, while the latter use personal experiences and draw on autobiography to comment on wider social questions as well.

In practice these subgenre separations blur together. For example, Daniel Clowes has an exceptionally ambivalent position on nostalgia. Superficially, it is possible to read his works as straightforward celebrations of the pop culture world and its tendency toward celebrating its own past. Like works by Katchor, Seth, and Deitch, Clowes's graphic novels feature characters who are collectors, curators, and commentators on the history of pop culture. However, his attitude is anything but nostalgic, and in *David Boring* there is a scathing treatment of the lifestyle informed by pop culture and nostalgia. Thus the main character, Boring, is the son of a minor comic creator. Clowes uses this device to then position Boring as a "lost son" adrift in a semi-fantasy world of obsession, sexual anxiety, and fetishism. Sections of the work read as standard romance narratives, while others drift into a film noir mode, encouraged by the fact that Boring makes cinema. Mixed into this complex plot is repeated reference to the father's comics and inclusion of panels from the father's old sci-fi strip. These pages are recreated by Clowes as "real" comics, yet because the panels are displaced through the strip, their only meaning is in relation to Boring's own chaotic and troubled misadventures. Clowes expresses himself quite clearly on his own ambivalence toward pop culture and retro recycling of old mass media forms as vintage chic, and such views help us better understand what he is saying in *David Boring*. He has explained that he dislikes all contemporary mass culture post 1966 and despises the nostalgia geeks. On the other hand, he has admitted to being fascinated by the 1950s and to liking the idea of collecting difficult-to-find ephemera. Yet he sees the idea of nostalgia as an escape from modernity and mass consumerism as "the trap." He states: "There are penalties to be paid for ignoring the past, but there are also penalties to be paid for ignoring the present."[29] Such guidelines make *David Boring* an easier work to engage with than might at first seem to be the case. Thus, one can interpret it as a work with a thesis on how too much obsession with the past (the father, his fragmented comics, cinema, pulp noir writings) is all a part of the contemporary malaise, rather than an escape from it. For Clowes, modern ennui is not generated because of a lack of cultural memory but because of its repetitive, psychologically exploitative presence. Rather than offering Boring a space for creativity or thought, nostalgia deepens his disturbed sense of reality.

Clowes's ambivalence toward retro culture is underlined in a panel in *David Boring* that catches the look and tone of Edward Hopper's famous work, *Nighthawks*. Here Boring is pictured sitting at the bar of a diner, reading his father's comic, *Yellow Streak*. For the first and last time in the graphic novel, two pages from the work are shown in conventional sequential order – on the actual page. They offer no narrative cohesion, and no volume of reading between the gutters could give them a sequential meaning. A fellow diner remarks sarcastically to Boring: "I'm glad to see they're still teaching the classics." What is going on here? It is possible to read the page as a sharp critique of the popular culture industry. The comic pages are situated in a landscape of ennui, and the ones we see as exemplary of the father's work are meaningless, empty. The comic does nothing to assist Boring's torment, and in fact the meaninglessness of its pages just chimes with the ennui evoked through the recreation of the famous painting by Hopper.

Producing his major works through the late 1920s to the 1960s, Hopper is a locus classicus of Americana, modernity, and kind of a national approach to imagining recent history that is deeply ambivalent towards nostalgia. His repertoire, including *Nighthawks*, casts everyday city life with a sense of uncanny mystery, notation of popular culture, and more than a little hint that people inhabiting this film-set world that is America are all rather drained and empty. Across his works there is also a strong tension between a modernist tone of abstraction and the use of reference to traditional and historical – old – Americana that is on the brink of seemingly fading into irrelevance. This is an ideal reference point for Clowes, whose own oeuvre points in this direction too. Hopper's ambivalence toward the past also captures metaphorically much of what we have said in this chapter: that the graphic novel is part of retro-culture and is also a critical reflection on it. There are plainly nostalgic graphic novels, but there are also quite insightful and critical interpretations of history too. Positioned neatly in the middle of these paths, Clowes plays with the tensions between the positions, making metacommentaries rather than siding fully one way or another.

By way of a final example, some of the complexities of the coexistence of retro-nostalgia and radical uses of history in the world of the graphic novel can be seen in two recent cover art contributions by Chris

Ware for *The New Yorker* magazine. This material is also a good point on which to conclude this work as a whole, as the covers confirm how graphic novelists are becoming central figures in public life, both political and literary. They remind us too how graphic novelists provide sequential material in many different venues, not simply for one-shot novel-like projects. Likewise the images indicate how pictures alone can generate narrative meaning; Ware's artwork produces a powerful message without need for detailed plotting.

On September 17, 2012, Ware provided an autumnal and very nostalgic image for *The New Yorker* of parents leaving their young kindergarten-age children at the gates of a school building. Titled "Back to School" the mood evoked is positive and happy, with the adults chatting with each other while the children walk in line through to the school, guided by a female teacher holding the door. Only one child is drawn looking back to her mother or father, and this focal point lends the image pathos. It seems rather glib, a one-shot image that offers a pretty cover, in its own unique way exemplary of how graphic novelists have tapped into the nostalgia business. Seeing the magazine on January 7, 2013, one discovers a second Ware depiction of the seasons and the school calendar, and it is a most startling and disturbing scene because of the context of its publication. Printed just weeks after the horrific massacre of children in an elementary school in Newtown, Connecticut (December 14, 2012), one comes to the image with a gasp. Ware and the editors here comment on that tragedy and its aftermath. In this scene now it is winter, and the perspective offered is of a shot from indoors looking to a group of now very frightened and concerned adults who are again at the school gate. Compared to their carefree appearance in the autumn edition, they are tense and anxious, eyes looking intently on their children rather than at each other or distractedly at their mobile phones. Moreover, Ware adds an almost spiritual dimension by painting the school floor black with dots of stars in the fabric of the concrete, implying an otherworldly, heavenly space, with some children ascending a stairway and others descending to a hall. Titled "Threshold," this is as powerful a comment on the tragedy at Newtown and the gun control question as one could imagine. While

Ware is sometimes seen as an introspective and self-regarding exponent of nostalgia, he is decidedly able to contribute subtly to a major national debate. This is the latest assertion of how graphic novelists speak to our difficult times. Ware's original conceit seems to have been to link images of seasonal change with memories of childhood/parenthood. The decision to publish the January 7, 2013, cover for *The New Yorker* demonstrated a more ambitious, brave, and critical orientation that marshalled aesthetics to provoke thought.

10   A Short Bibliographical Guide

The aim of this bibliography is not to list all the items that have been used in our book, but to provide the reader with a mapping of the field and initial advice on what we consider to be essential reading. For the presentation of the material, we will follow as much as possible the three-part structure of our book.

General information (Chapter 1)

As this book has implied throughout, it would be highly artificial and counterproductive to separate too drastically graphic novel studies and comics studies. Graphic novel studies are both an offspring of and a reaction against comics studies, and in many cases a good knowledge of the comics field is simply indispensable for anyone who is interested in the graphic novel. Yet given that the focus of this book is so heavily on the graphic novel alone, it may suffice to mention just some selected titles on comics as a key phenomenon of twentieth-century American culture such as Les Daniels, *Comix: A History of Comic Books in America* (Wildwood House, 1973); Jean-Paul Gabilliet, *Of Comics and Men: A Cultural History of American Comic Books* (University Press of Mississippi, 2010); Paul Lopes, *Demanding Respect: The Evolution of the*

American Comic Book (Temple University Press, 2009); Paul Williams and James Lyons, eds., *The Rise of the American Comics Artist: Creators and Contexts* (University Press of Mississippi, 2010); Jared Gardner, *Projections: Comics and the History of Twenty-First Century Storytelling* (Stanford University Press, 2011); and Charles Hatfield, *Hand of Fire: The Comics Art of Jack Kirby* (University Press of Mississippi, 2012). Two recent surveys of the field are Hillary Chute, "Graphic Narrative," in Joe Bray, Alison Gibbons, and Brian McHale, eds., *The Routledge Companion to Experimental Literature* (Routledge, 2012, 407–419); and the *Narratologia* series, Daniel Stein and Jan Thon, eds., *Theory and History of the Graphic Novel* (De Gruyter, 2013).

Most specialized series, journals, research centers, and Web sites do not distinguish very sharply between comics and graphic novels. It is difficult to overestimate the pioneering role of the University Press of Mississippi, whose "Comics & Popular Culture" series has been absolutely crucial in the development of the field. All major academic presses now have titles on comics and the graphic novel, and Leuven University Press recently has launched a further series. A special mention should go here as well to the new series linked with Project Narrative at The Ohio State University (Ohio State University Press). Among the most important journals, one should cite *The Comics Journal* (since 1977), *Inks* (twelve issues between 1994 and 1997), *International Journal of Comic Art*, aka *IJOCA* (since 1999), *European Comic Art* (since 2008), *Journal of Graphic Novels and Comics* (since 2010), *Image (&) Narrative* (since 2001, online), *ImageText* (since 2004, online), *Studies in Comics* (since 2010), and *Scandinavian Journal of Comic Art* (since 2012, online). Important research libraries are the Billy Ireland Cartoon Library & Museum (The Ohio State University, Columbus, OH) and the Comic Art Collection (Michigan State University, East Lansing, MI), and specialized programs are offered by the University of Florida and the University of Dundee, Scotland (in the European tradition, there have existed since the 1980s specialized BA and MA curricula in several fine arts schools; chief among them is the program of the CNBDI in Angoulême, France). In addition, more and more journals publish special issues on comics and graphic novels, for instance *MFS/Modern Fiction Studies* 52:4, 2006 ("Graphic Narrative," eds. Hillary Chute and Marianne DeKoven); *American Periodicals* 17:2, 2007 ("Cartoons and Comics," eds. Lucy Shelton Caswell and Jared Gardner); *English Language Notes* 46:2, 2008 ("Graphia: Literary Criticism and the Graphic Novel," ed. William Kuskin); and *SubStance* 40:1, 2011 ("Graphic Narratives and Narrative Theory," eds. Jared Gardner and David Herman). More and more professional organizations, such as the Modern Language Association (MLA), the International Association of Word and Images Studies (IAWIS), and Narrative, now host specialized comics/graphic novel groups and sections, scheduling special panels and sessions in their conventions. The international membership of these organizations is an important element in the academic interest in the American graphic novel outside the United States.

Part I: Historical Context (Chapters 2–4)

In the contact zone between comics and the graphic novel, particular attention should be paid to specific aspects. Certain forms of comics can indeed be seen as forerunners of the graphic novel: the woodcut novels of the 1920s and 1930s, for instance, as studied by David Beronå in *Wordless Books: The Original Graphic Novels* (Abrams, 2008) or the *Classics Illustrated* series, as presented by William B. Jones Jr. in *Classics Illustrated: A Cultural History* (MacFarland and Co., 2011), not to mention, of course, *Mad* magazine (see Tony Hiss and Jeff Lewis, "The 'Mad' Generation," *New York Times Magazine*, July 31, 1977) and the comix underground production, exemplarily surveyed and analyzed by scholars such as Roger Sabin (*Adult Comics*, Routledge, 1993; see also Roger Sabin and Teal Triggs, eds., *Below Critical Radar: Fanzines and Alternative Comics from 1976 to Now*, Codex Books, 2002, as well as Gary Groth and Robert Fiore, eds., *The New Comics: Interviews from the Pages of* The Comics Journal, Berkley Books, 1988, and Stanley Wiater and Stephen R. Bissette, *Comic Book Rebels: Conversations with the Creators of the New Comics*, Donals I. Fine, 1993).

Especially relevant for this book are the two moments when comics culture was first cut off from and then reintegrated into general culture. Psychiatrist Fredric Wertham's battle against the 1950s horror comics and the subsequent introduction of the Comics Code has attracted several publications. The essential titles are David Hajdu, *The Ten-Cent Plague: The Great Comic Book Scare and How It Changed America* (Farrar, Strauss and Giroux, 2008); Bart Beaty, *Fredric Wertham and the Critique of Mass Culture* (University of Mississippi Press, 2005); Amy Kiste Nyberg, *Seal of Approval: A History of the Comics Code* (University of Mississippi Press, 1998); John A. Lent, *Pulp Demons: International Dimensions of the Postwar Anti-comics Campaign* (Fairleigh Dickinson University Press, 1999); and the earliest work, dedicated to the British anti-comics crusade of the same period, Martin Barker, *A Haunt of Fears: The Strange History of the British Horror Comics Campaign* (Pluto Press, 1984). Regarding the "revival of comics" during the Pop Art era, there are many significant publications. Specifically of interest is the incorporation of Batman into mainstream and pop culture through the ABC television series in 1966 and Andy Warhol's fascination with the Batman and Robin characters. We suggest William Uriccchio, ed., *The Many Lives of the Batman* (Routledge, 1991) and Sasha Torres, "The Caped Crusader of Camp: Pop, Camp, and the *Batman* Television Series" (in Jennifer Doyle et al., eds., *Pop Out: Queer Warhol*, Durham University Press, 1996, 238–255); we also add here the edited volume by Jules Feiffer, *Great Comic Books Heroes* (Doubleday, 1977), which made a vital contribution to the demarginalization of comics. In the same vein, there are a long series of literary testimonies, if not full-fledged fictional reconstructions, of adolescents' fascination with pulp. These can be found in several books, both essays and fiction, by Jonathan Lethem (*The Fortress of Solitude*, Thorndike, 2002; *The Disappointment Artist*, Faber, 2005) and Michael Chabon (*The Amazing Adventures of Kavalier and Clay*, Picador, 2000; *Reading and Writing Along the Borderlines*, Fourth Estate, 2008) as well as in the very nostalgic, but far from uncritical *Give Our Regards to the Atomsmashers* (Sean Howe, ed., Pantheon, 2004).

Readers interested in the emergence of the graphic novel in the 1980s will read with great profit the collected interviews of Art Spiegelman (as edited by Joseph Witek in *Art Spiegelman: Conversations*, University of Mississippi Press, 2007; another interview collection with the same artist is *Comix, Essays, Graphics and Scraps*, Grafiche Renna/A RAW Book, 1998) or Michael Berry's piece "The Second British Invasion" for *East Bay Express* (1991, on the U.S. success of UK graphic novelists such as Moore and Gaiman; see also here Grant Morrison, *Supergods*, Spiegel & Grau, 2011). A detailed approach that explores terminological usage of the concept graphic novel is R. C. Harvey, "The Graphic Novel, Will Eisner and Other Pioneers," *Comics Journal* (May 2001, 103–106). A very good sense of the very recent past (2001–2010) is found in Ben Schwartz, introduction to *The Best American Comics Criticism* (Fantagraphics, 2010, 10–21); Charles McGrath, "Not Funnies," *New York Times* (July 11, 2004); and Douglas Wolk, *Reading Comics: How Graphic Novels Work and What They Mean* (Da Capo Press, 2007). From an institutional point of view, the edited collection by Paul Williams and James Lyons, *The Rise of the American Comics Artist: Creators and Contexts* (University of Mississippi Press, 2010), offers important insights on the 1980–1990s transition from comics to graphic novel.

Part II: Forms (Chapters 5–7)

The rapidly growing scholarship of the last two decades continues the first- and second-generation academic work on comics, which in the 1960s and 1970s had elaborated the first studies on the medium along lines that were both historical (since historical reflection is both cause and consequence of the first steps toward institutionalization) and semiotic (for that was, for better or for worse, the dominating intellectual current of that period). At the same time, graphic novel studies introduce vital shifts that can be observed in the broader domains of comics and visual culture. However, what remains deeply characteristic of the field is the importance of nonacademic voices. Just as one cannot study the nineteenth-century novel without close-reading Gustave Flaubert's private correspondence or Henry James's prefaces to his collected novels, one would commit a crucial mistake by preferring the material published in learned journals and by academic presses to the observations and reflections by authors, editors, publishers, or readers. Fiction remains an indispensable source of information: an introduction to the graphic novel will not be complete as long as one does not read the work of those graphic novelists who like to reflect within their own work on the techniques as well as the stakes of their profession. Authors such as Seth, Daniel Clowes, and Julie Doucet, for instance, have provided us with invaluable insights on the life and work of a graphic novelist. As already mentioned for Art Spiegelman, the interview genre remains a crucial aspect of graphic novel scholarship. (Mississippi has a specialized series, but publications such as *In the Studio: Visits with Contemporary Cartoonists*, edited by Todd Hignite and published by Yale University Press in 2007, are also recommended.)

Next to these interviews, it is worth mentioning also the introductions, often written by artists, editors, or librarians working in the comics and graphic novel field, to the new editions of forgotten or previously out-of-print classics. We have already mentioned David Beronå's commitment to the subgenre of the wordless woodcut novel. Other examples are Chip Kidd and Art Spiegelman's presentation of Jack Cole's superhero character Plastic Man (*Jack Cole and Plastic Man: Forms Stretched to Their Limits*, Chronicle Books, 2001), Chris Ware's editorial work for issue 13 of *McSweeney's Quarterly* (2004), and, in a less author-oriented perspective, the anthologies edited by Ivan Brunetti with Yale University Press (*An Anthology of Graphic Fiction, Cartoons, and True Stories*, vols. 1 and 2, in 2006 and 2008, respectively) or Paul Gravett (*Graphic Novels: Everything You Need to Know*, Collins, 2005).

In addition to the interviews and the editorial introductions, it is also necessary to stress the scholarly importance of many self-introductory, self-explanatory, self-legitimizing publications that have played an essential role in the communication of the field with the larger public. Two books by Will Eisner, *Comics and Sequential Art* (Poorhouse Press, 1985) and *Graphic Storytelling and Visual Narrative* (Poorhouse

Press, 1996), and the famous and bestselling *Understanding Comics: The Invisible Art* by Scott McCloud (Kitchen Sink Press, 1993) are still highly relevant to academic discussions, despite (or perhaps thanks to?) their willful refusal of scholarly jargon.

Today, the importance of the graphic novel in and for teaching is acknowledged widely, as one can best see in the initiative taken by the Modern Language Association to make its own handbook, *Teaching the Graphic Novel* (Stephen Tabachnick, ed., MLA, 2009; the Modern Language Association has also its own research group on the graphic novel, chaired by Charles Hatfield). A similar publication is *Critical Approaches to Comics: Theories and Methods* (Matthew J. Smith and Randy Duncan, eds., Routledge, 2011). The publication of comics and graphic novel readers, such as the one edited by Jeet Heer and Ken Worcester, *A Comics Studies Reader* (University of Mississippi Press, 2008), shows that there is definitely a large need, as well as a real market, for innovative classroom material.

A growing set of publications reflects on the specific features of the graphic novel, from a visual as well as a narrative point of view. For many decades, European, mainly Francophone, researchers have monopolized this kind of research. Some of this work is now available in English translation; see, for instance, Thierry Groensteen's *The System of Comics* (University of Mississippi Press, 2009) and *Comics and Narration* (University of Mississippi Press, 2013); Benoît Peeters's seminal article on page layout, "Four Conceptions of the Page" (in *Imagetext* 3:3, s.d., online); and Thierry Smolderen's *Births of the Comics* (University of Mississippi Press, forthcoming). All these translations have proven dramatically influential in the ongoing reflection on the medium. Most of this work remains relatively unknown, however, despite the efforts of scholars such as Ann Miller and Bart Beaty, who are both very active in their role as bridge-builders between Anglophone and Francophone culture (both coedit a collection of translated material published with Leuven University Press, 2014).

After the formative publications by Will Eisner and Scott McCloud, who showed that it was possible to find an audience for studies on comics and graphic novels, decisive contributions were made by other American-based scholars, notably, Charles Hatfield, *Alternative Comics: An Emerging Literature* (University of Mississippi Press, 2005); Jared Gardner and David Herman, who coedited an influential issue of the journal *SubStance* (40:1, issue 124, 2011); Robin Varnum and Christina Robbins, editors of an important collection on word and image relationships in comics and graphic novels (*The Language of Comics: Word & Image in the Comics* (University of Mississippi Press, 2001; one can complement this volume with the more recent collection edited by Bernd Herzogenrath, *Travels in Intermedial(ity) – ReBlurring the Boundaries*, University Press of New England, 2012, 92–110); Jane Marianna Tolmie, ed., *Drawing from Life: Memory and Subjectivity in Comic Art* (University of Mississippi Press, 2013); and Brian McHale, who has done pioneering work at the crossroads of narrative analysis and the study of poetry (see "Narrativity and Segmentivity, or Poetry in the Gutter," in Marina Grishakova and Marie-Laure Ryan, eds., *Intermediality and Storytelling*, De Gruyter, 2011, 27–48), a subfield that is not without intersections with the rising practice of nonnarrative, purely visual graphic novels. On these works, see Andre Molotiu, ed., *Abstract Comics* (Fantagraphics, 2009); for a narrative reading of abstraction, see Jan Baetens, "Abstraction in Comics," *SubStance* 40:1 (issue 124, 2011, 94–113).

Part III: Themes (Chapters 8–9)

The literary reuse of comics and graphic novel culture remains a key example of the new forms of reading/writing as studied by Jim Collins in his major study, *Bring on the Books for Everybody* (Notre Dame University Press, 2010). Although mainly focusing on the exchanges between novel and film, Collins's emphasis on the often very playful blurring of boundaries between traditional notions of high and low culture, and more particularly on the merger of words and images and the emergence of convergence and participatory culture, both online and offline, proves extremely helpful to a better understanding of what happens in the work of, for example, Michael Chabon and Jonathan Lethem. Also crucial in this regard are Henry Jenkins's *Convergence Culture* (New York University Press, 2006), which includes a study of fan culture and communities in gaming that has many echoes in comics and graphic novel culture, and Mark McGurl's *The Program Era, Postwar Fiction and the Rise of Creative Writing* (Harvard University Press, 2009), which stresses the impact of institutional features on "what" and "how" we read and write. Unfortunately, the significance of Pantheon editor Chip Kidd, whose importance for bringing together the worlds of trade publishing and graphic novel has been highly significant, is still awaiting academic recognition. Dave Eggers's commitment to comics culture, mainly through *McSweeney's Quarterly*, has been more widely acknowledged, although the critical reflection on the journal and its general editor is often enlarged (for it would be absurd to use here the word "reduced") to a study of Chris Ware, the guest-editor of *McSweeney's* special issue on comics and graphic novels (see, for example, Dave M. Ball and Martha B. Kuhlman, eds., *The Comics of Chris Ware: Drawing Is a Way of Thinking*, University of Mississippi Press, 2010).

In the area of globalized convergence culture, there is also a growing awareness of the importance of adaptation studies. Comics and graphic novels have always been an important adapting medium, as demonstrated by Martin Barker and Roger Sabin's *The Lasting of the Mohicans: History of an American Myth* (University of Mississippi Press, 1995), which contains a thought-provoking comparison of literary adaptations in comics and literary adaptations in other media (similar analyses, although more formally oriented, can be found in the above-mentioned books by Thierry Groensteen). But more and more comics and graphic novels are now also adapted themselves in film, literary fiction, and games, a phenomenon well acknowledged by scholars specializing in the field (*cf.* the Oxford University Press journal *Adaptations*) as well as in edited collections (see, for instance, Ian Gordon, Mark Jancovich, and Matthew P. McAllister, *Film and Comic Books*, University of Mississippi Press, 2007). The most interesting evolution, however, may have been the opening of the annual international Film Studies Conference of Udine-Gorizia to the subfield of comics and graphic novel adaptations (see, for instance, the special volume *Cinema and Comics*, edited by Leonardo Quaresima, Laura Ester Sangalli, and Federico Zecca, Forum: Udine, 2009).

Academic publications on graphic novel themes and culture cover a wide range of areas and fields of interest. In the U.S. context, there has always existed a strong relationship between graphic novel studies and identity and minority studies. The importance of Jewish culture for the field has been studied by, among others, Danny Fingeroth, *Disguised as Clark Kent: Jews, Comics and the Creation of the Superhero* (Continuum, 2008). In the case of women and gender studies, significant contributions have been made by Trina Robbins (herself a comix artist) in *Great Women Cartoonists* (Watson-Guptill, 2001) and Hillary Chute in *Graphic Women* (Columbia University Press, 2010). For Latino comics and graphic novels, a decisive publication is Frederick Aldama's *Your Brain on Latino Comics* (Texas University Press, 2009). On African-American comics, see, for instance, William Foster III, *Looking for a Face Like Mine* (Fine Tooth Press, 2005); Adilifu Nama, *Super-Black: American Pop Culture and Black Superheroes* (Texas University Press, 2011); and Sheena C. Howard and Ronald L. Jackson III, eds., *Black Comics: Politics of Race and Representation* (Bloomsbury, 2013). For interesting backdrop, see also Sam Durant, ed., *Black Panther: The Revolutionary Art of Emory Douglas* (Rizzoli, 2007). More generally speaking, the theme of identity has been studied by various others in the perspective of autobiographical or semi-autobiographical ("autofictional") narrative; see, for instance, Michael Chaney, ed., *Graphic Subjects: Critical Essays on Autobiography and Graphic Novels* (Wisconsin University Press, 2011); Elisabeth El Refaie, *Autobiographical Comics: Life Writing in Pictures* (University of Mississippi Press, 2012); and Jane Tolmie, ed., *Drawing from Life: Memory and Subjectivity in Comic Art* (University of Mississippi Press, 2013).

A second strand of publications is more historically oriented. In certain cases, the history in question is that of the field itself, but most authors are happy to establish careful links with history in general. One of the first academic publications, which is still very vital to a good understanding of the graphic novel today, is Joseph Witek's *Comic Books as History* (University of Mississippi Press, 1989), as well as "History in the Graphic Novel," a special themed issue of *Rethinking History*, 6:3 (2002) edited by Hugo Frey and Benjamin Noys. The already mentioned work by Jared Gardner, *Projections*, and Bart Beaty's *Unpopular Culture* (Toronto University Press, 2007) and *Comics versus Art* (Toronto University Press, 2012), are other excellent examples of an approach that cuts across the boundaries of comics history, cultural history, and history *tout court*. History, as demonstrated by Hillary Chute in the excellent survey article "Comics as Literature? Reading Graphic Narrative," in *PMLA* 123:2 (March 2008, 452–465), is one of the two subject matters, with reportage and journalism, that seem to match most naturally the medium-specific features of the graphic novel. It is not a surprise that many recent publications foreground precisely these aspects of the medium, such as *Graphic Subjects* (Michael Chaney, ed., Wisconsin University Press, 2011), which has a strong emphasis on memory, testimony, autobiography, and semi-autobiography. More recently, there has been a strong impulse toward the study of comics and graphic novels in adaptation studies and the so-called convergence culture (Henry Jenkins), with books such as Ian Gordon et al., eds., *Film and Comic Books* (University of Mississippi Press, 2007). On nostalgia culture – a ubiquitously present, yet highly ambivalent tendency in contemporary graphic novels – see the classic study of the general issue at hand by Simon Reynolds, *Retromania: Pop Culture's Addiction to Its Own Past* (Faber and Faber, 2011), as well as interesting contextual material in Mark McGurl, *The Program Era* (Harvard University Press, 2011), and Jim Collins, *Bring on the Books for Everybody* (Notre Dame University Press, 2010).

For nostalgia culture and comics culture in particular, see Jules Feiffer, *The Great Comic Book Heroes* (Fantagraphics, 2003 [1965]). See also the critical discussions that accompanied the publication of Art Spiegelman's *In the Shadow of No Towers* (Pantheon,

2004) and *MetaMaus* (Pantheon, 2011), *cf.*, for example, Hillary Chute, "Temporality and Seriality in Spiegelman's *In the Shadow of No Towers*," *American Periodicals* 17:2 (2007, 228–244), and Hillary Chute, "Comics as Archives: Meta*MetaMaus*," in *On the Subject of Archives* (2012), a special issue of *e-misférica* (published by the NYU Hemispheric Institute, online at http://hemisphericinstitute.org/hemi/en/e-misferica-91/chute).

The growing institutionalization of the graphic novel has inevitably, but with very lucky results, drawn attention to its major representatives, and some of them have become real stars. The U.S. field is, however, not monopolized by one major figure, as is still the case today in Europe, where an amazing percentage of the articles and books published on the subject are actually books on Tintin. On Hergé, we advise the American reader to start with the authorized but surprising biography *Hergé, Son of Tintin* by Benoît Peeters (Stanford University Press, 2011), or *The Metamorphoses of Tintin* by Jean-Marie Apostolidès (Stanford University Press, 2009), unless one prefers the more indirect and imaginary recreation of the Tintin character by Frederic Tuten in his novel *Tintin in the New World* (Minerva, 1993). Of course, the scholarship on Art Spiegelman is impressive, from the first readings still deeply rooted in trauma studies (Dominick LaCapra, *History and Memory After Auschwitz*, Cornell University Press, 1998 and James Young, *At Memory's Edge*, Yale University Press, 2000) to the more complete, almost exhaustive approach offered by the amazing multimedia presentation of *MetaMaus: A Look Inside a Modern Classic* (Art Spiegelman and Hillary Chute, eds., Pantheon, 2011); critical voices can be heard in Walter Benn Michaels, "Plots Against America: Neoliberalism and Anti-Americanism," *American Literary History*, 18:2 (2008, 288–302), and Andrew Loman, "Well Intended Liberal Slop," *Journal of American Studies*, 40:3 (2008), 551–571). But the graphic novel production is rich and diverse enough to make room for many other success stories: Marjane Satrapi (*Persepolis*), Alison Bechdel (*Fun Home*), Alan Moore and Dave Gibbons (*Watchmen*), Chris Ware (*Jimmy Corrigan, Building Stories*) (on

Ware, see, for instance, Daniel Raeburn, *Chris Ware*, Yale University Press, 2004), and Daniel Clowes (*Ghost World*, *David Boring*) (on Clowes, see Ken Pareille and Isaac Cates, eds., *Daniel Clowes: Conversations*, University of Mississippi Press, 2010) are also authors whose work is widely discussed and analyzed.

NOTES

1 Introduction: The Graphic Novel, a Special Type of Comics

1 Art Spiegelman, "Comix: An Idiosyncratic Historical and Aesthetic Overview," *Print* (November/December 1988), reproduced in Art Spiegelman, *Comix, Essays, Graphics and Scraps* (Palermo: Grafiche Renna/A RAW Book, 1998), 81.

2 The quote is reproduced in the growing literature devoted to Moore. It is found online at http://blather.net/articles/amoore/northampton.html (last accessed October 2012). Originally Moore made the remarks in an interview with Barry Kavanagh in 2000.

3 Jonathan Lethem with Karl Rusnak and Farel Dalrymple, *Omega the Unknown* (New York: Marvel, 2008); Chip Kidd and Dave Taylor, *Batman: Death by Design* (New York: DC Comics, 2012).

4 Script by Quentin Tarantino and artwork by R. M. Guéra and Jason Latour.

5 Stephen E. Tabachnick, ed., *Teaching the Graphic Novel* (New York: Modern Language Association of America, 2009).

6 The key predecessors avoid the nomenclature debate by using different terms to describe some similar "real world" cultural phenomenon. Hence we owe much to Roger Sabin's *Adult Comics* (London: Routledge, 1993) and Charles Hatfield's *Alternative Comics* (Jackson: University Press of Mississippi, 2005). We would also like to take this opportunity to draw attention to the excellent newer work by Bart Beaty, *Comics versus Art* (Toronto: University of Toronto Press, 2012).

7 See also Jan Baetens, ed., *The Graphic Novel* (Leuven: Leuven University Press, 2001) and Hugo Frey and Benjamin Noys, eds., "History in the Graphic Novel," special themed issue, *Rethinking History,* 6.3 (2002).

8 Art Spiegelman in Joseph Witek, ed., *Art Spiegelman: Conversations* (Jackson: University Press of Mississippi, 2007), 289. From a previously unpublished interview with Witek, 2004.

9   Harvey Kurtzman, *Jungle Book* (New York: Ballantine Books, 1959).

10 Marietta, GA: Top Shelf, 2009.

11 Frank Miller, *The Complete Sin City* (Milwaukie, OR: Dark Horse, 2005); Miller, *Holy Terror* (Burbank, CA: Legendary Comics, 2011).

12 See also Daniel Raeburn, *Chris Ware* (New Haven: Yale University Press, 2004), 14–16.

13 Daniel Clowes, introduction to *Ghost World: Special Edition* (Seattle: Fantagraphics Books, 2008), unpaginated.

14 Frank Miller in Gary Groth and Robert Fiore, eds., *The New Comics* (New York: Berkley Books, 1988), 63.

15 The work by Charles Hatfield, *Alternative Comics*, represents an important turning point in reflection on these issues.

16 A head shop is "a retail outlet specializing in drug paraphernalia used for consumption of cannabis, other recreational drugs, legal highs, legal party powders and New Age herbs, as well as counterculture art, magazines, music, clothing, and home decor; some head shops also sell oddities, such as antique walking sticks" (Wikipedia, accessed Dec. 26, 2011). Readers concerned with our use of Wikipedia should be reassured, for where better to find a definition of a head shop than a quasi-countercultural dictionary that is regulated by its own readers?

17 See Charles Hatfield, *Alternative Comics*, Chapter 6.

18 Both published with the University Press of Mississippi (Jackson, respectively, 2005 and 2011).

19 See, for example, R. A. Peterson, "Five Constraints on the Production of Culture: Law, Technology, Market, Organizational Structure and Occupational Careers," *Journal of Popular Culture* 16:2 (1982): 143–153, David Hesmondalgh, *The Cultural Industries*, 3rd ed. (London: Sage, 2012), and Pierre-Michel Menger, *Le travail créateur* (Paris: Gallimard, Seuil and éditions de l'EHESS, 2009).

20 It is a useful reminder that one of the first "serious" books on the U.S. graphic novel, Joseph Witek's still very readable *Comic Books as History* (Jackson: University Press of Mississippi, 1989), highlighted the historical rather than the autobiographical aspects of the graphic novel.

21 Notable examples of preserialization include *Maus*, *Ghost World*, *Jimmy Corrigan*, *From Hell*, *Watchmen*, and *V for Vendetta*. Moreover, a sense of serialization is maintained when graphic novels appear as trilogies or quadrilogies. This was always the case with Hergé's *Tintin* books, and is also important in work such as Alan Moore and Kevin O'Neill's *The League of Extraordinary Gentlemen*. In book form, this serialized work actually comprises *Volume 1* (La Jolla, CA: America's Best Comics, 2003) and *Volume 2* (London: Titan Books, 2003); *Volume 3* is only available in three separate one-shots from Top Shelf (but as yet not collected). The actual Volume 3 in sequence of publication is *The League of Extraordinary Gentlemen: The Black Dossier* (La Jolla, CA: Wildstorm Productions, an imprint of DC Comics, 2007); it was published as a graphic novel, with no pre-issues.

22 Fanzines and their circulation of adult comics are dealt with in Roger Sabin and Teal Triggs, eds., *Below Critical Radar: Fanzines and Alternative Comics from 1976*

to Now (Mesquite, TX: Codex Books, 2002), which includes a detailed discussion of how Charles Burns, Daniel Clowes, and Chris Ware published work before being contracted to major literary publishers.

23 For a recent critical discussion, see Thierry Smolderen, *The Origins of Comics* (Jackson: University Press of Mississippi, forthcoming).

24 This decision is not the a priori result of some repressed Eurocentrism of the authors (one British, one continental). It is fully acknowledged in works mapping the global influences of comics and the graphic novel, a good example being Scott McCloud's *Reinventing Comics: How Imagination and Technology Are Revolutionizing an Art Form* (New York: Perennial, 2000), one of the first attempts to chart the non-U.S. influences on the transformations of the U.S. production, in which the author brings to the fore mainly the impact of the European production.

25 The best and most detailed approach that explores terminological usage of the concept "graphic novel" is R. C. Harvey's "The Graphic Novel, Will Eisner and Other Pioneers," *Comics Journal* 234 (June 2001): 92–97. An excellent sense of the very recent past (2001–2010) is found in Ben Schwartz's Introduction to *The Best American Comics Criticism* (Seattle: Fantagraphics, 2010), 10–21.

26 See his anthology *Wordless Books: The Original Graphic Novels* (New York: Abrams, 2008).

27 Novelist Jonathan Lethem recalls that growing up with artistic parents, he was drawn to pop culture as a way of countering parental expectations, although as he notes too, ironically, the material he selected was drifting toward art. He writes: "Growing up in an artist's family, I seized on comic books and science fiction as a solution to the need to disappoint my father's expectation that I became an artist like himself.... The cartoonist I settled on lastly, Robert Crumb, was of course as late-modernist and literary as they come, a Philip Roth or Robert Coover of comics." Earlier he had been drawn to Marvel comic books, which he described as "inchoate 'graphic novels' before the invention of the term." See Lethem , *The Disappointment Artist* (London: Faber, 2005), 146.

2 Adult Comics before the Graphic Novel: From Moral Panic to Pop Art Sensationalism, 1945–c.1967

1 David Hajdu, *The Ten-Cent Plague: The Great Comic Book Scare and How It Changed America* (New York: Farrar, Strauss and Giroux, 2008), 112.

2 See Bart Beaty, *Fredric Wertham and the Critique of Mass Culture* (Jackson: University Press of Mississippi, 2005), 82–86.

3 Art Spiegelman and Chip Kidd, *Jack Cole and Plastic Man: Forms Stretched to Their Limits* (San Francisco: Chronicle Books, 2001).

4 See Charles Hatfield, *Hand of Fire: The Comics Art of Jack Kirby* (Jackson: University Press of Mississippi, 2012) and for further on Marvel's updating of the comics post-Wertham, herein Chapter 2.

5 Hajdu, *The Ten-Cent Plague*, 112.

6 Hajdu, *The Ten-Cent Plague*, 165.

7 See the actually quite subtle article by Joe Queenan, "Drawing on the Dark Side," *New York Times* (April 30, 1997). More recently the violence of recent publications in comics/graphic novels is a cause for concern; see Dave Itzkoff, "Behind the Mask," *New York Times* (Nov. 20, 2005).

8 Joseph Witek, *Comic Books as History: The Narrative Art of Jack Jackson, Art Spiegelman and Harvey Pekar* (Jackson: University Press of Mississippi, 1989), 37.

9 *Frontline Combat*, no. 5 (May 1952), reproduced in complete black and white in Les Daniels, *Comix: A History of Comic Books in America* (London: Fusion-Wildwood House, 1973), 75–78.

10 Joe Sacco, *Safe Area Gorazde* (Seattle: Fantagraphics, 2000).

11 Spiegelman wrote a student term paper on Krigstein's "Master Race" that was subsequently published in an EC fan magazine. It has been reprinted several times. A full account of this fascinating connection is given in Spiegelman's article "Ball-Buster: Bernard Krigstein's Life Between Panels," *The New Yorker* (July 22, 2002). The storyline of "Master Race" was provided by scriptwriter and EC editor Al Feldstein.

12 Bernie Krigstein, "Master Race," *Tales Designed to Carry an Impact*, no. 1 (April 1955).

13 See Tony Hiss and Jeff Lewis, "The 'Mad' Generation," *New York Times Magazine* (June 31, 1997).

14 Harvey Kurtzman, *Harvey Kurtzman's Jungle Book* (New York: Ballantine, 1959).

15 See Harvey Kurtzman, *The Jungle Book* (Princeton, WI: Kitchen Sink Press, 1986), preface by Art Spiegelman.

16 Jonathan Miller in Tomi Ungerer, *The Underground Sketchbook of Tomi Ungerer* (New York: Viking Books, 1964), 3.

17 See Richard L. Graham, *Government Issue: Comics for the People, 1940s–2000s* (New York: Harry N. Abrams, 2011), 54–58, which reproduces Neal Adams's "I am the Guard" (Johnstone and Cushing for the U.S. National Guard, 1960).

18 An excellent history of the genre is found in William B. Jones Jr., *Classics Illustrated: A Cultural History* (Jefferson: MacFarland and Co., 2011), 111.

19 Jones, *Classics Illustrated: A Cultural History*, 137.

20 Jones, *Classics Illustrated: A Cultural History*, 111; "Shakespeare Bows to 'Comics' Public: Play Texts Will Be Produced in Picture Form to Interest World's Popular Audience," *New York Times* (March 9, 1950), 24.

21 Jean-Paul Gabilliet, *Of Comics and Men: A Cultural History of American Comic Books* (Jackson: University Press of Mississippi, 2010), 58.

22 The reprints ran 1964–1966 and included the titles *Tales from the Crypt* and *The Vault of Horror*. At the time, Ballantine was making its name publishing J. R. R. Tolkien's *Lord of the Rings* for the U.S. paperback market.

23 Thomas Crow, "For and Against the Funnies: Roy Lichtenstein's Drawings in the Inception of Pop Art, 1961–1962," in, *Roy Lichtenstein: The Black-and-White Drawings 1961–1968,* ed. Isabelle Dervaux (New York: The Morgan Library and Museum, 2010), 31. Readers should note that our own analysis offers a less focused emphasis on Lichtenstein and a less causal relationship, including the role of television and cinema remakes of comics, as well as comics' own historical developments. We would also not hold such a black-and-white view of the power of Wertham; drug

imagery sneaks into some strips very quickly, and EC horror never really dies out, having a quick rebirth through fast reprints as books not comics.

24   Adam Gopnik, "Comics," in *High and Low: Modern Art and Popular Culture* eds. Kirk Varnedoe and Adam Gopnik (New York: Museum of Modern Art, 1990), 208. See also Roger Sabin, *Comics, Comix and Graphic Novels: A History of Comic Art* (London: Phaidon, 1996), 74.

25   Andy Warhol and Pat Hackett, *Popism: The Warhol Sixties* (San Diego: Harcourt Brace Jovanovich, 1980), 39–40 (italics added).

26   Henry Jenkins and Lynn Spigel, "Same Bat Channel, Different Bat Times," in *The Many Lives of Batman*, eds. Roberta Pearson and William Uricchio (London: Routledge, 1991), 123. The best descriptions are found in Lynn Spigel, *TV by Design* (Chicago: Chicago University Press, 2008), 259–260; and Sasha Torres, "The Caped Crusader of Camp: Pop, Camp, and the Batman Television Series," in *Pop Out: Queer Warhol,* eds. Jennifer Doyle et al. (Raleigh: Durham University Press, 1996), 238–255.

27   Will Brooker, *Batman Unmasked* (New York: Continuum, 2000), 193.

28   West, cited in Michael Kackman, *Television, Espionage, and Cold War Culture* (London: University of Minnesota Press, 2005), 89.

29   Warhol and Hackett, *Popism*, 139.

30   Jean-Claude Forest, *Barbarella*, trans. Richard Seaver (New York: Grove Press, 1966).

31   Detailed context is provided in the biography of strip writer Michael O'Donoghue, Dennis Perrin, *Mr Mike: The Life and Work of Michael O'Donoghue* (New York: Avon Books, 1998). Thanks here to go to Richard Ellis for his fascinating insights on *Evergreen Review*.

32   Charles Hatfield, *Hand of Fire: The Comics Art of Jack Kirby* (Jackson: University Press of Mississippi, 2012), 122.

33   That is to say, Clowes draws his graphic novels in a style that is deliberately close to the preexisting comics and popular animation shows of the 1960s and 1970s.

34   Ware, cited in Andrea Juno, *Dangerous Drawings* (New York: Juno Books, 1997), 42.

35   Bart Beaty, *Comics Versus Art* (Toronto: Toronto University Press, 2012).

36   See Lawrence Alloway, *American Pop Art* (New York: Whitney Museum of American Art, 1974), 16.

37   John Broom and Sid Green "The Art Gallery of Rogues," *Batman* (Dec. 1965, no. 117), and Bill Finger, "Two Batmen Too Many," *Batman* (Dec. 1965, no. 117), both reproduced in *Showcase Presents Batman*. Vol. 2 (New York: DC Comics, 2007), 86–109.

38   Daniels, *Comix*, 142–144.

39   Neil Gaiman and Andy Kubert, *Marvel 1602* (New York: Marvel, 2006).

3 Underground Comix and Mainstream Evolutions, 1968–c.1980

1   Justin Green, *Binky Brown Meets the Holy Virgin* (San Francisco: Last Gasp, 1972), and Jaxon, *Comanche Moon* (San Francisco: Rip Off Press/Last Gasp, 1979).

2   See Jean-Paul Gabilliet, *Of Comics and Men: A Cultural History of American Comic Books* (Jackson: University Press of Mississippi, 2009); Paul Lopes, *Demanding*

Respect: The Evolution of the American Comic Book (Philadelphia: Temple University Press, 2009); Charles Hatfield, *Alternative Comics: An Emerging Literature* (Jackson: University Press of Mississippi, 2006); Mark James Estren, *A History of Underground Comics* (Berkeley: Ronin Publishing, 1993); Patrick Rosenkranz, *Rebel Visions: The Underground Comix Revolution, 1963–75* (Seattle: Fantagraphics, 2008).

3 Lopes, *Demanding Respect*, 76–78.

4 Robert Doty, *Human Concern/Personal Torment: The Grotesque in American Art* (New York: Whitney Museum of American Art/Praeger, 1969).

5 See also album art for Big Brother and the Holding Company's *Cheap Thrills*.

6 Harvey Pekar, "Rapping about Cartoonists – Robert Crumb," *Journal of Popular Culture* 3:4 (1970): 683.

7 The secondary literature on Crumb is relatively limited. This is changing with the important new work Jean-Paul Gabilliet, *R. Crumb* (Bordeaux: Presses Universitaires de Bordeaux, 2012).

8 See Art Spiegelman and Alfred Bergdoll, *Cascade Comix Monthly* (Feb. 1979), 11–12, reprinted in Joseph Witek, ed., *Art Spiegelman: Conversations* (Jackson, University Press of Mississippi, 2007), 4.

9 See, for example, Robert Crumb, *The Book of Genesis* (London: Jonathan Cape, 2009); Kim Deitch, *Alias the Cat* (London: Jonathan Cape, 2007).

10 Eisner cited in Michael Schumacher, *Will Eisner: A Dreamer's Life in Comics* (New York: Bloomsbury, 2010), 167.

11 Will Eisner, *A Contract with God* (New York: Norton, 2004), xii.

12 Eisner's early comic book series *The Spirit* was original too, but it was closer to convention than this work.

13 Readers with a penchant for media trivia might enjoy learning that Skip Hinnant, who provided the voice for Schroeder in the musical adaptation, was subsequently cast to lend his voice to the lead character of Bakshi's *Fritz the Cat*. For what it's worth, Hinnant's brother made his career playing Snoopy, first on stage and then in the first *Peanuts* television special, *You're a Good Man, Charlie Brown* (1973).

14 For more on Trudeau, see the important work Kerry Soper, *Garry Trudeau: Doonesbury and the Aesthetics of Satire* (Jackson: University Press of Mississippi, 2008).

15 R. C. Harvey, "The Graphic Novel, Will Eisner and Other Pioneers," *The Comics Journal* 234 (June 2001): 92–97.

16 Richard Corben, *Bloodstar* (New York: The Morning Star Press, 1976), 5.

17 Archie Goodwin and Walter Simonson, *Alien: The Illustrated Story* (New York: Heavy Metal, 1979).

4 "Not Just for Kids": Clever Comics and the New Graphic Novels

1 See Spiegelman, Introduction to *Garbage Pail Kids,* The Topps Company, Inc. (New York: Abrams, 2012), 5–10.

2 Art Spiegelman cited in Joseph Witek, *Art Spiegelman: Conversations* (Jackson: University Press of Mississippi, 2007), 165.

3 Roger Sabin, *Comics, Comix, and Graphic Novels: A History of Comic Art* (London: Phaidon, 1996), 165.

4   Peter Novick, *The Holocaust and Collective Memory: The American Experience* (London: Bloomsbury, 2001).

5   Holocaust denial anti-Semitism gained attention in the late 1970s and early 1980s. In 1985 former Director General of the United Nations Kurt Waldheim was revealed to have concealed aspects of his life and work for Nazi Germany during his war service in Greece; also in 1985 President Ronald Reagan attended a commemoration of the fortieth anniversary of the Second World War in Bitburg, West Germany, which became controversial for taking place in a military cemetery that included graves of German SS personnel. American pop culture tackled several of these events, notably through rock music including Lou Reed's "Good Evening Mr Waldheim" (1988) and The Ramones' "My Brain Is Hanging Upside Down (Bonzo Goes to Bitburg)" (1985). Klaus Barbie was tried for crimes against humanity in Lyons, France, in 1987.

6   See Dominick LaCapra, *History and Memory after Auschwitz* (Ithaca: Cornell University Press, 1998); James Young, *At Memory's Edge* (New Haven: Yale University Press, 2000).

7   See several versions reprinted online including http://web.ics.purdue.edu/~felluga/holocaust/villagevoice2.html (last accessed August 2013).

8   John Carlin and Sheena Wagstaff, "Beyond the Pleasure Principle: Comic Quotation in Contemporary American Painting," *The Comic Art Show: Cartoons in Painting and Popular Culture* (New York: Whitney Museum of American Art/Fantagraphics, 1983), 62.

9   For more general context on comics and art world interactions, see the excellent Bart Beaty, *Comics versus Art: Comics in the Artworld* (Jackson: University Press of Mississippi, 2012).

10 Many of these books are excellent overviews. See, for example, the works from Stephen Weiner, which are all very useful snapshots of a period of publishing, including *Graphic Novels for Public Libraries* (Northampton Mass: Kitchen Sink Press, 1996), *The 101 Best Graphic Novels* (New York: NBM, 2001), and *The Rise of the Graphic Novel* (New York: NBM, 2003), and from Paul Gravett, *Graphic Novels: Stories to Change Your Life* (London: Aurum, 2005).

11 For an analysis of the impact of McCloud's work, see Beaty, *Comics versus Art*, 34–35.

12 The article commonly cited is Michael Berry, "The Second British Invasion," which is still available online at http://www.sff.net/people/mberry/gaiman.htm (last accessed January 2013). This was not the only report of this type, but it is now much cited because of its availability online.

13 See Karen Berger's interview available from www.juliaround.com (last accessed August 2013). For Round on Berger, see "Is This a Book? DC Vertigo and the Redefinition of Comics in the 1990s" in *The Rise of the American Comics Artist*, eds. Paul Williams and James Lyons (Jackson: University Press of Mississippi, 2010), 14.

14 Moore cited in Gary Spencer Millidge, *Alan Moore: Storyteller* (Lewis: Ilex, 2011), 108.

15 See the useful commentary in Qiana J. Whitted, "Of Slaves and Other Swamp Things: Black Southern History as Comic Book Horror," in *Comics and the US South*, eds.

Brannon Costello and Qiana J. Whitted (Jackson: University Press of Mississippi, 2012), 202.

16 See John Newsinger, *The Dredd Phenomenon: Comics and Contemporary Society* (Bristol: Libertarian Education, 1999).

17 Best known as the author of the *Blueberry* western series, Giraud had already received a special award from the National Cartoonists Society as "Best Realistic Artist" in 1972. He later moved to the United States and worked with the film industry. See also Stanley Wiater and Stephen R. Bissette, *Comic Book Rebels: Conversations with the Creators of the New Comics* (New York: Donald I. Fine Inc, 1993), 145–188.

18 Roger Sabin, *Adult Comics* (London: Routledge, 1993), 71.

19 Gary Groth and Robert Fiore, eds., *The New Comics: Interviews from the Pages of* The Comics Journal (New York: Berkley, 1988), 288.

20 Frederick Luis Aldama, *Your Brain on Latino Comics* (Austin: University of Texas Press, 2009), 4–5.

21 Chris Ware, cited in Andrea Juno, *Dangerous Drawings: Interviews with Comix and Graphix Artists* (New York: Juno Books, 1993), 50.

22 Art Spiegelman, *In the Shadow of No Towers* (New York: Pantheon, 2004), 1.

23 Hillary Chute, "Comics as Literature? Reading Graphic Literature," *PMLA* 123:2 (2008): 453–465; quotation page 456. The reference to Felman and Laub is to page xv of Shoshana Felman and Dori Laub, foreword to *Testimony: Crises of Witnessing in Literature, Psychoanalysis, and History* (New York: Routledge, 1992), xiii–xx.

5 Understanding Panel and Page Layouts

1 This selection is far from exhaustive, as shown by the excellent contributions of, among various others, Pascal Lefèvre in "Mise en scène and Framing. Visual Storytelling in Lone Wolf and Cub," in *Critical Approaches to Comics: Theories and Methods*, eds. Randy Duncan and Matthew J. Smith (London: Routledge, 2011), 71–83, and "The Conquest of Space: Evolution of Panel Arrangements and Page Lay Outs in Early Comics," *European Comic Art* 2:2 (2009): 227–252.

2 For a detailed discussion of the issues raised by single-frame narrative, see Lew Andrews, *Story and Space in Renaissance Art: The Rebirth of Continuous Narrative* (New York: Cambridge University Press, 1995), and Jan Baetens and Mieke Bleyen, "Photo Narrative, Sequential Photography, Photonovels," in *Intermediality and Storytelling*, eds. Marina Grishakova and Marie-Louise Ryan (Berlin: De Gruyter, 2010), 165–182.

3 See Jean-Christophe Menu in *La Bande dessinée et son double* (Paris: L'Association, 2011).

4 Scott McCloud's *Understanding Comics* is the most influential spokesman for this approach.

5 Pierre Fresnault-Deruelle, "Du linéaire au tabulaire," *Communications* 24 (1976): 7–23. A good overview of the discussion concerning linearity versus tabularity is given by Harry Morgan in his book *Principes des littératures dessinées* (Angoulême: Editions de l'An 2, 2003).

6   H. Porter Abbott, *Cambridge Introduction to Narrative*. 2nd ed. (New York: Cambridge University Press, 2008), 56.

7   Marjorie Perloff, "Screening the Page/Paging the Screen: Digital Poetics and the Digital Text," in *New Media Poetics: Contexts, Technotexts, and Theories*, eds. Adelaide Morris and Thomas Swiss (Cambridge, Mass.: MIT Press, 2006), 143–165.

8   Benoît Peeters, "Four Conceptions of the Page," trans. Jesse Cohn in *Image Text* 3:3 (n.d.), available at http://www.english.ufl.edu/imagetext/archives/v3_3/peeters/. All further quotations from Peeters's essay are quoted from this (unpaginated) source.

9   Hugo Frey, "For All to See: Yvan Alagbé's *Nègres jaunes* and the Contemporary French Social Crisis," *Yale French Studies* 114 (2008): 116–129.

10 An intertextual argument should be added here as well. The book reworks the famous *The New Yorker* cover design by Art Spiegelman, which did only feature the black-on-black illustration, not the string of flying comics characters. The addition of this element, which perturbs the overall composition of the page, achieves thus even more importance. Jeet Heer underlines in his recent work that the original design concept was from Mouly.

11 Here as well, the intertextual layering is intense, for the monstrous combination of an animal's body and a human's head inverts the allegorical structure of *Maus*, which presented human figures with animal heads.

12 For a detailed analysis of this dimension, see Hillary Chute, "Temporality and Seriality in Spiegelman's *In the Shadow of No Towers*," *American Periodicals* 17:2 (2007): 228–244.

13 London: Humanoids, 2001 (French original 1990).

14 See, for instance, their long-running series *The Dark Cities* (since 1983). For more information on this work, which has expanded into various media formats, each of them with their own fictional universe, see http://www.urbicande.be/.

15 See the anthology of forgotten works by Dan Nadel, *Art Out of Time: Unknown Comics Visionaries 1900–1969* (New York: Abrams, 2006).

16 For a detailed analysis, see Thierry Groensteen, *The System of Comics* (Jackson: University Press of Mississippi, 2007), 97–102.

17 Craig Thompson's *Blankets* (Marietta, GA: Top Shelf, 2003) might be a more recent application of the same procedure.

18 That is, the elements that surround the work in the book without being part of the work in the narrow sense of the word; see Gérard Genette, *Paratexts. Thresholds of Interpretation* (New York: Cambridge University Press, 1997).

19 Benoît Peeters and Jacques Samson, *Chris Ware: L'invention de la bande dessinée* (Brussels: Les Impressions Nouvelles, 2009).

20 The most detailed survey can be found in Groensteen's *Theory of Comics*, 112–115, but it is important to realize that the gutter is almost a routine theme in most critical speculations on graphic storytelling.

21 The adaptation symptomatically tries to remediate this problem of the "original" by speeding up the rhythm of the second half of the film (the "action movie" half of the work). We will not discuss the specific aspects of this work, which fall outside the domain of our study.

22 We follow here the translation of "discret" proposed by Bart Beaty and Nick Nguyen. The French term "discret" is the antonym of "osentatious" and refers to forms of layout that are so mainstream and common that the reader hardly notices them.

23 In *Understanding Comics* (see chapter 3: "Blood in the Gutter"), McCloud lists and discusses six types of panel transitions: (1) *Moment to moment*: a single action portrayed in a series of moments; (2) *Action to action*: a single subject (person, object, etc.) in a series of actions; (3) *Subject to subject*: a series of changing subjects within a single scene; (4) *Scene to scene*: transitions across significant distances of time and/or space; (5) *Aspect to aspect*: transitions of one aspect of a place, idea, or mood to another; and (6) *Non-sequitur*: panels with no logical relationship.

24 Charles Hatfield, *Alternative Comics: An Emerging Literature* (Jackson: University Press of Mississippi, 2006), 48.

25 New work on materiality is found in Ian Hague, *Comics and the Senses: A Multisensory Approach to Comics and Graphic Novels* (London: Routledge, 2014).

26 Many examples of this technique of iteration can be found in the work of the experimental Oubapo group (see http://www.oubapo.fr.st/), although repetition with a small difference also defines all American classics, such as *Peanuts*.

27 Meir Sternberg, "Reconceptualizing Narratology," *Enthymema* IV (2011): 40.

6 Drawing and Style, Word and Image

1 See Chris Ware, "Introduction" *McSweeney's*, 13 (2004): 11–12. Similar stances can be found in Thierry Groensteen, *Bande dessinée et narration* (Paris: PUF, 2011; an English translation is forthcoming from University Press of Mississippi), 124–129, and Gert Meesters, "Les significations du style graphique: *Mon fiston* d'Olivier Schrauwen et *Faire semblant, c'est mentir* de Dominique Goblet," *Textyles. Revue des lettres belges de langue française* 36–37 (2010): 215–233 (although with a stronger and more exclusive focus on "graphic style").

2 According to Roland Barthes, the link between style and individuality is rooted in a kind of "biological" approach of the literary craft: the style of an author refers to his or her body, and since all bodies are different, each "authentic" style can only be different from that of other voices, other authors, and other bodies. See *Writing Degree Zero*, transl. Annette Lavers (New York: Hill and Wang, 1968).

3 Most authors and critics stress the fact that graphic novel artists should not confuse drawing and copying the world. Drawing is less a matter of reproducing someone or something that exists or may exist in the world outside, but of catching their essence with a few well-chosen lines. The Swiss comic-pioneer, Rodolphe Töpffer, insisted very much on the crucial distinction between naturalistic reproduction (which for him did not work in cartooning) and the more stylized way of drawing that enabled the viewer to seize immediately the essential idea of a person, an object, or an event (and which made him prefer a more naive way of drawing to the academic canons of his time). Ever since Töpffer, the link between graphic novel drawing and either caricature or children's drawings has been discussed quite intensely, but in a way such a discussion should not take as its goal the defense of such an unconventional and much less prestigious style, but the reflection on the real motivations of this nonrealist approach

(once again, to use "realism" in a very general, nontheoretical sense). Drawing must not copy life, but inflate life to the represented figure and action.

4 See Julie Doucet, *My New York Diary* (Montreal: Drawn and Quarterly, 1999).

5 "Art School Confidential," in *Twentieth Century Eightball* (Seattle: Fantagraphics, 2002), 8, later remade as an amusing film. Similarly the Hollywood adaptation of *Ghost World* includes very witty sections on culture and value of fine art teaching.

6 The concept of graphiation was coined by Philippe Marion in *Traces en cases* (Louvain-la-Neuve: Académia, 1993). An English presentation was given by Jan Baetens, "Revealing Traces: A New Theory of Graphic Enunciation," in *The Language of Comics: Word & Image in the Comics*, eds. Robin Varnum and Christina Robbins (Jackson: University Press of Mississippi, 2001), 145–155.

7 Lewis Trondheim, *Désoeuvré* (Paris: L'Association, 2005). The most frightening point of Trondheim's theory, which seems indeed to apply to all great (European) comics artists and graphic novelists, is that things can only get worse: once begun, things always go downwards, and graphic novelists have no hope to make a new start. Instead they have the discomforting certitude that their later work can only be worse than what they have been doing until then.

8 When they appear, they are traditionally put down as surviving traces of the former studio system and its division of labor. In the later Corto Maltese adventures by Hugo Pratt, one can easily see that the cars have not been drawn by the same hand that produced the "typically Pratt" characters.

9 See Meesters, *Les Significations*, and Groensteen, *Bande dessinée et narration*, for this stereotypical view of stylistic change.

10 This series is an ongoing project of Benoît Peeters and François Schuiten that questions the status of the notion of "series;" each volume is simultaneously a totally independent book and a part of an overarching series; see www.urbicande.org.

11 For a detailed reading of *Asterios Polyp*'s idiosyncratic use of color and style, see Groensteen, *Bande dessinée et narration*, 126–128.

12 New York: Vertigo/DC Comics, 1995.

13 We will come back to Seth in our discussion of nostalgia in the graphic novel.

14 Raymond Queneau, *Exercises in Style,* transl. Barbara Wright (New York: New Directions, 1981). Basic information on the Oulipo group can be found on the website www.oulipo.fr and in the edited anthology by Harry Mathews and Alistair Brotchie, *The Oulipo Compendium*, rev. edition (Los Angeles and London: Make Now Press and Atlas, 2005). For an indepth reading of *99 Ways*, see Jan Baetens, "Not Telling, but Retelling: From Raymond Queneau's *Exercises in Style* to Matt Madden's *99 Ways to Tell a Story*, and Back," in *Graphic Novel Adaptations*, ed. Stephen E. Tabachnick (Jefferson, NC: MacFarland, forthcoming).

15 See his (unpublished) PhD (supervisor Roger Sabin), defended at the University of the Arts London in 2011.

16 The two illustrations by Simon Grennan are redrawings of pages 145 and 146 of Mike Mignola's *The Chained Coffin and Others* (Milwaukie, OR: Dark Horse Comics, 1998).

17 For an overview, see Jan Baetens, "Words and Images in the American Graphic Novel," in *Travels in Intermedial(ity) – ReBlurring the Boundaries*, ed. Bernd Herzogenrath (Hanover, NH: University Press of New England, 2012), 92–110.

18 "Rhetoric of the Image," in *Music Image Text*, transl. Stephen Heath (London: Fontana, 1974), 32–51.

19 In *Sleepwalk and Other Stories* (Montreal: Drawn and Quarterly, 2002).

20 See the "Dialogue" section of the Comics Code, as available on http://www.comicartville.com/comicscode.htm.

21 See also Hatfield's *Alternative Comics*, which studies these concepts with the help of indepth close readings of, among others, *Maus* and *Love and Rockets*.

22 See *McSweeney's* 13 (2004): 42. The "'review" is from 1939.

23 *"Le Coeur révélateur" et autres histoires extraordinaires* (Genève: Les Humanoïdes associés, 1995).

24 In France, the adaptation of Proust's *Remembrance of Things Past* by Stéphane Heuet has been an amazing bestseller – and for that reason sometimes looked down upon by a certain, more snobby, BD readership.

25 On this new form of cross-mediality, see Henry Jenkins, *Convergence Culture: Where Old and New Media Collide* (New York: New York University Press, 2006).

26 Posy Simmonds, *Gemma Bovery* (London: Jonathan Cape, 2000).

27 See Thierry Groensteen, "Histoire de la bande dessinée muette," *9e Art* 2 (1997): 60–75, and "Histoire de la bande dessinée muette," *9e Art* 3 (1998): 92–105.

28 *Ex-Foliations: Reading Machines and the Upgrade Path* (Minneapolis: Minnesota University Press, 2008), 88–89.

29 Montreal: Drawn and Quarterly, 2008 (transl. Noah Stollmaan).

30 We will not discuss the (many) other forms that Ware's material, richly and systematically serialized before publication in book form, can take. This serialization, however, is much more than a simple prepublication. Given the complexity of the question and the sometimes very confidential status of some of these serializations, our analysis will focus exclusively on the book version.

31 We refer here to the Russian Formalist concept of "ostranenie." See the recent collection of essays edited by Annie van den Oever, *Ostrannenie* (yes, with double "n") (Amsterdam University Press, 2011).

7 The Graphic Novel as a Specific Form of Storytelling

1 *Living to Tell About It: A Rhetoric and Ethics of Character Narration* (Ithaca: Cornell University Press, 2004), 18.

2 Roland Barthes, "An Introduction to the Structural Analysis of Narrative," transl. Lionel Duisit, *New Literary History* 6:2 (1975): 237–272.

3 See, for instance, Ian Gordon et al., eds., *Film and Comic Books* (Jackson: University Press of Mississippi, 2007).

4 See, for instance, David Herman, "Narrative Worldmaking in Graphic Life Writing," in *Graphic Subjects*, ed. Michael A. Chaney (Madison: Wisconsin University Press, 2011), 231–243.

5 *Substance* 40:1 (2011): 53–69.

6 Walter Benjamin, "The Storyteller," transl. Harry Zohn, *Illuminations* (New York: Schocken, 1969), 83–109.

7   Jared Gardner, "Storylines," *Substance* 40:1 (2011): 56–57.

8   Charles Hatfield, *Hand of Fire: The Comics Art of Jack Kirby* (Jackson: University Press of Mississippi, 2012), 59.

9   Hatfield, *Hand of Fire*, 47.

10 And as for *Peanuts*, setting is plainly there, albeit in highly symbolic images – the kennel, the baseball mound, a child's piano – out of which the animated adaptations added classic small town America. *The Simpsons*' Springfield *avant la lettre.*

11 In Robert Crumb, *Robert Crumb's America* (San Francisco, Last Gasp, 1995). "A Short History…" was first published in 1979 (in black and white; later versions are in color).

12 Chris Ware's *Building Stories* (New York: Pantheon, 2012) plays in various ways with this basic structure.

13 See Kim Deitch, *A Shroud for Waldo* (Seattle: Fantagraphics, 2002), 50.

14 Toronto: The Coach House Press, 1975. Actually, the book only became famous via its French translation: *La Cage*, transl. Marc Avelot (Paris: Les Impressions Nouvelles, 1985).

15 In the following paragraphs, we rework some fragments borrowed from Jan Baetens, "Uncaging and Reframing *The Cage*," in *Drawing from Life: Memory and Subjectivity in Comic Art*, ed. Jane Marianna Tolmie (forthcoming with University Press of Mississippi, 2013).

16 See our analysis of the page and panel structure of this scene in Chapter 6.

17 *Cf.* the final chapter ("Conclusion: What Does It Mean to Be Posthuman?") of her book *How We Became Posthuman* (Chicago: Chicago University Press, 1999).

18 For a detailed example, see Jan Baetens, "Dominique Goblet: The Meaning of Form," in *Graphic Subjects*, ed. Michael Chaney (Madison: University of Wisconsin Press, 2011), 76–92.

19 Jacques Rancière, *The Politics of Aesthetics: The Distribution of the Sensible,* transl. Gabriel Rockhill (New York: Continuum, 2004).

20 Charles McGrath, "Not Funnies," *New York Times*, July 2004.

21 Other critics such as Charles Hatfield (see *Hand of Fire*, 35–38) defend a more positive approach towards cartoonish depictions, but their point of view does not seem to be dominant in recent scholarship.

22 Sam Leith, "Hope in the Final Panel," *The Telegraph*, Aug. 2, 2007, available at http://www.telegraph.co.uk/culture/books/fictionreviews/3666885/Hope-in-the-final-panel.html (accessed Jan. 11, 2013).

23 Douglas Wolk, *Reading Comics: How Graphic Novels Work and What They Mean* (New York: Da Capo Press, 2007), 203.

24 The story is part of the collection *Sleepwalk and Other Stories* (Montreal, Drawn & Quarterly: 2002), 65–75.

25 For a more detailed and slightly different framed analysis, see Jan Baetens, "Abstraction in Comics," *SubStance* 40:1 (2011): 94–113.

26 Seattle, Fantagraphics, 2009. Earlier collections had been made in Europe, for instance by the Swiss author Ibn al Rabin. Both Andrei Molotiu and Ibn al Rabin refer to the same historical sources.

27 Opening page of the introduction in *Abstract Comics*, ed. Andrei Molotiu (Seattle: Fantagraphics, 2009), n.p.

28 For a survey of the current discussions, see Thierry Groensteen, *Bande dessinée et narration* (Paris: PUF, 2011), 195–198 (an English translation by Ann Miller will appear soon from University Press of Mississippi).

29 Douglas Wolk, "Comics," *New York Times Book Review*, Holiday Books Edition, December 6, 2009, p. BR14.

30 Molotiu, introduction to *Abstract Comics*, n.p. (but actually p. 8).

31 Lev Manovich, *The Language of New Media* (Cambridge, Mass.: MIT Press, 2001), 218.

32 The digital comics promoted by Scott McCloud go into a totally different discussion, which we will not go into here (see his *Reinventing Comics*, 2000).

33 For a detailed reading of the "queer" use of the list-principle, see the already mentioned article Baetens, "Dominique Goblet: The Meaning of Form."

34 N. Katherine Hayles, "Narrative and Database: Natural Symbionts" *PMLA* 122, no. 5, 2007, pp. 1603–1608.

8 The Graphic Novel and Literary Fiction: Exchanges, Interplays, and Fusions

1 Iain Sinclair, *Edge of Orison* (London: Hamish Hamilton, 2005), 217; for Sinclair writing further on Moore, 224–234. Earlier in his career Sinclair worked with Dave McKean as illustrator on *Slow Chocolate Autopsy* (London: Phoenix House, 1997).

2 Jim Collins, *Bring on the Books for Everybody* (Durham, NC: Duke University Press, 2010).

3 With apologies to Jürgen Habermas. We do not propose a major discussion and simply mean the society at large wherein literature is appreciated and commercially bought and sold. For context on the modern publishing industry see John B. Thompson, *Merchants of Culture* (Cambridge: Polity, 2012).

4 Michael Chabon, *The Amazing Adventures of Kavalier and Clay* (New York: Picador, 2000).

5 Jonathan Lethem, *The Disappointment Artist* (London: Faber, 2005).

6 Grant Morrison, "Foreword," in Robert Mayer, *Superfolks* (New York: St Martin's Press, 2005 [1977]).

7 See, among others, Frederic Tuten, "Tintin on Love," *Fiction* 3.2/3.3 (1975).

8 Jay Cantor, *Krazy Kat: A Novel in Five Panels* (New York: Knopf, 1987); Rick Moody, *The Ice Storm* (New York: Little Brown, 1994).

9 Umberto Eco, *The Mysterious Flame Queen of Loana: An Illustrated Novel* (Orlando: Harcourt, 2005).

10 Lev Grossman, "Who's the Voice of This Generation" *Time International* (10/7/2006): 44–47, and for a similar discussion also Grossman, "Pop Goes the Literature," *Time* (12/13/2004): 71–72.

11 *The Paris Review* (2012), at http://www.theparisreview.org/interviews/6127/the-art-of-fiction-no-216-bret-easton-ellis (last accessed October 2012). Since the novelist was born in 1964, long after the horror comics were first printed one can assume he is referring to 1970s reprints – or suffering from a false memory syndrome.

12   Michael Chabon, *Reading and Writing Along the Borderlines* (London: Fourth Estate, 2008).

13   Included in the collection Jonathan Lethem, *The Ecstasy of Influence* (New York: Doubleday, 2011), 135.

14   Nick Hornby, *Fever Pitch* (London: Gollancz, 1992); Nick Hornby, *High Fidelity* (London: Gollancz, 1995).

15   Lethem cited in Grossman, "Who's the Voice of This Generation?", 44–47.

16   These are two otherwise very useful collections that are highly recommended.

17   Kidd in Chip Kidd, *Book One: Work 1986–2006* (New York: Rizzoli, 2006), 388.

18   Ibid., 365.

19   Chip Kidd, *The Cheese Monkeys* (New York: Scribner, 2003); Chip Kidd, *The Learners* (New York: Scribner, 2008).

20   For a helpful discussion of Eggers's career, see Caroline D. Hamilton, *One Man Zeitgeist: Dave Eggers, Publishing and Publicity* (New York: Continuum, 2012).

21   Martin Barker and Roger Sabin, *The Lasting of the Mohicans: History of an American Myth* (Jackson: University Press of Mississippi, 1995), 146.

22   Stéphane Heuet, *Remembrance of Things Past* (three volumes translated with Nantier Beall Minoustchine Publishing since 2003). In French, five volumes have already appeared (seven more are announced).

23   Presentation of the work on the *Ulysses "Seen"* website at http://ulyssesseen.com/landing/ (consulted August 2013).

24   The magazine made an explicit use of the label "novel" to identify its stories.

25   Pratt (or his ghostwriter) has even novelized one of the books of the *Corto Maltese* series, as if the literary ambitions of his work had not been sufficiently acknowledged by the recognition of his graphic novel!

26   Raymond Queneau, *Zazie in the Metro*, transl. Barabara Wright (London: Penguin, 2011; French original: 1959).

27   Contrary to the recent and quite uneventful graphic novel adaptation by Clément Oubrerie, *Zazie dans le métro* (Paris: Gallimard, 2008), the Carelman book reprints the complete text.

28   Joseph Moncure March and Art Spiegelman, *The Wild Party* (New York: Pantheon, 1994).

29   Art Spiegelman and R. Sikoryak, eds., *The Narrative Corpse: A Chain-Story by 69 Artists* (New York: RAW Books, 1995).

30   He now also teaches seminars under the Oulipo umbrella in well-established institutions for fine arts such as the Wexner Museum, Columbus, OH (linked to The Ohio State University, whose importance for the field has become paramount – and whose Billy Ireland Cartoon Library hosts many treasures of American comics).

31   Zadie Smith, "Introduction," Smith, ed., *The Book of Other People* (London: Penguin, 2008 [2007]), vii.

9   Nostalgia and the Return of History

1   Useful context on retro culture is provided in Simon Reynolds, *Retromania: Pop Culture's Addiction to Its Own Past* (London: Faber and Faber, 2011).

2 Jared Gardner, *Projections: Comics and the History of Twenty-First-Century Storytelling* (Stanford: Stanford University Press, 2012), 149–179. See also Gardner, "Archives, Collectors, and the New Media Work of Comics," *Modern Fiction Studies* 52:4 (2006): 787–806.

3 Chapter 8 of this book offers a subtly different explanation. Here we argue that literary culture's increased concern with visual culture provided a rich space wherein the graphic novel could flourish. Themes treated in graphic novels (autobiography, history) were also aligned to mainstream literary values, as described by Mark McGurl in *The Program Era* (Cambridge Mass: Harvard University Press, 2009).

4 Art Spiegelman, *Meta-Maus* (New York: Pantheon, 2011).

5 Chris Ware, *Building Stories* (New York: Pantheon, 2012).

6 Tardi is a leading graphic novelist in France. This product commemorates the memory of the May 1968 student uprising. Tardi's illustrations are inspired by protest songs from the era, and these can be heard on the accompanying CD, sung by his partner, Grange.

7 For example, Chute writes: "Because comics represents time as space on the page, additionally, authors such as Spiegelman have been able to push on the conventions of comics' spatial representation to powerful effect, by, say, palimpsesting past and present moments together in panels that are traditionally understood to represent only one temporal register.... In this sense it builds a productive recursivity into its narrative scaffolding." *Graphic Women: Life Narrative and Contemporary Comics* (New York: Columbia University Press, 2010), 7–8. As Chute acknowledges, this angle on time on the page is often linked to the claims of Scott McCloud, *Understanding Comics* (New York: Harper Collins, 1994).

8 See Jerry Moriarty, *The Complete Jack Survives* (Oakland: Beneventura Press, 2009).

9 Janwillem van de Wetering and Paul Kirchner, *Murder by Remote Control* (New York: Ballantine, 1986); see also Gahan Wilson, "Paperbacks: Little Nemo Meets Dick Tracy," *New York Times* (May 4, 1986).

10 Shotaro Ishinomori, *Japan Inc.* (Berkeley: California University Press, 1992). The first edition is noted in Edwin McDowell, "The Region: America Is Taking Comic Books Seriously," *New York Times* (July 31, 1988). Special thanks here to Benjamin Murphy for his excellent term paper on a course exploring history and the graphic novel.

11 Both titles appeared after *Maus* but did not make the same impact as the next set of works of the early 2000s by Ware, Katchor, Clowes, Satrapi, et al.

12 Stephen Bissette and Rick Veitch, *1941: The Illustrated Story* (New York: Heavy Metal, 1979).

13 Academics play their part, too, in making these important considerations a topic. See the work of Mark McKinney in his book on colonial heritage in French language comics and graphic novels, *The Colonial Heritage of French Comics* (Liverpool: Liverpool University Press, 2011).

14 Art Spiegelman in "Art Spiegelman Interview: Part II," *The Comics Journal*, 181 (October 1995): 106.

15 See Mark Alexander, "Wah-hoo: SGT Fury and His Howling Commandos" at http://www.twomorrows.com/kirby/articles/24fury.html (last accessed January 2013).

This real-life theme may or may not be the backdrop to the plotting of Chabon's novel *Kavalier and Clay*.

16   These titles are collected together in Alan Moore and Eddie Campbell, *A Disease of Language* (London: Knockabout Books, 2010).

17   Chip Kidd, in Kidd and Dave Taylor, *Batman: Death by Design* (New York: DC Comics, 2012), 7.

18   See Constance M. Greiff, *Lost America: From the Atlantic to the Mississippi* (Princeton: The Pyne Press, 1974). See also Thomas C. Wheeler, ed., *A Vanishing America: The Life and Times of the Small Town* (New York: Holt, Rinehart and Winston, 1964).

19   Jerome de Groot, *Consuming the Past* (London: Routledge, 2008), 217.

20   Jay Kantor, *Krazy Kat* (New York: Knopf, 1987).

21   Jules Feiffer, *The Great Comic Book Heroes* (Seattle: Fantagraphics, 2003 [1965]), 78. We note that already in 1962, the writer Philip K Dick imagined comics and pop culture as future nostalgia items. See his novel, *The Man in the High Castle*.

22   And, we might note, commercially owned with the apparatus of copyright law, even for the most scholarly and unprofitable publications needing to reprint images as examples.

23   Roger Sabin's *Adult Comics* gives a brilliant flavor of the UK publishing scene's hyped thinking on the graphic novel in the 1986–1992 era.

24   Jim Collins, *Bring on the Books for Everybody* (Durham, NC: Duke University Press, 2010).

25   We are not suggesting *Maus* caused this shift in museum practice. It simply is a significant antecedent and a very early example of the popularization of autobiography. The worldwide reception and importance of Anne Frank's *Diary* indicates how societies preferred to account for the Holocaust through emphasis on individual or family experiences rather than other terms.

26   Derf Backderf, *My Friend Dahmer* (New York: Abrams, 2012), 84–85.

27   See also the excellent article by Andrew J. Kunka, "Intertextuality and the Historical Graphic Narrative: Kyle Baker's Nat Turner and the Styron Controversy," *College Literature* 38:3 (2011): 168–93.

28   Art Spiegelman, *In the Shadow of No Towers* (New York: Pantheon, 2004), 11.

29   Clowes in Ken Pareille and Isaac Cates, eds., *Daniel Clowes: Conversations* (Jackson: University Press of Mississippi, 2010), 139.

INDEX

Printed in Great Britain
by Amazon

81935053R00169